ENDORSEMENTS

"In her compelling book, *Direct Hit*, Kathleen Klawitter takes us on a transformational and captivating journey from chaos to complete recovery. From the first few pages to the final paragraph, she completely redefines the meaning of the word 'drive' for a golfer, as her real-life challenge was to be found away from the green courses. Written in an epic cinematic style, her true story unravels with fascinating twists and turns. A must-read if you want to live your life in full swing."

~ Nabil Doss
Expert in Influential Communication

"*Direct Hit* is a deep, profoundly healing saga. It shows that the practices of Skydancing® Tantra can play a big part in regaining one's psychic and emotional health. This book is a must for those who want to find new and powerful ways to heal traumatic injuries, as well as recover from the wounds of sexual abuse. I honor the courage of the author who shows us it is possible to heal yourself, if you apply perseverance and devotion to the task. She has become the heroine of her life."

~ Margot Anand
Best-selling author of *The Art of Everyday Ecstasy* and others, including *Love, Sex and Awakening*

"In her comeback journey, *Direct Hit*, Kathleen is the acknowledged master of one facet of her life: staying in the moment while being true to herself."

~ Mark Eaton
NBA All-Star, Best-selling author of, *The Four Commitments of a Winning Team*

"Kathleen Klawitter's heart-wrenching, yet hopeful, story takes you on an emotional rollercoaster as she discovers who she is and what she must do to recover after a tragic accident. After reading about her journey, both literally and figuratively, I believe I can do anything I set my mind to, based on her example. I highly recommend it!"

~ Libby Gill
Award-winning author of *The Hope-Driven Leader*

"In her book, *Direct Hit,* Kathleen Klawitter embodies the Divine Feminine in her courageous journey of birthing herself through traumatic brain injury and beyond. Her 20-year transformation is huge, and she offers her best gifts to the world with much energy and enthusiasm. Kathleen exudes pure spirit burning brightly as the flame that dances and peeks through all of existence, providing pure feminine nourishment to all."

~ Laura Cornell, PhD
Author of *Moon Salutations: Women's Journey Through Yoga to Healing, Power, and Peace*

"Think of golf, life, and 'Yoda' all combined to give you astonishing wisdom and insights into what it means to be a persevering human. Kathleen Klawitter, who learned to recalibrate her brain following a devastating traumatic brain injury, hits a hole-in-one with her amazing story that gives us real lessons in golf and life."

~ Scott G. Halford
Emmy Award–winning writer, producer, and *Wall Street Journal* Best-selling author of *Activate Your Brain*

"Kathleen Klawitter has written a most engaging memoir, with a storyline revolving around a devastating brain injury she incurred, followed by a long and phenomenal recovery period. Alternately tragic and happy, uplifting, yet profoundly unsettling, the book is her story of the courageous healing journey she continues to make, a kind of travelogue through the multitude of disciplines and modalities available in our time. Inspiring!"

~ Vicki Noble

Author of *Shakti Woman: Feeling Our Fire, Healing Our World* and *Motherpeace: A Way to the Goddess,* co-creator with Karen Vogel of *Motherpeace Tarot*

"Kathleen Klawitter's amazing and inspirational story is a shining beacon for anyone looking to be guided out of a life-shattering trauma."

~ Patrick J. Sweeney II

Adventurer and author of *Fear is Fuel*

"In this inspiring, poignant, and sometimes humorous survivor's memoir, Kathleen takes us on a remarkable journey. She teaches us how to view life's changing experiences in new ways so we can live one precious and wild life. Whether the reader has experienced a brain injury, knows someone with a brain injury, or has an interest in this area, this book is an invaluable resource in terms of treatment, and it is a significant contribution in the field of traumatic brain injury research."

~ Cheryll A. Smith, PhD

Clinical Neuropsychologist

Kathleen

DIRECT HIT

DIRECT HIT:

A GOLF PRO'S REMARKABLE JOURNEY

BACK FROM TRAUMATIC BRAIN INJURY

KATHLEEN KLAWITTER

DIRECT HIT:
A Golf Pro's Remarkable Journey
Back from Traumatic Brain Injury

Copyright © 2020 by Kathleen Klawitter

ISBN: 978-1-7330393-0-7
ISBN: 1-7330393-0-9
Library of Congress Control Number: 2019916997

Cover design by: Bill Van Nimwegen
Drawing images by Kathleen Klawitter
Brain Image Biasa.org
The Moon Salutation "Expression of the Feminine in Body, Psyche, Spirit"
© 2000 Laura Cornell

Printed in the United States of America

To my Spiritual Guides, Traditional Healers, and Nature Spirits, including the air I breathe, the sun that shines, the water that flows, and our precious Mother Earth, who have always been there for me and continue to inspire and amaze me.

To all who are open and receptive to live their lives fully and embrace the sacredness and oneness of all.

CONTENTS

CHAPTER 1

SILENT SHOT—
THE MOMENT THAT CHANGED MY LIFE

"Permanent?" I asked.

Frontal lobe, brainstem . . . ," the doctor said, barely audible. Then, she cleared her throat and added, "Permanent *injury*, not permanent *impairment*. The quality of your life will be somewhat different."

I straightened up in my chair, tears streaming from my eyes. "Bullshit! I cannot live like this!" I barked, as if the firmness in my voice could erase her words. I stood, ready to grab my backpack and rush out the door of her office.

"The days will get better," she said with a smile, obviously trying to make the diagnosis not seem so bad.

I leaned over and growled at her. She remained positive, despite my abrupt behavior, although it could not quell the uneasiness spawning in my belly. How did this happen? I had always believed in my heart that the side effects of my accident were only temporary; it's what kept me going. Has it really been over a year?

I recalled the inciting moment that turned my world upside down, wishing I could rouse from this terrible nightmare. It was a warm summer day in late July. The mid-afternoon sun cast long shadows from tall redwood trees onto the first fairway. The aroma

1

of freshly cut grass was everywhere as I started to walk from my car in the parking lot to the Sebastopol Golf Clubhouse, a nine-hole course in beautiful Sebastopol, California. I had already pulled out a scorecard and one of those short green pencils with an eraser.

I glanced over at the putting green where women from my golf league were practicing for their round of golf. I took a deep breath to yell, "Hello, girls!" but instead, I exhaled quickly so I would not interrupt their concentration. I smiled contentedly, knowing I would join them on the links later.

I continued down the path to the clubhouse, stopping momentarily to finish writing names on the scorecard. Without warning, something struck me in the head. It felt like a railroad tie had been driven through the top of my head, into my skull, and out my left eye socket. The pain was excruciating, as if a bowling ball had fallen on my head, and shuddered through my whole body.

My hands went up and the scorecard and pencil fell. The black asphalt and the green grass were spinning like a plate atop a long, thin stick, knowing it would eventually fall was just a matter of time. In seconds, darkness consumed me as I fell to the ground, crumpled in a heap.

Another golfer ran over and cradled my head in his lap. "Help is on the way. You've got to stay awake," he said repeatedly.

His words were heavily muffled by a loud, humming noise that resounded in my ears. I lay motionless, glassy-eyed, and drooling.

Loud sirens pierced the air and an ambulance arrived a few minutes later. Paramedics automatically checked my vitals. I heard distant voices asking me questions, yet I could not speak. They started to place a cervical collar around my neck when I was suddenly overcome with nausea and struggled to roll on my side to vomit. One of the women from the golf league was sitting beside me and quickly wiped my mouth with a tissue. The paramedics rolled me back onto a gurney and placed me in the ambulance.

As we raced to the hospital, a man's voice kept asking me the date, and I kept telling him June 24, which is my birthday. It was, in fact, July 28. I lay strapped to the gurney in a painful stupor with my eyes fixated on a screw embedded in the ambulance ceiling. Any movement of my eyes or head brought on nausea, dizziness, and the feeling of falling into an abyss.

I found myself encased in a large, hollow tube with loud thumps and ringing echoing through my head.

"We're almost finished, ma'am," said a muffled voice from behind the glass window. "We just need to get one more x-ray."

My head was pounding, and I was confused and disoriented. All I knew was that I needed to sit up and elevate my head. And ice—was anyone going to put ice on my head? Was anyone there?

Hello? Can anyone hear me?

Apparently, I was not saying these words aloud.

A golf companion and close friend held my hand as we waited for the doctor. She looked in my eyes, her lips forming a half smile. Although her presence comforted me, I could see she was preoccupied. No doubt she was wondering how this had happened. Later, I learned a golfer was hitting from the ninth tee with his comrades. He had been drinking a few beers and thought he could drive the green. His aim was dangerously off, and he managed to hit the golf ball over the clubhouse, a mere 200 yards away. To my misfortune, it struck me on the head with the force of something much larger. My young, vibrant, and motivated life, as I knew it, changed in an instant.

The emergency room doctors concluded that I had a contusion on the top of my head, along with a concussion and an altered state of consciousness that should be carefully monitored for a few days. Against doctors' orders, I apparently insisted on leaving the hospital and asked my friend to help me into her car and drive me home.

I slept for almost 20 hours before my two orange kittens, Maple Leaf and Jack, woke me up. I had acquired them two months earlier. Maple Leaf was nestled on my head, licking my eyebrows, while Jack played in an open closet, climbing all over my clothes. I tried log rolling to get out of bed, but my head felt so heavy, and the pain was unbearable, and the room started to spin. Slower, I thought. I must move very slowly so my brain can catch up. I felt like one of those bobblehead dogs you put on a car's rear dashboard.

I spied the litter box on the floor under a window, shuffled toward it, and dropped to my knees to grab the scooper. When I leaned forward, I felt liquid flow to the front of my brain, followed by a vibrant light-green inkblot that kept growing. I quickly pulled my head up and sat back on my knees until everything settled down. Nauseated, I dry heaved a couple times. I'll clean the litter box later, I thought, and crawled back to bed.

The following months were exhausting as I tried to function as if everything were normal. I attempted to drive, but each time I looked left or right, the scenery moved in waves in slow motion to catch up to my brain and eyes. I was overwhelmed by vertigo and had to pull over to vomit or dry heave. I even tried to teach golf, only to double-book clients or forget that I booked lessons at all. Even worse, when I did teach, I would get confused about golf shots and strategies. I was a golf professional, yet information that I once knew inside and out was completely scrambled in my mind.

I became increasingly frustrated and angry. Why couldn't I figure out what was wrong? Time was passing, often without my realizing what day it was. Talking with friends was difficult. I

4

could not keep up with conversations, especially with more than one person. I could not formulate questions or add to the discussion because the pace of my thoughts was so delayed. My brain became so fatigued that I no longer cared about anything.

Simple tasks became monumental nightmares. A short trip to vote turned into a long, nerve-wracking experience. The voting booths were conveniently located just around the block from my house. I jumped into the car, and I was suddenly overcome with dizziness when I tried to look left and right. I kept driving, thinking I would get there shortly. But something went wrong. Much time passed, and I had no clue where I was. It was now dark outside, and I was lost. I caught a whiff of ocean water, which was at least a half-hour away from my home. Frightened and confused, I pulled over and cried.

An angel surely must have heard my desperation as a young couple in a van, with surfboards tied to the top, stopped to check on me. They were wearing beach attire and asked if they could help. I explained that I needed to get home to my apartment in Sebastopol, and they instructed me to follow them in their van. They took me to the local grocery store, which I recognized, but they insisted on following me all the way to my home, less than a minute away. I thanked them as they helped me out of the car and into the house. I was safe for the time being.

A friend introduced me to a neuropsychologist in Santa Barbara, California, who instructed me to stay in bed for three weeks without any type of visual, audio, or environmental stimulation. In our first meeting, she was surprised by how many months had passed before I saw a doctor.

"You look so fresh," she said. By *fresh*, she meant that my head injury looked like it had just happened.

I followed her instructions and rested in bed with my head elevated on two pillows, getting up only to eat or go to the bathroom. Everything seemed to slow down, and some of the headache pain diminished from unbearable to almost tolerable.

I started noticing a strange recurring phenomenon. Any stimulation provoked a liquid feeling inside my brain. It felt like I had a blood fountain extending from the base of my neck, the brain stem, and up into the top of my head. The fountain would spill over, but it felt like all the blood had to filter through a strainer at a dripping pace when it came back down.

I thought my brain was going to explode from the pressure. With no place to go, I feared it would burst open, like a whale spouting, so I stopped anything that I was doing and waited until all the blood passed through the strainer. The process took hours, even days, depending on how quickly I ceased what I was doing. Sometimes I didn't realize the stimulation was happening. An overhead fan, the flames in a fireplace, fluorescent lighting, an action movie, sunlight, a crowded restaurant, a car radio playing, two or three people talking, any driving, the hum of the refrigerator, raindrops on the roof—pretty much everything prompted the painful fountain to drip.

I returned to my neuropsychologist for extensive therapy and evaluations. The process was grueling, and many times, the testing had to be broken into smaller time frames because I would get nauseated and dizzy and my brain would just flood out. I would literally stop what I was doing, like a windup doll grinding to a halt.

Diagnosis: Traumatic Brain Injury

After consulting with several other doctors over the course of several months, I was diagnosed with a traumatic brain injury (TBI), which caused impairments to my cognitive function, including executive functioning; language (slowed, delayed, slurred); balance (vertigo); short-term memory loss; inability to tolerate stimulating environments of any kind; optical problems (convergence insufficiency, double vision, and tracking); very slow and disorganized thinking; and difficulties with reading, studying, and behavioral functioning.

My disoriented way of my life persisted. While shopping at the Von's Food Store in downtown Santa Barbara, I was overcome by the visual stimulation of constantly scanning for items on the shelves. Everything became a kaleidoscope of colorful shapes and images that blurred into each other. I passed rows of canned creamed corn, stacks of lemons and apples, and bottles of salad dressing. Delicate pink carnations at the edge of the floral department seemed to pop out and reach for me. I saw the checkout line and the clerk, but he didn't see me. I couldn't speak. I heard the distant ringing of cash registers and the muffled sound of voices. Finally, I spotted the automatic glass doors. I made a beeline for them and staggered outside with the breeze in my face.

I sat down on the hot cement to rest. A bearded man wearing old, tattered clothes was lying on the sidewalk in front of the store next to a grocery cart filled with bags and boxes of his personal possessions. I walked over and lay next to him, despite getting a whiff of the stench of his body odor and the alcohol on his breath. I closed my eyes and was immersed in a dark tunnel. I don't know how long I had lain there. Eventually, the homeless man nudged me and offered what looked like a blanket, as the setting sun brought cooler temperatures. When I reached out to grab it, I realized it was just a plastic garbage bag. As I fumbled with it, a young grocery clerk approached.

"Ma'am, ma'am, you have been out here for quite some time. May I help you to your car?" he asked.

I sat up. "No, I can't drive. I mean I'm *unable* to drive."

The kind clerk looked confused. "Well, I will call you a taxi."

Irritated, I snapped, "I can't afford a taxi. I can't even work anymore."

"Well, you can't just sit here all evening," he said, somewhat sternly.

Overhearing the conversation, the homeless guy mumbled something about this being his spot and shouted, "I can stay here as long as I want!"

It's evening? I pulled myself up in disbelief. "I need to go home. My cats are still outside."

"Yes, I'm trying to help you get there," the clerk said.

Many other times, I would lie down wherever I was because of mental fatigue. Some of my favorite resting spots were Von's Food Store, downtown State Street, or any park bench. I was pretty much at home with the homeless. I wasn't aware of what was happening, so nothing mattered at the time. In fact, my pride in my appearance and fastidious grooming habits all went by the wayside. I did not attempt to comb my hair or apply makeup. I wore the same light-blue sweatshirt and rust-colored jeans every day because it was too difficult to make clothing selections without taxing my brain. I was exposed, raw, uninhibited, and meandered the streets like a homeless person.

I didn't realize that I was doing these things. I kept fumbling ahead as if everything were normal. I didn't know the confusion inside my head was affecting what was happening outside. I compared the way my brain accessed and processed information to trying to grab a red radish on a Lazy Susan while six other people were reaching for the pickles and black olives. Soon, I was not hungry for that radish after all—especially when the process nauseated me. Eventually, I figured out how to pluck those radishes from a tray that was standing still. Then, I would go back for the pickles and then the olives.

It works like spokes on a wheel. When I am on the perimeter and come back to the hub on the same spoke, it makes sense to me, and I can get things done. However, if I get caught on the perimeter, I don't know which spoke I am on, and I lose the thought altogether, or I retrieve information that is out of context. It was quite frustrating and downright embarrassing, particularly in my interactions with others. I knew what I wanted to say, yet my thoughts scattered like sand in a dust devil, forever lost in a field of uncertainty.

"What day is it?"

"Where are we?"

"Why am I so hungry?"

"Oh, I started that last week, or was it yesterday? Oh, it was two months ago."

"Yes! Of course! It's Valentine's Day, not Thanksgiving."

"Happy New Year! I mean Happy Birthday, Dave, er, uh . . . I mean Matt."

"Paper or plastic?" the grocery clerk cheerfully asked.

"Hi . . . wooden is fine . . . sorry, I mean the . . . umm . . . oh, for gosh sakes, the brown ones there!" I replied, pointing to a paper bag.

"I'm sitting here with my groceries waiting for my pickup ride. The van is late, so I thought I'd call." The EZ Lift operator informed me the ride was scheduled for a different day. "No, that can't be right. I am here now, you know, with my groceries. My Tofutti Cuties are melting, and the red snapper is going to spoil . . . ."

And, so it went, day after day.

One afternoon, I walked on a foot trail with my friends. They didn't seem to notice the depth of my difficulty in navigating the path. But how could they? It wasn't like I had a broken leg. You would be able to see that. The broken part was inside my brain. Invisible. My pace was slow. I barely shuffled my feet because the landscape kept shifting in my head. My friends walked ahead, disappearing out of sight. I came upon a clearing and sat motionless on a park bench staring at the trees against the blue-gray sky. I would have been quite content to just sit there for the rest of my life. *Now, how did I get here again?*

CHAPTER 2

LIFE BEFORE THE DIRECT HIT (1989–1998)

I was born and reared in Indiana and grew up playing sports. I especially loved softball and went to college for that very reason. I was a gifted athlete and did quite well academically. I graduated with a bachelor's degree in psychology, but to my dismay, a career in professional softball was not a viable option. Disillusioned with the theories of the mind—and being financially desperate—I accepted an entry-level position as a recorder at the Midwest Stock Exchange (MSE) in Chicago.

My sister, a manager on the trading floor, had enough influence to get me on board and offered the job to me. I jumped at the opportunity to make good money. Unfortunately, I knew the stressful job and the frenzied atmosphere weren't for me within two weeks. My gnawing stomach reminded me daily how much I disliked working there. Despite the pain, I earned pay-grade increases and worked my way up to a manager in corporate marketing within a few years.

While at MSE, I met Christine, who worked at the brokerage firm on the trading floor. A free spirit herself, we gravitated to each other because of our mutual love for sports. She immediately enlisted me to play on her company's softball team. I was thrilled! Playing shortstop made me feel alive again. By the end of the season, we became lovers.

I shared my mission with Christine to move to California soon and play on the Ladies Professional Golf Association (LPGA) Tour. When I confessed that I hadn't played since I was a teenager, she immediately suggested that we go hit some balls. That weekend, we drove to a driving range in a small town in Illinois. With woods in hand and a large bucket of balls, we started smacking the balls past the 225-yard marker.

When I noticed a large water tower just to the left of the range boundary, I grinned at Christine and said, "I double dog dare ya!" She obliged and, on her first try, smacked the tower with a wailing sound! We laughed so hard, and I just had to try, too. It took a couple of times before I heard that glorious wailing sound echo. My short-lived victory ended moments later when the manager of the range came out yelling. We quickly gathered up our clubs and scurried off to the parking lot, giggling the whole way.

Even though softball and beach life were healthy and welcome diversions in the Indiana Dunes community where I resided, the stress from the fast-paced, cutthroat corporate world continued eroding my body and spirit. I had been diagnosed with Crohn's disease, an inflammatory condition of the intestinal tract, at an early age. While I was in high school, my belly usually was distended, and at times, I suffered from constipation. It would be many years before I adopted a diet that served me better. But now, surgery was imminent. I remember sitting on the South Shore train one morning on my way to work in the Chicago Loop, watching the sun come up over the trees. An inner voice whispered Psalm 121: "I will lift my eyes unto the hills from whence cometh my help."

The train continued to rock with the words resounding in my mind. Instinctively, I sensed that my life as a corporate businesswoman was about to end and that my whole life was about to change. My health and happiness were more important than a prestigious, high-profile job. Even though I had amassed many material possessions, including a sports car, a truck, a boat, a house, antiques, and even a financial portfolio, I felt something was missing. That something was *me*.

Days later, I was admitted to the Mayo Clinic in Rochester, Minnesota, with a bowel obstruction that required surgery to remove 12 inches of diseased intestine and part of the ileum, the final section of the small intestine. I prayed in the hospital chapel the night before my surgery, promising God I would do better instead of stuffing everything into my gut. Bad food and beverage choices, thoughts like "I am not good enough," and being a people pleaser continued to press my boundaries. My poor gut took the full brunt of the negative energy and responded with this inflammatory condition. The prognosis: more surgeries and a colostomy bag by the age of 40. I knew nothing of how to change this situation. But I knew one thing for sure: I refused to have a bag dangling from my hip for the rest of my life!

While recovering from the intestinal surgery, I walked the beach where I lived every morning and contemplated my life, wanting to live my passion for sports instead of working for money and prestige. I lived in a charming two-story beach house nestled in the Indian Dunes National Lake Shore. Interestingly, I could see the Chicago skyline across the lake on the horizon. It looked so small, so still. How could I let the pace of the city eat me up? Money and prestige were still within reach, like a golden carrot dangling in full view right in front of me at arm's length. But, enough was enough and, at the age of 29, I resigned from the MSE. I donated most of my possessions to a local church and sold the rest, including my home. I packed what I could in my car and drove cross-country to Palm Springs, California. Freedom.

My family and friends thought I was nuts, but I had a vision. I dreamed of becoming an LPGA professional, playing on the golf tour. The days of walking on the beach evoked fond childhood memories of frolicking outdoors; playing basketball, volleyball, and track in high school; and playing softball during the summer months. A gifted athlete, I had even dreamed of going to the Olympics in the late 1970s. The thought of returning to sports full-time reignited my passion to be a professional athlete. I narrowed my options to bowling, tennis, or golf. I chose the latter as it was a lifelong sport and my office would be outdoors . . . walking barefoot every day on freshly cut grass amid trees, birds, sand traps, and water hazards. In my heart, I knew this was my calling.

Getting in the Swing

The aesthetic beauty of Palm Springs, with sunny skies and warm temperatures, was a welcome escape from the sleet, slush, snow, and rain in the Midwest. With golf clubs in hand and sporting perfectly pressed shorts and a designer collared golf shirt, I proceeded to the row of golf carts in front of the golf course. Christine had just flown in for a vacation, and we chattered incessantly as we placed our clubs on the back of the cart and plopped down on the seat. I had not played golf in years, so this first round in a desert paradise was very exciting. I have relished the smell of freshly cut grass ever since I was a little girl playing in the backyard. Now, it had even more meaning to me. It meant the fairways and greens were ready for grown-up play. I couldn't wait to kick off my cleats and run barefoot in the grass.

Christine tore open her bag of M&Ms as I opened my Doritos. (Obviously, I had not considered healthy food choices yet.) Suddenly, she hit the accelerator without putting it in reverse. We bumped into the rail, and both sets of clubs went flying off the back end. Colorful M&Ms plunked and tinkered all around us, and my bag of Doritos flipped in the air across the front of the cart! We were laughing hysterically and then paused, noticing a group of men staring at us from the restaurant patio. We waved, and they obliged in the comical entertainment. This is how my illustrious golf career began; unfortunately, it wasn't going to be as easy as I thought it would be.

The rest of the afternoon went more smoothly as we settled into the game. I began to play with more intention as I selected clubs for making creative shots. My swing felt light and natural, and I felt so high to be playing on freshly cut fairways. Christine and I both excelled at driving the ball off the tee. She would pull out her big Flintstone "Bamm-Bamm" club, and with her 5-foot-11-inch frame, her swing plane was huge, creating more velocity and distance. She would drive that ball a country mile. I would use a 3-wood and drive almost as far with more accuracy, although the beauty was just watching the ball soar.

We attracted several spectators by the end of our round. I loved feeling the energy of the crowd. They motivated me to hit even farther! We finished our game of golf pretending we were playing on the tour. In my head, I heard the voice of a sports announcer: "And now putting out for $300,000 . . . and the winner is Kathleen Klawitter from Highland, Indiana. And from Punxsutawney, Pennsylvania, it's Christine Burke." I sank my putt, tipped my visor, and waved to the imaginary crowd. I proudly walked off the course, redeeming my golfing debut earlier that day. I played well for my first round in a long time. I was sore and tired but thrilled to be on my way.

After Christine left for Chicago, I focused on my job hunt. Decked out in a tailored business suit and matching pumps and my leather briefcase in hand, I proceeded to call on the high-end country clubs in Palm Springs in hopes of landing a job quickly. Seriously, a golf pro parading around in pumps? Not only did I not have the right look; I had no luck at all. The head professionals at the clubs took one look at me and shook their heads no. Finally, one of the pros sat me down and asked what my handicap was.

"I don't have a handicap. The last time I played golf regularly was with my dad when I was 14 years old," I confessed.

"You don't play golf?" His eyes bulged. "How do you expect to get a job at a country club if you don't play golf?"

I stared at him, dumbfounded. I was embarrassed but grateful for his direct approach. I returned to my hotel room to redesign my strategy for becoming a golf pro. The first order of action was to gather up my business suits and pumps and take them to a consignment shop. Then, I headed to a discount golf shop and bought golf attire, my new uniform for the coming years.

After being rejected by several high-end golf courses, I lowered my sights significantly. Eventually, I landed a job as the "cart barn girl" at a low-profile country club in a mobile home park. The name suggests a place where people go to have a shot and a beer and do the two-step. But it was where I washed the golf carts, collected range balls, and performed other menial tasks. It was a perfect place to start: a nine-hole, short-yardage course with a good driving range, putting green, and sand bunker for practice after work.

That's when I started to play and practice golf. I'd hit balls late into the night. I'd rise with the sun and majestic mountain views and continue my practice around the green with chip and pitch shots. At lunch, I'd practice putting on the green. In about a year, I had my LPGA apprentice card. I was well on my way to a happier and healthier new life and career.

My goal was to play on the women's golf tour, although hitting hundreds of balls all day and night became a time for me to inspire other golfers to hit better themselves. After two years of playing and competing, I felt more fulfilled helping other golfers to play better. I realized my true passion was to become a teaching pro rather than a touring pro. My entrepreneurial skills flourished in this realm. I was free to create fun ways to play and learn the game of golf.

Little did I know at the time that my holistic approach to golf, combined with my talent for creating games to improve performance, would later play major roles in my rehabilitation for a traumatic brain injury.

CHAPTER 3

STRATEGIES FOR GOLF . . . AND LIFE

News of my innovative golf teaching techniques spread, and my golf career flourished over the next few years. I designed several clinics on all aspects of the game, including mental strategies and on-course instruction. I formed women's golf leagues for beginner and intermediate players. I was hired as head coach of the College of the Desert Women's Golf Team. Under my tutelage, we claimed two winning seasons and a state championship, when I was also voted "Coach of the Year." I also hosted golf trips for women, created a golf newsletter, and wrote numerous articles for local golf magazines.

I developed and facilitated a one-of-a-kind league for women golfers. I took a few moments with each group on the course and taught different golf shots, golf strategies, rules and etiquette, and club selection. It was incredibly fulfilling to see the women learn so much more with on-the-course instruction and by watching a professional in action. No score was kept, and I offered each player one free throw per round if she became frustrated after several swing attempts in hitting the ball, especially from the sand trap. These became memorable weekly evenings that we all enjoyed during the beautiful summer months, and it was a cutting-edge learning approach for the woman golfers. After hearing a touching, yet frustrating, story from my mother, I also created a new scoring system for these women that I call the "3–4–5 Rule."

The 3–4–5 Rule

My mother phoned one evening, sniffing through her words about how embarrassed she was playing golf with my dad and Dan and Deanna, their best friends. Deanna was my mom's maid of honor some 40 years ago, and they have remained the best of friends. They were so excited to be together again, as they lived in northern Illinois and my parents lived in central Indiana.

They all loved golf, and for the first time, they played together. My mom was in a golf league in Indiana and played a decent game, but she knew she was the novice player of the foursome. Her golf shots were even worse compared to how she usually played. She started picking up her ball in the middle of the fairway instead of finishing out the hole. She followed with another poorly hit shot and picked up her ball prematurely again. By the third hole, she panicked. "I can't do this. I can't keep up. You guys are so much better than me."

The others tried to encourage her to keep playing, but their attempts were futile. She was disgusted with herself, and everyone felt uncomfortable for the remainder of their visit. This story is typical among married couples. It can be easily remedied with one simple rule or exercise I developed called the "3–4–5 Rule." On a par 3 hole, you allow yourself three shots in the fairway. If you don't make it to the green side (20 yards and in), then simply pick up the ball and give yourself a chip shot from anywhere on the fringe. From here, continue honoring the player farthest from the flagstick to hit his or her ball until everyone has putted out.

Hearing the ball has dropped in the cup gives a person such a feeling of completion. This is the object of the game of golf. There is no other sound like it: *plop-pa-pa-pa-pa-pa* . . . and silence. Done! And on to the next hole.

The same procedure holds true on the next hole. If it is a par 4, you allow yourself four shots in the fairway. If it is a par 5, then you allow yourself five shots in the fairway. Play your whole round of golf this way, concentrating on your swing routine in the fairway without rushing to keep up. You will automatically keep up without even having to think about it because of the number of shots you are taking on the fairway. No score is kept here. Before long, you will be reaching the green easily along with your other family and friends.

Give yourself time to develop mentally and physically. You also can piggyback from another player. Hit your shot from where they are hitting theirs until you reach the green side. Then, take your pitch, or chip shot, and putt out. Maneuvering around the golf course in this way not only develops confidence but also results in great shot making and merriment with friends or family. My mother can attest to this, as the next time she played with her husband and best friends, they all had a wonderful outing using the 3–4–5 Rule. Deanna even prodded my mom a couple of times, using her putter to her buttocks after putting out with the rest of them. This system caught on with many women players and even a few instructors.

I particularly liked putting games, which are the fastest way for golfers to lower their scores, and my mom soon found this out with the new 3–4–5 Rule. Golfers can practice their putting virtually anywhere, including the living room. One of my favorite games—which my parents and their golfing friends love to play— is called Stop Your Wining, which requires two wine glasses and a bottle of unopened wine. It goes like this.

Lay the wine bottle on its side. Set two wine glasses approximately five inches apart about a foot in front of the wine bottle. Pace off about three steps (six to nine feet) from your set up and mark this spot with a coin, tee, or tape. Take turns putting from the mark until you reach a score of 21 points. The ball must land between the two wine glasses and ideally stop just before the wine bottle. This is how the scoring works:

- Touch wine glass = 1 point
- Stopped ball within space between the wine glasses and wine bottle = 6 points
- Ball touches back bottle = 3 points

If the bottle breaks, the game is over. The winner gets to pour the wine, and the loser buys dinner. But, truthfully, the game is such a fun and effective learning exercise that everybody wins!

Another putting game is called Stacked Quarters. Place two quarters on top of each other. Take your putting stance and make your stroke to hit the top of the quarter without moving the bottom quarter. If you try to do this, it will not work, However, if you visualize in your mind's eye that the top quarter is already in front of the bottom quarter and then take your putting stroke, your body will fill in the details, and the top quarter will move a few inches in front of the bottom quarter. Now, that's good sense! When you get *really* good, try dimes.

For long putts on the green, I instructed my students to visualize a large bucket of water being poured on the green. Then, I asked, "Which way would the water flow?" Their answer determined where they would aim the putt. This simple tip worked wonders to reduce the number of putts and their final scores.

I also created a women's golf pledge that I had typed out on a colorful index card and handed out to each new woman who joined the golf leagues and for the ladies' golf team. It added a bit more integrity to the player and the game. It went like this:

Women's Golf Pledge

As a woman golfer, I gracefully acknowledge the greatest values in the game of golf. Further, I hereby claim these values in my golf performance and in my daily life. I am thankful for the opportunity to play golf, especially with other women evolving in this sport.

Truth . . . in being true to myself; in being honest about my score and in following the rules of golf to the best of my knowledge.

Loyalty . . . in the courtesy and care of the golf course I am playing.

Patience . . . with myself and my golf swing, and with the other players and their individual golf styles and personalities.

Joy . . . in having fun playing the game of golf with my family, friends, co-workers, and even players I have never met before.

Peace . . . in quieting my mind, I stay relaxed and confident.

Wisdom . . . with purpose and genuine sincerity, I create exactly what I desire by "thinking the thought."

Love . . . in loving golf, in loving nature, in loving life, and in loving myself.

This is my pledge; a pledge I proudly share with all women.

The High-Five System

My next foray was into teaching deep-breathing techniques to golf students and my "High-Five System" to help them cultivate a more relaxed state and present-moment awareness. When you are in the moment, you are more consciously aware of your thoughts. I wanted my students to experience the mental part of the game, showing how contrasting thoughts affect the power of the mind. Purposeful and meaningful thoughts, not negativity, will result in improved golf performance. Plus, a positive mental attitude, combined with an inner smile, would result in a happier state of mind, making you stronger and more confident.

I taught this system to golfers in individual and group lessons on the course, in the classroom and gave talks on holistic golf at country clubs and conferences. My presentation attracted the attention of other golf professionals, and went like this:

> *The High-Five System is based on living your thoughts from the higher vantage point where you live from a place which allows the feeling place of being on top of the world, where all goes well with ease and grace. It's kind of like when athletes, like NBA star Michael Jordon, make a great shot and then they jump up high, slapping hands together with another player, in a high-five motion. "Yes, that was awesome!"*
>
> *When is the last time you felt like you were on top of the world? When you were in the zone and everything went your way? Or how about that effortless golf shot you made? Or that round of golf that just made your day? When is the last time you ever felt so high? Well, this is what we're going to talk about tonight.*
>
> *I devised the High-Five System with five steps that are going to help you reach this state of mind more often, which will only require a willingness and a passion for practice on your part. I know many of you are thinking how hard it is to break an old habit. The easiest way to release an old habit is to overlay a more meaningful new habit. And that is what the first step in the High-Five*

System is about: creating a solid routine to stabilize a more purposeful foundation in your golf swing. No more scattered thoughts driving you crazy! This is a step-by-step routine that will keep you focused and in the flow.

The routine is basically mechanical with grip, stance, alignment, posture, and then clearing the mind before you swing. The last thought will be based on your individual learning, for instance, either focusing on the target, the ball, getting a feeling within your body, or a sense of rhythm. The whole process only takes about 10 to 15 seconds, though it is best done with relaxed confidence. So, your "homework" before you play your next round of golf, is to write out your routine, practice it in your mind, the living room, or outdoors. If you're not a golfer, then work on a daily routine, including scheduling in quiet time, exercise, or dance, things to do, such as work or school, fun time, or block out an hour for reading or playing a musical instrument. Being consistent is key in creating a new habit and positive motion forward in your life.

The second step in the High-Five System to stay in the present moment. How often do you race ahead in your mind or dwell on the past? Come on, give me some good examples of this! How about when you think of the putt you missed on the last tee while you're standing in the tee box of the next hole? Or, how many of you have thought about the group of players behind you and how you might be holding them up? In your daily lives, do you simmer over thoughts like, "I can't believe I made such a fool of myself at the party last night" or "I'm not good enough for this crowd." The power is always in the present moment, so allow yourself to just keep your thoughts focused on what you are doing in that moment.

If you're putting, then do your routine and put that ball in the cup! Then, you can turn to your friend and ask her what she's having for dinner tonight. The third step is to focus on exactly what you desire. You know that little voice that creeps in and starts saying, with all the false bravado." Oops, I think I will just pick up the ball so they won't think I'm so slow," or "Gosh, how did I get stuck in this group?" *or "Is she going to talk the whole round of golf?"*

(One of the biggest distractions today is *ding!* "Answer your text." *Ding!* "Answer your text." *Ding!* "Answer your text." Millions of people are demonstrating the classical conditioning of Pavlov's anticipatory response of "psychic secretion" every time that phone makes a peep.)

These types of thoughts are only distracting and draining, whether in your daily life or in your golf performance, and they are always going to be there. So, it's up to you to stay focused on what you truly want. Choose purposeful and uplifting thoughts that keep the momentum moving in your direction, such as "I love being out on the golf course with my friends," "I putt the ball right down the line and into the cup," and "I have a solid routine I can always count on."

(After the round, you can watch a movie, eat dinner, go for a walk, or answer your texts.)

The fourth step in the High-Five System is to believe in yourself. This may be hard for some people as we're now talking about your self-esteem. I know because I've been there, too. I thought I was truly a failure after I graduated from college. I only went to college to continue with sports, and then ended up with

26

a degree in psychology. I loved being an athlete, and I loved helping people . . . but I ended up working at the stock exchange. I was literally dying there because I got caught up in money, material things, prestige, and perks. I had everything I wanted, until I realized I had everything but myself. In June 1989, my life came to a screeching halt, as I had urgent surgery for Crohn's disease. After that, I changed everything and started to live my life. I changed the way I thought, the way I ate, what I did for a living, and where I lived.

My family and friends thought I was nuts to give up such a lucrative job, but I believed in myself more than anything, and I focused on my dreams and desires to become a professional athlete. You, too, have the power to change almost any situation just by deciding to do so. It only takes a thought, and the power of your choice then sets into motion a new set of waves that accommodates the desire. So, make it heartfelt and meaningful! I did, and it got me where I am today.

Start believing in yourself more than anything in the world, no matter where you're at or where you want to go in life, and no matter what anyone else says! You deserve to be happy in life and have fun on the golf course. And you truly can play the kind of golf you want, too. So, repeat after me: "I believe in myself more than anything in the world," and again!

The last step in the High-Five System is to give yourself some good, old-fashioned, tender loving care. When was the last time you pampered yourself? When was the last time you gave yourself a compliment? Did you know that when you feel good about yourself, you are stronger in body and mind? What will that do for your golf performance? Yes, it gets you to those higher

*states of mind that allow the very best to flow to you!
Great shots, lower scores, more fun, and more confidence.*

*Start using the High-Five System today! Play golf
like you were on top of the world. Love yourself and love
being out on the beautiful playing field with family and
friends. What could be better? And, finally, be thankful
for everything and everyone, appreciating all that is.*

How to Improve Your Game after Age 50

I believe that purpose and positivity can keep people strong
and active into their senior years. I wrote the article below, "How
to Improve Your Game After Age 50," about the power of the
mind, a spin-off from my High-Five System. It appeared in two
golf publications in California in the mid-1990s: *Golf News
Magazine* in Palm Springs and another in Sacramento.

*Move over, John Daley, the new old-age is
sprouting wings, and they're not on their way to
heaven! Recent studies have shown "old age" is
primarily a habit of the mind—which happens to be the
single most important ingredient to a successful golf
swing, whether you're five or 85. The secret lies in
staying physically and mentally active. As my
grandfather Robert Koontz says, "Life is for the living!
So, stay active!" He was still swinging well into his
eighties.*

*You have unlimited potential if you use your minds
correctly. For instance, how many of you are
accomplished water finders on the golf course?
Practicing ball slicers? Natural complainers? You are
using your mind perfectly; however, you are using it in*

28

a non-productive way. You can improve your golf game by dedicating yourself to new mental skills.

First, focus on exactly what you want, instead of what's wrong or what usually happens. For example, let your last thought be of the target, instead of the irresistible water. Ultimately, what you think about, you bring about. So, change the thought to exactly what you desire.

Second, stay in the present moment, instead of clutching onto the past. What happened on the last hole, happened on the last hole. It is of no value to dwell on the putt you just rimmed out. Seize the moment with complete concentration and on the here and now. Play each ball as if it were your last. Present-moment awareness never ages!

Third, give yourself some good old TLC. Allow yourself the freedom to do well, to change old and negative thought patterns, and to create a perfect golf routine that is best for you. Be patient and easier on yourself. You deserve the best, so start expecting the best!

Finally, believe in yourself, for you are the mind in action. Believing you can improve your golf performance is the first step in doing it. Hitting the ball straighter, hitting the ball farther, or just feeling comfortable playing golf with your family or friends is just a thought away. So, trust yourself, know it, and do it! By becoming aware of what you are thinking, and by practicing the positive and useful portions of these thoughts, you will bring dynamic results to your golf game, as well as in your daily life.

In the 49-and-over gang, the great Chicago Cubs pitcher, Satchel Paige, put it this way: "How old would

> *you be if you didn't know how old you are?" Old age is*
> *the product of the mind, and the mind can be changed.*
> *Playing golf with youthful verve is now the "way to go."*

My Mission

As I grew and developed as a golf professional, I continued
to incorporate what I was learning in my spiritual journey into my
golf teachings. My mission statement was "To be the best I could
be in body, mind, and spirit, and to share this with others." Golf
was my vehicle. All my golf students improved their golf game
by listening, integrating, and demonstrating my holistic approach
to their golf performance and then implementing these strategies
on the golf course. Helping and watching them succeed filled me
with joy and a sense of accomplishment.

A major coupe was receiving an invitation to speak at the Fall
Health Classic in October 1992, a four-day workshop at the Westin
Mission Hills Resort in Palm Springs. I presented a four-part
series on my innovative approach to golf performance and
engaged the audience in the inner game of golf with relaxation
exercises to reclaim their inner power, anchoring it with a good
routine and combining it all with simple golf fundamentals.
Attendees learned strategies to allow them to be their best in
body, mind, and spirit in their golf game, and in their personal
lives as well. I also introduced my golf meditation tape, "Utilize
Divine Power and Swing Right into Action!" Here's a snippet:

> *You are about to take a journey like none other*
> *before. A creative process filled with an awareness about*
> *your golf game, with exciting new choices, and a new*
> *way of thinking about your golf swing and yourself.*
>
> *This tape was created to help you utilize Divine*
> *power to discover your own special golf swing and to*
> *guide you to your true self. What is Divine power? A*

power which is ever present running in, through and around you. It is mind in action. By using this power, you can bring dynamic results to your golf game and you can transform your life! Believe you can do anything! Anything and everything you have always wanted to do; whether hitting the ball straight, hitting farther, or just feeling comfortable playing golf with your family or friends. Being happier about your golf performance is just a thought away.

So, open your mind and follow your heart, and come with me on this adventure into an exciting and refreshingly new golf domain! The Divine power is within you.

The golf meditation tape and the four-day workshop were well received, and I fit right in with the theme of the Fall Health Classic, which focused on the fields of holistic and preventive health, the environment, and macrobiotics.

I shared the speaking agenda with Dr. Benjamin Spock, a renowned pediatrician whose book, *Dr. Spock's Baby and Child Care* (New York: Pocket Books), is one of the best sellers of all time and currently in its ninth edition; Dr. Saul Miller, a noted sports psychologist and author; Cesar Chavez, founder and president of the United Farm Workers of America; and Michio Kushi, best-selling author and founder of macrobiotics. Kushi's presentation motivated me to learn more about a macrobiotic diet and integrate it into my healthy lifestyle.

The week was buzzing with health and wellness, and when I wasn't speaking, I was listening to other leading experts. I was attracted to the macrobiotics sessions, as this new way of eating was proved to prevent disease and maintain good health. After the diseased sections in my gut were removed during abdominal surgery, I needed a strategy to stay healthy. Macrobiotics seemed to be the ideal solution. I even had a personal consultation with Dr. Martha Clayton Cottrell, a pioneer in holistic medicine and one of the conference speakers who specializes in women's health, suppressed immunity, and disease prevention. We discussed meal planning for my Crohn's disease. I was on my way to a healthier eating lifestyle.

CHAPTER 4

NOURISH THE BODY
TO NOURISH THE SPIRIT

When I moved to California to launch my golf career in 1989, I vowed to adhere to a healthy diet to alleviate symptoms or cure myself of long-term diseases. As in all things in life, attitude is everything. I was determined to improve my health from the inside out. I became increasingly aware of the different symptoms in my body after eating certain foods.

I constantly asked myself, "How is this food serving me?" and "Is it nourishing and sustaining or heavy, blocking, and depleting?" I realized it was up to me to change my eating habits before I suffered physical maladies and reached another critical situation. For instance, I was told early on to eliminate white flour and white foods (bread, rice, pasta, potatoes) from my diet to help alleviate the inflammation in my intestines. I did the best I could; however, at that time, other viable food options were not as recognized or available as they are today. Simply substituting cow milk with rice milk would have been easy, but I was not educated or aware of this option, among others. Plus, I was working in a stressful environment, with fast foods and fast eating, trapped in an unhealthy cycle.

At the Fall Health Classic in 1992, I heard Michio Kushi speak about a diet called macrobiotics, which literally translates to "broad life" or "long life." Macrobiotics encompasses a more complete and whole way of choosing, preparing, and eating whole foods. I committed to this healthy-eating lifestyle and found the only macrobiotic center on the west coast in Oroville, a small town just north of Sacramento. There, I met Cornelia and Herman Aihaira, a Japanese couple who were pioneers in macrobiotic cuisine and health programs. They wrote the best-selling book, *Natural Healing from Head to Toe: A Comprehensive A to Z Guide to Treating Health Problems Using Whole Foods, Medicinal Preparations & Massage* (Garden City, NY: Avery, 1993). I took several of their hands-on macro classes, staying on-site at their center, the Vega Institute, for a couple of weeks at a time to absorb and feel the full effects of changing from one way of eating to another.

At times, I felt flu-like symptoms, and then there were the sugar cravings, which were promptly extinguished with chewing on a piece of Kombu seaweed. Unfortunately, in the first program, I learned this piece of information later in the day. Earlier at lunchtime, I sneaked off in my car to the nearest gas station and wolfed down a chocolate peanut bar. It helped for only a half-hour or so, and then the sugar cravings returned. "I guess I'm walking through the door on this one," I said aloud, as I remembered the promise I had made in the Mayo Clinic Chapel. I was determined to live a more purposeful life, including intentionally making healthy food choices.

During the first workshop, I shared a small dorm room with a woman who was being treated for cancer. There were two single beds, with a small shared dresser and one nightstand. The community bathrooms and showers were down the hall, along with a dry sauna room and bathtub room for salt soaks each night. There was a rotating schedule for all the participants in the dorm, usually about a dozen, so we were all able to follow the macro protocol of releasing toxins from the body through a salt soak, then a dry sauna visit, followed by a cold shower to alkalize the blood and other body fluids. Done daily, this kept the assimilation process in the body moving, like a pool filter, allowing fluids to be purified and oxygenated.

This reminded me of reading about actress Katherine Hepburn's life story and how she would emerge from the Long Island Sound where she lived, tiptoeing across ice and snow after a short daily swim in the winter months. Apparently, she had repeated this plunging ritual since she was a child. Obviously, Hepburn instinctively knew this was a healthy practice for her.

Water is life. It is the creative, connective tissue of all life. We may not realize how true this is until we think about how we live, eat, and move through our day and plan our towns, communities, and cities. At birth you are 96 percent water and at death about 70 percent water. Your bones, 25 percent water. Your brain is 85 percent water! We're more alike than we think.

Water must also move; it must breathe, and it must be free of toxic substances or it cannot function for life. We are only alive as much as our waters are alive. Masaru Emoto, author of *Messages from Water and the Universe* (New York: Hay House, 2010), takes this a step further with his discovery that water holds vibrational energies and that these subtle energies can be altered by our negative or positive thoughts, intentions, and even our prayers.

At the institute the next morning, we would rise before dawn to walk barefoot on the lawn, which stimulated the body, especially the kidneys. Then, we came in for morning tea and talked with the Aiharas. We all sat on pillows on the floor around a long wooden table and listened to the Aiharas review the day's menu and our individual roles in preparing the foods for the day. I was learning a new slow, serene, and spiritual way to approach foods, unlike the frenzied pace of a corporate woman in a corporate world. This extensive technique of preparing natural foods would influence me for the rest of my life.

Whole Foods = Whole Health

Macrobiotics promotes homeostasis in the body, a place where balance and stability thrive. It is important to note macrobiotics is not a cure, yet it allows the perfect container for the body to right itself. In the Western World, it is typical to call chronic fatigue or an immune deficiency a "virus." When you stay in balance with your food and thought choices, your body builds a natural immune system and adapts more easily to change. Whole foods lead to whole health. This was originally called the Science of Foods for Health and Happiness by Dr. Sagen Ishizuka, founder of Japanese Medicine and Diet, who was one of the first to investigate the nutritional value of whole grains. It was later adopted in the early 1900s by George Osawa, founder of present-day macrobiotics.

Herman Aihara studied extensively with George Ohsawa, the founder of the macrobiotic diet and philosophy, from 1941. He wrote several macrobiotic books and became the president and founder of the George Ohsawa Macrobiotics Foundation (GOMF) in San Francisco in 1970. He moved GOMF to Oroville, California, in 1974. Aihara was continually active in research, study, writing, translating, lecturing, and giving personal consultations in the United States and abroad until his death in February 1998. Cornelia continued the macrobiotic school until her death in 2006.

After studying with the Aiharas, I returned to Palm Springs to continue my learning curve. Shortly thereafter, I met Eli, a strikingly handsome man, at the Religious Science Church. In conversation, he confided that he was bolstering his immune system with a balanced macrobiotics diet while his cousin was successfully healing from cancer with the same diet. He impressed me with his vast knowledge and creativity, and we struck up an instant friendship.

Eli was tall with jet-black hair, hazel eyes, an engaging smile, and a thin, well-toned physique, and he loved the performing arts. We shared our love of song in a voice class together, along with our knowledge of macrobiotics. To meet someone who was already living the macrobiotic lifestyle was a tremendous advantage for my own healing process with Crohn's disease and endometriosis.

Eli single-handedly created a macrobiotic community in Palm Springs and was instrumental in local health food stores ordering and carrying essential macrobiotic staple foods. His MacroMeals program, comparable to the Meals on Wheels concept, targeted mostly wealthy people who were healing in some capacity. I quickly became his assistant and did some of the prep work, such as washing and cutting vegetables for the main dishes and preparing a big pot of short-grain brown rice, a staple in macrobiotic cooking, along with a big pot of miso soup.

I learned many recipes from Eli, and just cooking with him helped me to embrace this new harmonious way of eating. Selecting land and sea vegetables with the seasons and weather; food combining; getting used to a diet without sugar, caffeine, dairy, and processed meats; and substituting those with foods that were unrefined, whole, and natural, in addition to taking the time to locate and purchase locally grown foods, were all challenging changes.

The most notable shift was the balance between yin and yang, a physical interpretation of the ancient Chinese meta-physical system of natural balance, similar to the concept of acid and alkaline in the body. Sodium and potassium are the primary antagonistic and complementary elements in food. They most strongly determine its character, or "yin–yang" quality. The human body runs more efficiently with a slightly higher alkaline level, so adding plenty of greens, seaweed, and miso are musts. We also followed Aihara's directive to "chew your liquid, drink your food." Chewing food 75 to 100 times could get quite boring . . . and disgusting. We did the best we could and then swallowed.

Getting Creative in the Kitchen

We had fun in Eli's lively kitchen. There was always music playing while we created healthy dishes and individual dinner plates. Eli and I would each grab a wooden spoon, pretending they were microphones, and start singing show tunes or Barbra Streisand songs. After we finished cooking, we would cover the plates, review the address list, and Eli would be on his way to deliver the happy food. The delivery part only lasted a week or so before Eli devised a schedule of dates and times for people to come and pick up their own MacroMeals, as it was a bit much to cook *and* deliver.

Thanksgiving was a most memorable celebration and the dietary highlight of the year. Eli hosted quite a food extravaganza that was a bit different than a traditional Thanksgiving. Over 40 people attended his inaugural event. A Kabocha squash substituted for a roast turkey and made to look like the great America bird with purple kale plumes coming out the back. (Kabocha is an Asian variety of winter squash, and in some cultures, it is revered as an aphrodisiac.) For mashed potatoes, we simply cooked and combined cauliflower and millet and whipped it up like "real" mashed potatoes. Gravy? Simmered shiitake mushrooms, onions, Tamari soy sauce, and wild kuzu root starch for thickening, with lots of pepper. And my favorite recipe for steamed green wraps, which are like stuffed cabbage rolls, was mustard greens and kale with sauerkraut and sesame seeds on top, all rolled up in a large collard green leaf. Kukicha tea, roasted twigs, and stems from select tea bushes, was the beverage of choice (not alcohol), and complemented the sweet squash pie, which is delicious and surpassed the bland taste of pumpkin pie. No wonder I ate dessert first! The best part of the holiday dinner was Eli and I breaking out into the polka while singing "Shall We Dance" from the musical *The King and I.*

Beyond Eli's healthful cooking classes, I practiced balancing acid/alkaline levels of the body and how to regulate them with food to cultivate good health instead of symptoms of disease. Within my own constitution, I started eating smaller portions five to six times daily, thereby increasing my metabolism and reducing stress on my digestive tract. I allowed my appetite to rule and control my portions. I enjoyed a variety of foods at each meal, sometimes rebuffing traditional macro-breakfast fare for roasted chicken.

It reminded me of when I was having some toxic release symptoms while at the Vega Institute (Macro Center). Herman Aihara saw me doubled over with a stomachache and said, "On one hand, you are in some discomfort, which does not feel good, though, on the other hand, it is showing you a more positive aspect of your body and how it deals with release. The contrast will set you free." On a deeper level, there is an overall pearl of wisdom here that Aihara used to call "happy even when sick": "Such is the key to happiness and the state of well-being, where the little compass of yin and yang teaches the art of adaptability."

Little by little, within a year, I accomplished my goal of no longer being afflicted with Crohn's disease, which, in Science of Mind, is called a demonstration. Giving thanks to this manifestation completed the circle of the treatment. Some may call this a miracle, yet it is a product of mastering the mind. I followed this holistic lifestyle to a tee for a couple of years, I lost weight and felt healthier and lighter instead of so dense with a distended belly. Most of all, I felt clean from the inside out. I had indeed reversed the process from my earlier days with a more complete healthy lifestyle. The macro lifestyle was excellent as a *healing* diet for me in those beginning years.

As I continued to evolve in my life, I utilized the macrobiotic lifestyle and methods as a beneficial foundation, and I made decisions moment by moment as to what my body wanted, and I obliged gracefully, such as enjoying fish, fowl, and even some desserts, like organic chocolate. I could always tell when I moved away from mindful eating habits, as my body gave me signals, such as bloating, being anxious, or being angry. I took note, usually by pausing, breathing, returning to a place of awareness, and then making any necessary adjustments.

The simplest and quickest way to tap into your own body is to just sit or stand still for a few moments, following your breath, with eyes closed. Take deep breaths from your belly. Just tune into your body and listen. Your body will give you some signals if anything is happening, and you will notice and feel it. Make some mental notes, adjust your foods, and create the changes that will lead you on the path to better health. It just takes a willingness to make the change, to fill your body temple with more love, and soon you will simply return to this natural way of living and enjoy a sense of well-being and boundless energy.

Baring My Enthusiasm

I have a fun and adventurous spirit, so I like to mix things up when I'm doing anything, even cooking. I attributed my heightened vitality to a more natural way of living. For example, I find fun in the simplest of tasks, even in the kitchen. I slip on dance shoes or high heels, or I wear an apron. Yes, only an apron. I am sure my zany gramma, Claire Elsie Mae, who now dances in heaven, did this once or twice in her lifetime. Cooking naked is a blast. I recommend that everyone try it at least once, if just for the sheer pleasure of the experience.

One hot summer day, I had just finished a couple of golf lessons. I went home, stripped off my clothes, dropping them on the ground just before diving into my swimming pool at my house in Palm Springs. The water felt so refreshing and soothing. While floating on a long raft, I thought about preparing an exotic lunch meal—well, as exotic as you can get for macrobiotics. I was dreaming of getting my fingers in sweet, warm, sticky rice and rolling asparagus tips in toasted seaweed sheets to make nori roll-ups. That was enough to get me out of the pool and into the kitchen.

Dripping wet, I put on my grandmother's half apron with the small strawberry print. I pulled my hair up with a comb, and then ran to the closet in my bedroom and grabbed my red, yellow, and blue psychedelic pumps. I slipped them on and tiptoed back down the hallway like I was walking the catwalk. Hips first, swaying from side to side, singing "I'm too sexy for my cat!" I strutted back into the kitchen where I began concocting my exotic meal, pausing to nibble and savor on a piece of Tanzania dark chocolate bar.

When I heard the low whistle of sweet rice simmering and asparagus steaming, I screamed with delight and ran over to the CD player to pop in *Barry White's Greatest Hits*. Immediately, I moved and undulated to the rhythms of seduction in "Your Sweetness Is My Weakness." Oh, yeah, baby! I peeled sweet potatoes and, in a perfect lilting action, tossed their skins into the sink and then washed their naked bodies under the faucet. I lined them up on the cutting board and split and quartered them with a knife. Then, I tossed them into a pot of boiling water and watched them tumble from rawness into softness. I tapped two steel lids together, as if marching in a band with crashing symbols, and then strained out the water from the pot and began my brew of sweet potato pudding. I danced as I added a couple of teaspoons of agar flakes (*cha-cha-cha*), a pinch of salt (*cha-cha-cha*), and then I mixed and turned (*cha-cha-cha*), heated (*cha-cha-cha*), and cooled (*cha-cha-cha*).

I continued to conduct the symphony of sensual delight. The soft melodic hum of my voice escalated to the syncopation of the sexy songs, and I glided across the floor in anticipation of this exotic feast. I turned off the burners in time with the beat and picked up a spatula to test the pudding. I twirled and spun, with my apron flying. Just as I prepared for a taste, I let out a scream.

There, through the back window, was the pool guy watching me with unbridled curiosity. I screamed again, and he screamed back! I ran to the window (as best as I could in my high heels) and snatched the curtains closed in a sweeping motion. I heard his deep laughter as he continued vacuuming the pool floor. I should have told him to put a 10-dollar bill in the slot and the curtain would open for another show. Instead, I grabbed the sweet potato pudding, dipped my spatula into its soothing sauce, and, ever so slowly, savored the flavor.

Sometimes, I would forgo music from the CD player and rely solely on the cooking preparation itself to fill the air with symphonic delights, such as the sizzle of onions in olive oil, the snap of the knife cutting through the potatoes, the smooth unveiling of apple skins, the fragrance of freshly roasted chicken, a spoonful of yellow curry sauce passing through my lips to my tongue, the anticipation of chocolate damiana sauce dripping down asparagus, the rumble and bubble of lentil stew, the clatter and chatter of pot lids, and dipping spoons and flipping spatulas.

Healthy foods became my passion, and I carried my healthy-eating habits into the golf arena and lectured students on making their bodies stronger and more vibrant. When you are in a state of love, joy, and appreciation, you create an energetic field around you that allows more of the good stuff to flow your way. That high vibration ends up in the food you prepare and eat, the people you encounter, and how you present yourself in the world, whether a golfer or a working woman.

Some would say this is good luck, but I believe it is an art that requires cultivating, like a well-tended garden. Watch what happens if you leave your garden without water, compost, or fertilizer, and do not weed for a while. Conversely, watch what happens when you give more loving attention to your garden by watering daily, weeding, pruning, singing, and watching it grow. It becomes fortified, nourished, strong, and bountiful. This is how our minds and bodies will react to constant tending. Nourish the body to nourish the spirit!

CHAPTER 5

MY SPIRITUAL AWAKENING

From 1989 to July 1998, I had transformed my life, not only as a career woman in golf, but physically and spiritually as well. I had been reared a devout Catholic to sit, stand, kneel, and recite the rosary. When it came time for Communion, I always dreaded the phrase "The Body of Christ," recited in a deep melodic voice by the priest. Then, he would plop the wafer on my tongue with his thumb and index finger. From there, the wafer bobbed and stuck to the roof of my mouth like a Band-Aid. I'd walk back to my pew making loud sucking noises. Then, I'd sit and stare at the crucifix—the man with the thorn hat still bleeding on his face and hands and feet.

When I arrived in Palm Springs, I had no intention of attending services every Sunday, but my strict Catholic upbringing forced me to go to church somewhat regularly. Eventually, I meandered into a Religious Science Church one Sunday morning. Everyone was so happy and festive. The songs were joyous and full of life. The message focused on co-creating with God, not pain and suffering. I looked over my shoulder feeling somewhat fearful. I swore lightning would strike any moment because I was having so much fun in church.

In 1990, when Dr. Tom Costa, minister of the Religious Science Church, found out I was a golf professional, he handed me a book titled *Golf in the Kingdom* by Michael Murphy (New

York: Viking, 1972). It was the first book I had ever read about golf, and my first real connection with the game and its truest values, especially the mystical realm. Murphy's interpretation of golf as an "inner body sport" was astounding. He wrote: "From the stillness arises the answers in a most subtle and profound way, exploring the journey in a round of golf, and even more so about the journey in life, golf was the place for transformation to unfold" I resonated with the warmth of his words, and read and reread the chapters, especially the second half of the book, expanding more into this spiritual aspect of golf and the powers of the unseen. It coincided with the metaphysical teachings of the Science of Mind and, later, with my own journey to India.

Golf on the Moon

Murphy also talked about the future of golf, and golf on the moon. Could there be a Fra Mauro Country Club for the elite? In 1971, Fra Mauro was the intended landing site of the ill-fated Apollo 13 mission and the eventual landing site on the moon of Apollo 14. Upon landing, astronaut Alan Shepard placed both feet firmly on the moon surface and quietly unfolded a long aluminum/Teflon instrument—a makeshift 6-iron golf club he had concealed in his spacesuit! He placed a golf ball on the moon dust links and proceeded to hit the infamous golf shot on the moon. The ball sailing for miles and miles and miles was his "golf-god" mantra. Aided with one-sixth gravity, it never came down . . . or is that the one that eventually landed on my head?

Who knows? One thing was for sure: As a dominant visual learner, I practiced the visualization of the ball's path after reading about Murphy's "actual streamers of energy" that are produced and emanate from the golfer to the target, streamers that the golf ball traveled. I found great success in this with shots where I could not see the actual flagstick on the green, which subtly forced me to visualize it in my mind. It also was beneficial to my short game, especially putting and chipping, where I could easily lay an illumined track. I remember this approach during my nighttime range practice, when all was dark, while using my driver to smack balls effortlessly over the oleander bushes, a mere 250 yards away.

I began taking weekly Science of Mind classes at this church, using the teachings of Ernest Holmes, the founder of the worldwide Religious Science movement. He wrote the classic guide on how people could master their own lives by utilizing the subtle powers of the mind and distilled basic truths of the enlightened beings into basic principles. I studied these dynamic principles for two years by doing in-depth personal growth assignments. As an example, I would answer questions from a reading assignment in the Science of Mind textbook. After that, I would write a personal "treatment" from that assignment to anchor myself in the lesson.

A treatment is a definite conscious idea or intention set in motion in the subjective world, based in pure love, knowing that creative spirit is always at work. It is a five-step process that always begins with silence and meditation:

1. Recognize God.
2. Unification by becoming one with God.
3. Realization, the purpose of the treatment.
4. Thanksgiving.
5. Release into the Universe, knowing in the mind of God it is already done.

Over the course of the first year, I wrote over a dozen treatments for myself on the topics of joy, peace, balance, and relationships (especially with myself): "I discover God's Divine order that is always in order, and I center upon this truth. I am in harmony with everyone and everything through the presence and power of God in me." And then, the "I am" treatment, which is the realization that "I am God, the center of all creation I dwell. I am goodness, truth, beauty, peace, harmony, and joy. I am the creative principle. I am power, the source of all strength. I am still and know that I am." I admit I had to move beyond parts of my old belief system to embrace this ideology. I have a bachelor's degree in psychology, which cost my dad tens of thousands of dollars for my college education.

One of the basic principles I studied is what you place in your subconscious mind must appear as your experience. Buddha said it like this: "The mind is everything. What you think, you become." Said another way, "You reap what you sow." In the *Holy Bible*, "As a man thinketh in his heart, so is he." (Proverbs 23:7). The law of personal limits says you cannot go beyond your self-accepted image. Said another way, you cannot go beyond what you believe or are aware of. Jesus simply said, "It is done unto you as you believe." (Matthew 9:29).

I applied these two laws faithfully and turned entirely away from an "incurable" diagnosis of inflammatory bowel condition called Crohn's disease. If I believed I had it, I could not overcome it. The word *incurable* means that a condition cannot be cured by outer methods and that we must go within to affect the healing," per author Louise L. Hay in her book *You Can Heal Your Life* (Carlsbad, CA: Hay House, 1984). The healing revelation became conscious, allowing the eternal truth that my Divine birthright is health and happiness. I did not will it to happen but merely opened a path by which it may happen, removing doubt and fear, replacing it with love and goodness. I conceived this natural law of a healthy well-being as already accomplished. This is expanded consciousness, letting the light shine in as the presence of spirit. "The tongue of the wise is health," according to Proverbs 12:18.

During this time, I also realized the full meaning of the word choice. I had the right to choose what I wanted to experience. I certainly did not want to physically suffer any longer, so I chose the law of life and creative power, taking the steps necessary to change my condition. I participated in the "You Can Heal Your Life" intensive workshop offered at the Religious Science Church, where self-acceptance, unconditional love, and forgiveness of past conditioning were key in moving forward in my healing. In spring 1992, I was inspired to create a golf meditation tape, *Utilize Divine Power and Swing into Right Action*, based on the works of Louise Hay, which I presented at the Fall Health Classic and spoke of in the last chapter.

In every moment of every day, I was choosing my life. The law of cause and effect is put into motion here. One is the inside and the other is the outside of the same thing. A healthy mind, a healthy body. I began to deliberately choose more purposeful thoughts that produced more positive outcomes in all aspects of my daily life.

Dan Millman, a recognized gymnastics coach, Olympic trainer, best-selling author, and lecturer on personal development, later expressed this beautifully in his 1995 book, *The Laws of Spirit: A Tale of Transformation* (Tiburon, CA, and Novato, CA: H J Kramer in a joint venture with New World Library). Millman wrote, "We are both burdened and blessed by the great responsibility of free will—the power of choice. Our future is determined, in large part, by the choices we make now. We cannot always control our circumstances, but we can and do choose our response to whatever arises. Reclaiming the power of choice, we find the courage to live fully in the world." His book, *Way of the Peaceful Warrior* (Tiburon, CA, and Novato, CA: H J Kramer in a joint venture with New World Library, 1980), a personal favorite, also helped with the inner questions of my mind.

I always had been told what to do by an authoritative, or seemingly authoritative voice, usually male, and sometimes perceived as the "Voice of God." Up to this point, this persuasive—and sometimes scary—God lived outside of me and resided somewhere in the sky. Science of Mind taught me that I am surrounded by an Infinite Intelligence, which I can choose to tap into at any time, by thinking the thought, idea, or concept and then moving toward that thing. It is infinite and impersonal. Dr. Costa always said, "There is no spot where God is not!" And from the *Holy Bible*, "Be not conformed to this world, but be transformed by the renewing of your mind." (Romans 12:2).

I was a practitioner, becoming totally immersed and demonstrating some of the principles of Science of Mind. I was well on my way to becoming a Religious Science minister when I put on the brakes. "I'm too young to become a minister!"

Inner Truths

Even though this "academic verbiage" was feeding my mind and body, I felt there had to be something more to the action and reaction game. I continued to apply some of the laws and principles into my golf repertoire, which helped me integrate all I was learning intellectually. I had already been teaching the mental part of the game to enhance the golfer's personal performance. Now, I would introduce the body, mind, and spirit approach, treating the whole person instead of concentrating on golfing mechanics. In 1994, I even gave a speech to my colleagues at an LPGA Golf School in Reno, Nevada, titled "The Inner Truth about Golf," which magnified this trinity. I had the honor of being one of three golf professionals selected to speak at the LPGA Golf School. I was already teaching the principles of holistic golf at a time when people were unaware of the connection among body, mind, and spirit in the golf industry. At that time, golf performance was believed to be 90 percent mechanics and 10 percent mind.

I walked on stage to present to about 50 colleagues and began:

I respect and appreciate each one of you because we are all so unique, and each one of us brings her own experience to the table, her own integral part to this group. So, with an open heart and an open mind, I will expose myself to you. The title of my mission statement is 'The inner truth about golf and about you.' Now, I'm going to ask everybody to breathe with me. Take a breath in for six counts, hold it for six counts, and blow it out for six counts. If everyone would just breathe in 1, 2, 3, 4, 5, 6. Hold it 1, 2, 3, 4, 5, 6. Blow it out 1, 2, 3, 4, 5, 6. I don't know about all of you, but I'm feeling much more grounded.

I am an eternal student of life and love. My vision is to be the very best I can be in body, mind, and soul. As an LPGA teaching professional, I cultivate this trinity into each individual lesson I give into every individual who comes to me.

Most of you are aware of the body and the mind; you practice this daily, whether in your personal life or your golf game. But you can only move the furniture around so many times. Same stuff, different arrangement. Until you become aware of and connect with the soul, the very heart of your being, you will be limited to the power of your mind . . . which becomes tiresome and boring. When you embody the most essential element of your true existence, the soul, the possibilities become endless and the process becomes an act of love. Let's all breathe again."

Glancing around the room, I could see many of the attendees were completely engaged in my presentation, whether they understood it or not. They were still practicing the breathing exercise. I smiled to myself, breathing in sync with them, and continued:

Now, here are my three strategies:

With the first strategy, you must look deeply into your own eyes to reveal your truest desires. The eyes are the windows to the soul. You need a mirror for this exercise. In a dimly lit room, gaze into the mirror while listening to Bette Midler's "Wind Beneath My Wings." Then, notice what happens.

I instructed the attendees to notice their mouths. Cultivating a mental attitude with an inner smile for happiness is a state of mind. Smile from the heart, and it will be a genuine reflection of their state of joy. Were their lips pursed with tension or relaxed in peaceful contentment? Are they hiding behind a big fake smile, only to be filled with sorrow? I remember practicing this physical smile, with the corners of my mouth curving slightly up instead of slightly down. I worked new cheek muscles I did not know I had. Now it feels quite natural for me to have this inner smile that reflects on my physical smile. Practicing this daily will make you stronger, live longer, and play golf better. Imagine playing a round of golf for the sheer joy of being out in nature with other friends, not preoccupied with the score or competing. "Happy to be happy," I always say.

A special note about mirror work: The mirror often symbolizes a woman's vanity, although many cultures believe the mirror represents the human heart and the Goddess in the Goddess religion. In my own work, the mirror has been invaluable in showing my true reflection of self, especially from the emotional plane, and where I am in any moment. I remember a simple exercise I did from the works of Louise Hay in her book, *You Can Heal Your Life*. I had to look in the mirror and say, "I love you."

Sounds simple, right? I invite you to try it for yourself. I found the exercise quite challenging at the time. It took several attempts of creeping up to my dresser mirror before I could gaze into my own eyes and say those magical words. When I finally did, tears were streaming down my cheeks.

I integrated mirror work into my golf profession as head coach of the College of the Desert Women's Golf Team, using the strategy outlined earlier, where I had each woman look in a handheld mirror while I played the "Wind Beneath My Wings." Many women cried, others stared blankly, yet all learned something that day. They each realized they were their own best friend and in control of their lives and their golf games. By following the body–mind–soul approach to golf, the team won a state championship and was undefeated both years when I was head coach. I also was honored with the Coach of the Year award.

> *The second strategy calls for taking more quiet time to connect with the Eternal Source of your being, allowing the 'how' and the 'why' to present itself to you. Personally, I like to hike in the mountains, sit under the night sky, or listen to the birds in the early morning sun. You may have some favorites of your own, such as hitting golf balls in the morning or the evening, taking a walk, or just sitting in your room.*
>
> *The third strategy is to embrace this Divine guidance with all your heart and facilitate this truth with genuine love and sincerity.*

Then, Lynn Marriott, one of the facilitators at the LPGA School, said, "I sense that your mission is to treat the whole human being, the whole deal, and golf is the vehicle. It's not just this person doing golf; it's this human being doing golf, and all those issues and all the things that make up a human being are represented in their golf. It comes out in their golf. Golf is not separate from the human being. That's what I hear coming through Kathleen's stuff, similar to professional golfer and coach Harvey Penick's simple and direct teachings in his *Little Red Golf Book* (New York, NY: Simon & Schuster 2012, 1992).

I finished my speech talking about the perfect golf model:

> *It's the model that one of the facilitators had put up on the chalkboard from the LPGA school showing golf schools, club fitting, and swing mechanics. I have these three parts in my model, but I added something to bond it all together, and that is soul, which comes from the heart."*
>
> *Golf, from my perspective, may be 90 percent mind and 10 percent mechanics, but it's 100 hundred percent soul! I sat down after this courageous unveiling, and let out a big exhale of relief, knowing I had just shared something completely different in the golf teaching arena.*

I continued my golf instruction using the holistic model for years, including being a contributing writer to local magazines and guest speakers at various events.

Revving Up with Reverend Ann

I continued my holistic quest when I entered the Unity Church in Palm Springs to experience the magic and vivaciousness of Reverend Dr. Ann Bodenhamer Martin, a remarkable woman who regaled worshippers in her little white church in the desert with tales of her wild adventures. Filled with wisdom and encouragement, she was well received, well loved, and touched everyone with her powerful sermons and message of love. Long after her services ended, she would hug every person at the door before they left.

Dr. Martin, or "Dr. Ann" as I called her, was an attractive former model with strawberry blonde hair and a quiet humor that had the churchgoers rolling in the pews. Her presence was authentic and passively bold, and her message from the pulpit was gleaned from a pioneering and adventurous life. Her creative expression was endless throughout her teaching, not only in the structured metaphysical principles of Unity but also in her meditations and special class projects. Indeed, Dr. Ann had a colorful past. In the 1950s, she was known as "Jacqueline the Kitten" and was married to Ken Elliott, a well-known Louisiana radio personality called "Jack the Cat." They conceived, produced, and hosted all sorts of radio and TV shows, including *New Orleans Bandstand* and *Hospitality House*, which were broadcast live from their own home.

Around 1960, Dr. Ann was credited with introducing *The Ann Elliott Show*, a lighthearted morning TV show that mixed feature stories, news, and weather. The show format is very common today. Perhaps her most notable, but forgotten, accomplishment was being the first filly to ever "call the horse races." In a highly competitive profession dominated by exclusively male voices, "Ann Elliott" was hired as the voice of Jefferson Downs outside New Orleans for four years in the early 1960s. She even stumped the panelists on *What's My Line?* a popular prime-time TV show hosted by John Daly, where celebrities tried to guess the off-beat occupations of the show's contestants.

Can you begin to imagine how she spoke from the pulpit? I was always thoroughly engaged in whatever Dr. Ann had to say, especially in her personal guidance to me on my spiritual journey. She was one of the first people to help me in applying the body, mind, and spirit approach to my golf career, and suggested that I call myself the "Golf Minister" in a golf column in a local magazine. I wrote articles, but I never embraced the minister concept. She also recommended that I obtain an 800-GOLF number.

What I had learned most from Unity Church of Palm Springs, and especially Dr. Ann, was compassion and love. In these two years, I learned to love myself fully and to share this love with others. I also learned that "God" is a part of me, not some booming voice in the sky. Dr. Ann performed a holy union or symbolic marriage ceremony, where we united our higher/ cosmic self to our lower/earth self. Each one of us has a higher self, a part of us that is stronger, clearer, and more loving. This essential part of us is for our normal everyday use, but most of us only use it in emergencies, turning to it as last resort.

During this ceremony, I made personal sacred vows of fidelity to my "super mind." Most notably, I vowed to live each day as it comes, release the past, and allow the future to unfold from the highest vantage point; to pledge myself to silence for some part of the day; to retire to the my most high secret place, my dimension of grace, and glory; to accept renewal of body, mind, and spirit; and to accept a life of conscious awareness of the high watch.

This small, but powerful, ceremony helped me feel the availability and connection with my higher self and, like any rite of passage, allowed that sense of full integration to take over, achieving a sense of spiritual oneness.

Becoming whole, becoming "one with the one." I still have the double gold wedding band that was blessed at this ceremony, and it constantly reminds me of my commitment to move from the higher vantage point.

Dr. Ann also taught me the value of "I am worth it!" I participated in her 10-week prosperity class and learned how to expand my consciousness in all aspects of my life, from keeping my office neat and organized to making the bed to picking flowers and writing "thank you" on my checks to pay the bills, or, as she had stated, "my blessings." I learned to tithe, in other words, planting one-tenth of my money crop to assure my next crop, although I could also tithe my talents, skills, and energies into the "cosmic bank."

I opted to give some golf talks and clinics for free to fulfill this investment. Abundance and unlimited supply became my new state of mind. I leased a new white Mazda Miata convertible and bought a beautiful home in Palm Springs, complete with a swimming pool, desert garden, and guesthouse. With renewed faith, strength, and love, I filled my days with purposeful living, including prayer, meditation, expression through movement, such as dance, speaking, proper nutrition, adopting a healing diet of macrobiotics, nature hikes, and giving to all people. I practiced metaphysics and the teaching of Unity for another two years before Dr. Ann asked me to be a lay minister. I was delighted, but I held this position for only one month. Another great calling propelled me to yet another church.

I learned about another female minister, who was creating The Capitol Religious Science Church of Sacramento, California, in a "Religious Science" news bulletin. I moved to Sacramento during the summer months, as temperatures in the desert were consistently over 100 degrees, making it unbearable to teach and play golf. After a brief interview with this minister, I was invited to facilitate the meditations during the weekly Sunday service.

I loved creating guided meditations and selected the perfect background music for each one. A couple of favorites were "The River of Life," with Whitney Houston's "One Moment in Time," and "A Candle My Friend," accompanied by live piano music, "You'll Never Walk Alone." They were memorable experiences for all, which reached the audience at the core of their hearts. Perhaps the love of Dr. Ann had seeped into my being to be shared and amplified.

When I left the Unity Church, Dr. Ann's parting words to me were "You're in the gate, the flag is up, and you're off! Now get out there and express yourself. You're walking in the light, honey. Scatter your Christ blessings everywhere. You give me cosmic shivers! Your love and your timing are always in tune with the infinite. Honest. I love you, baby girl."

Dr. Ann and I continued our friendship via phone calls and letters. Occasionally, I was compelled to reach out to her to share a special thought or experience, like the time I was enjoying the night sky in Palm Springs. Suddenly, I observed flashing circular lights in the distance. I was certain it was a visit from light beings from the other side, wherever the other side was. I immediately called Dr. Ann to tell her to look up at the sky near the church and reel in this amazing phenomenon. At the next Sunday service, she informed me the circling light beams, otherwise known as "spotlights" here on Earth, were calling attention to a new car dealership in town. Later, she wrote a letter telling me this was one of her fondest moments of our relationship. "Keep looking toward the light, honey!" Humility and humor are our best teachers.

My personal growth was all beginning to make sense. I realized I could make conscious choices in my life, and take responsibility for them, good or bad, and change my decisions at any time. I could co-create with God, life force, and Source energy. I could make many things come true by thinking with genuine, heartfelt intention. And, more important, allow them to come true. This became very evident in my golf career. I manifested visions quickly and easily because I had set those thoughts in motion from the higher vantage point.

My work was no longer the struggle it had been at the stock exchange in Chicago. I seemed to be in a flow of infinite goodness much of the time, connected from the inside out. I do know that this is part of my personality as well. I have always been a happy person, focusing on the positive and purposeful. But there was more expansion in this work I was doing, knowing, and using the laws and principles of the Universe. This could not have been more apparent than in the experience I'm about to relate.

CHAPTER 6

INDIA, HERE I COME!

After hiking for a couple of hours in the foothills of Palm Springs one afternoon, I paused to rest. I sat Indian style on a large rock, arms resting on my knees with my palms facing up. I sat motionless staring into the hills when, suddenly, an image appeared. It was a small man of color with bushy black hair wearing an orange robe. Smiling, he motioned with his hand and beckoned to me, "Come to India. Come to India." Within seconds, he vanished as quickly as he had appeared. My hands now rested on my knees, and my neck was craned forward to see where this man had gone.

"That's it," I muttered as I stood up and dusted sand off my pants. "I'm going to India!" Some athletes go to Disneyland, but I was heading to India. When I shared this story with two friends, their eyes widened, and their jaws dropped. They informed me that *their* friends were traveling to India to see an avatar who wore an Afro and an orange robe. They put me in touch with these friends, who also were shocked when I told them about the apparition. "Oh, my gosh! You were summoned!" they exclaimed. "That is how it usually happens." They shared his whereabouts, and my vision was confirmed.

I quickly put the wheels in motion. I sold my car, lined up a house sitter, paid my bills a couple of months in advance, got a passport, and received my airline ticket in front of LAX about three hours before I was to board the plane. After a 12-hour flight, I boarded another plane in Bombay, where I was greeted by soldiers with machine guns, not a friendly flight attendant. I ended up in a small town called Madurai, at the southern tip of India, where I stepped into a "taxi." This vehicle was slightly larger than a red Radio Flyer wagon. The taxi driver maneuvered skillfully through masses of people, an oxen cart, and double-decker buses on a wide one-lane road, like Shriners at a St. Patrick's Day parade on Lake Shore Drive in Chicago. It was pandemonium, to say the least.

The three-hour trek to Kodaikanal via the steep and winding Ghat roads was a miserable but memorable experience. Although there were many turnouts on the road, the taxi driver never stopped once to enjoy the scenic beauty of the Palani Hills. Instead, I got the blurred view out the open window of a small speeding car, with an Indian-speaking driver who occasionally sounded his horn to announce his approach around the upcoming bends. Uphill traffic gets the right of way on these mountainous roads leading from the Madurai's arid plains up to Kodaikanal, a city in the hills of the Dindigul District in the state of Tamil Nadu, India. Its name in the Tamil language means "the gift of the forest." Kodaikanal is referred to as the "princess of hill stations" and has a long history as a retreat and popular tourist destination.

The Palani Hills of Kodaikanal are surrounded and pro-tected by thick forests, rich flora, and high-jinksing monkeys, specifically, the gray langur. These langurs are mostly gray, some more yellowish, with a black face and ears. I enjoyed several sightings of these curious long-tailed monkeys from the backseat as I jostled along. They swung and leaped from tall vine trees and darted across the street for bits of morsels to eat.

The road narrowed even more. There was a steep hill on one side and a gradually deepening drop on the other side, which indicated to me we were getting closer to the top. Large tamarind trees with dense foliage flanked the two-lane road, providing thick shade and relief from the scathingly hot taxi, which had no air conditioning. We slowly crept up on the horizon to see the hillside packed with colorful houses nestled amongst cypress, eucalyptus, and other big trees.

There were more people and activity on this stretch of road now, including vegetable vendors, fruit sellers, tea and pop kiosks, and coconut vendors with heaps of tender yellow coconuts ready to be cut open for their rich, thirst-quenching milk. Children were playing along the street, and women in saris were squatting in front of iron sheets above hot wood coals, flipping *chapatis* (unleavened flatbreads) with long silver spatulas. I immediately noticed around the base of large trees several figurines of Gods and Goddesses adorned flower garlands and other offerings.

Small groups of men also had gathered, perhaps to discuss Sathya Sai Baba's upcoming visit. Sathya Sai Baba was one of the most revered spiritual teachers in the world. He quietly transformed the world by reestablishing the eternal values of Truth (Sathya), Right Conduct (Dharma), Peace (Shanti), Love (Prema), and Nonviolence (Ahimsa) in everyday living. The mission of Sathya Sai Baba was to "cultivate the attitude of oneness between people of all creeds, all countries, and all continents. This is the message of love I bring. I come to light the lamp of love in your hearts."

Through the Sathya Sai Organization, Sai Baba established a network of free hospitals, clinics, drinking water projects, auditoriums, *ashrams* (praying altars), and schools. The organization has more than 1,200 branches in 126 countries. Clearly, these villagers hoped to catch a glimpse of this renowned guru and philanthropist.

My eyes turned to the star-shaped Kodaikanal Lake, which was in full view now, and I could see people in rowboats and *pedalos,* or paddle boats as they are called in the United States. A pedalo is a small human-powered watercraft propelled by the action of pedals turning a paddle wheel. The paddle wheel of a pedalo is a smaller version of that used by a paddle steamer. A two-seat pedalo has two sets of pedals, side by side, designed to be used together.

A path skirted around the lake, and there were several people walking or riding their bikes. I also noticed people on horseback trotting along near rows of pear trees and a park-like area with rhododendron and magnolia bushes and hundreds of roses and dahlias. It was a kaleidoscope of color to behold after my arduous journey. I even sighted a Bodhi tree, which added to the religious significance of the park. Peering out the taxi window for closer inspection, I saw beautiful water lilies floating in the pond. Oh, how I imagined peacefully resting on a patch of those fragrant flowers in that moment.

The driver slowed on a gravel turnout up a small hill where a one-story bungalow appeared amid a rich floral garden. It was my first accommodation, with a common kitchen and two adjacent bedrooms with a "bathroom" in each. I checked into my hotel room—a small cottage with a dirt floor, a cot, and a wooden table and chair. There was a fireplace but only cold running water—unfiltered, of course.

A young Indian boy assisted me with my luggage and showed me to my bedroom. Then, he lit the stone fireplace with gasoline, which promptly emitted a choking stench in the air. The toilet was an Indian-style hole in the ground with two boards on either side to place my feet on for squatting. The term *squat* only refers to the expected defecation posture, not any other aspects of toilet technology, such as whether it is water flushed or not. Squatting slabs can be made of porcelain (ceramic), stainless steel, fiberglass, or, in the case of low-cost versions in developing countries, with concrete, ferro cement, plastic, or wood covered with linoleum.

I was advised to bring my own toilet paper if I preferred to wipe myself with something other than my bare hand and water. There was a very small sink with cold running water that I very much appreciated. There was no flooring in the whole house. My single bedspring cot rested on a damp dirt floor.

Cold, sore, and exhausted, I unpacked a few things and gave myself a sponge bath for some cooling relief. I quickly dressed and slipped under the white-gray sheets and huddled closely with the cotton blanket. I was glad I reached my destination safely, yet in that moment, I did not feel safe. I felt chilled and depleted from the 22-hour journey. What was I doing here? Sickness and death were all around me, and I wished I had the time to get required vaccinations before I left. However, Divine intervention prevailed.

The skills, prayers, and affirmations that I had learned at the Religious Science and Unity Churches were my only hope of survival—I'm not kidding! I was in a third-world country on a whim, prompted by an image that appeared in the foothills of Palm Springs. What was I thinking? If I remained focused and sustained a position of well-being, all went well. The continuous mantra begins, "There is only love and goodness, my body is a body of well-being." Throughout the next two months, I felt like I was hovering above the stench of disaster and disease.

I began to imagine something happy so I could drift off to sleep. I started waltzing with every friend and relative I could think of. I heard the lilting symphony of Johann Strauss's "The Blue Danube" circling in my mind with every step I took. One by one, round and round, uplifted and relieved, I drifted off to sleep for a little while, then awoke in a surprising dream of skating in an ice rink. I was effortlessly doing spins and turns and dancing on ice in front of a large audience.

One minute later, I was Brian Boitano at the 1988 Calgary Winter Olympics. I'm not kidding. I *was* Brian Boitano, skating the performance of a lifetime, wearing a soldier costume with a burgundy sash. I even remember leaping into a difficult jump, then wiping the snow off my blade, and flinging it joyously into the air! It is said the test of the Olympic games is an athlete's ability to call on himself for the best he has at the time he needs it most. This was my underlying message in this dream: Do not be afraid. I had to summon the courage to be the best I could be in this moment, in this third-world country, sleeping on a damp dirt floor.

The next morning, I awoke to the clatter of the village, with moving vehicles, honking horns, the hum of distant voices, and the aroma of smoke rising from black kettles cooking food or boiling clothes clean. The air and water were relatively clean, although the diesel fumes from truck traffic added to a distinct pungent stench. Reflecting more than 20 years ago, I still remember this fact about India. I cannot imagine how it is now with all the growth and the problems with rising temperatures, drought, and pollution.

I spent the next several days walking to the ashram for *darshan* (devotional prayer). It was customary to take off your shoes at the door of the ashram to leave the "dust of the world" behind. Men and women sat on the floor separately and observed a code of silence. During this time of darshan, Sathya Sai Baba would walk among the assembled people taking letters, giving advice, or granting personal interviews. We also sang devotional songs to God called *bhajans*. It is scientifically proven that classic bhajans have a soothing effect on the mind, body, and spirit.

Cows on Parade

A funny thing happened to me on my way back from darshan one afternoon. I was chomping on an apple as I walked along a path near a fence. A cow standing on the other side was watching me with big brown eyes, so I held out the rest of the apple in my palm for her to eat. She happily gobbled it up. As I moved along, she began to follow me, her cowbell dinging. With that, other cows joined in. I picked up my pace and looked back to see a parade of cows following me with great anticipation. I started laughing until a local resident, who was watching in amusement, advised me to run and hide or they'll be waiting for me at my back door. I did just that, quickly darting behind a mound of used coconut shells to outsmart them. Another lesson well learned in India.

Heavenly Dining Experiences

Frequently, I would venture into the village to have a bite to eat in a restaurant. The best deal was a *thali*, an extra-large single plate piled with liberal helpings of rice, *sambhar*, *kootu* (vegetable curry cooked with lentils), *kosumalli*, *papri chaat*, and curd. Chapatis were made of wheat flour rolled with little oil and water and then thrown into a tandoori oven. The high heat makes them blow up soft and fluffy. The cooks slapped butter and garlic on while they were still hot, and you used those to lap up any extra curry sauce. And for dessert, there was *akkaravadisal* (a sweet made with rice, lentils, and milk) to complete the meal.

Sometimes I purchased my meal for a few rupees at the street vendors in the bazaar, like savory curry stewed over large black kettles on open flames. Petite dark-skinned women served the bowl with plenty of rice. In as much as the dish tasted like food from the gods, I was almost more captivated by the women's colorful saris pulled up slightly and tucked at the waist.

Young men in white long shirts and white pants wielded long machetes and skillfully chopped away the hard shells of coconuts, until a little square of coconut shell popped up like a trap door to expose the raw juicy core. They inserted a plastic straw at the top before handing it over to a waiting customer. The soft, meaty flesh from the inside was delectable, especially on such hot summer days. In fact, Sathya Sai Baba urged everyone to enjoy one a day.

Hot chai was my favorite hot beverage made with black tea and several savory spices, like cardamom pods, star anise, cinnamon, milk, and sugar. Another culinary delight of the East Indians is the artful and functional display of their spices. They use these spices in significant quantities as a food additive for flavor and color or as a preservative that kills harmful bacteria or prevents their growth. The spices are placed in small tins in a large circle tin, which makes the whole thing brilliantly colorful and functional.

Occasionally, I felt a sense of urgency to satisfy my sweet tooth. A housemate joined me for a jaunt into the village on such an occasion. We stumbled on a confectionary store, tucked among other small-business buildings, which was no larger than a walk-in closet. We drooled over the trays of chocolate, brownies, and lemon bars in the display case. I purchased a half dozen of each. We carried our precious cargo to a bench with an idyllic view of the lake, made ourselves comfortable, and ate every sweet morsel. We skipped back to the bungalow singing freely on a sugar high, as the sun cast its last rays across the lake. Ah, life's simple pleasures!

Upon our return, the other housemates had congregated in the kitchen to discuss the news of Sathya Sai Baba heading to the next town. We jumped at the chance to see him a bit longer and packed it up the next day to hitch a ride together in a larger taxi. I was curious if my next accommodations would be any better than the first.

My second hotel stay was in a three-story stone structure sandwiched between other hotel buildings. It was hard to tell where one began and one ended. The accommodations were primitive but livable. I had a very small brick room with a single bed, a small desk and chair, and a small shower. There was a newer Indian toilet, which was only a foot off the ground. But, at least, it had a toilet seat. I still had to squat over it, and I used my own toilet paper.

There were no screens or glass panes for the open windows in my room, so bugs flew in freely and regularly. The room, however, was equipped with a small fan at the foot of the bed. I kept it on "high" while I slept to prevent mosquitos from landing on me and infecting me with diseases.

The unfiltered water was still a major concern. I showered very cautiously below the chin to prevent water from entering any orifices, which could lead to dysentery. I also inspected every bottle of water that I purchased to ensure it was sealed properly. To make money, street-smart local children filled used plastic water bottles with tap water, screwed the caps back on, and then sold them as bottled spring water.

Some Indian boys earned tips by making the rounds to politely gather dirty clothes to wash them, as there were no laundromats in the village. My neatly folded clothes always came back a shade darker than when they left. Apparently, the clothes were washed in big black kettles over an open fire, which explained the ashen color and smoky stench.

The ashram and grounds of a Sai Baba Center were across the street from my hotel. I would sneak up and sit on the hotel's roof to get a glimpse of Sathya Sai Baba in the gardens. Lots of monkeys joined me, even though I did not give them anything to eat. At this center, there was an Indian canteen where meals were served. I loved arriving early just to watch the men unload the truck full of fresh vegetables from the fields. Frequently, I witnessed the beautiful singing and prayer over the food being prepared by the men and women. It was not just human resources but a Divine power, as well, that was working through the making of this special food.

Beggars usually approached me on my way to the canteen. Beggary is an age-old social phenomenon in India, due to abject poverty, unemployment, and migration from rural villages. On one occasion, an older woman, who had previously gouged out one of her eyes, asked for a rupee for a flower she had just picked in the nearby field. I was perplexed by her simple gesture and made the mistake of giving her a rupee. She waited for me the next morning to begin the process again. This time, I said, "Bless you, dear one. No more," and then I walked away.

I loved the Indian cuisine and how it was prepared at the canteen. The people sang and prayed over the food from field to meal. There was, however, the expectation of cultural obedience, where men sat on wooden benches at tables, while women were relegated to the cold floor. We sat on thin mats, with our food on silver platters, using our fingers to bring such heavenly morsels to our mouths. I savored every delectable bite and vowed to bring these culinary delights back to the States with me.

I can still hear the words of the elder Indian echo: "Eat with the right; wipe with the left." There was no toilet paper in many of the places I stayed, so it was very important to remember this basic rule. We dined under the watchful eyes of playful monkeys, who entertained us with their rooftop high jinks while they waited to salvage food scraps.

I will always remember the unfamiliar sights and aromas of India, such as the smell of nuts wafting in the morning air. Life there is a study of contrasts that ignite the senses: the stench in the air, a corpse lying on the ground face-up with coins covering the eyelids, and an ashram on almost every corner, covered with flowers and other sacred offerings, to worship a God or Goddess. The majestic mountains magnified the beauty above, and thousands of people lived in tiny shanties below. It is a remarkable experience to behold such polarity.

An Audience with Sathya Sai Babi

The highlight of my trip was being chosen for an interview with Sathya Sai Baba, although the whole process tested my patience and devotion to life. There were thousands of people everywhere. Men and women were divided in the large devotional area, and then they received chits, or numbered coins, to enter the ashram in an orderly way. They stood in long rows of the appropriate chit and were led, row by row, into the sacred ashram. Most of this was outside, where it was quite hot in the sun. The sick or disabled were given priority into the ashram and sat near the front of the altar where Sathya Sai Baba was seated.

After much devotional singing followed by darshan, Sai Baba slowly walked around to bless everyone. He gestured to those people who would receive a private interview. A friend whom I met there had been chosen and was allowed three more people, so she motioned to me, and that is how I met and had an interview with Sathya Sai Baba, the "man in the orange robe in the mountain," God incarnate. His universal message is "To love and to *be* love." He is comparable to Jesus of the Western world and still walks the Earth demonstrating his immeasurable love and endless miracles. Sathya Sai Baba died, April 24, 2011.

What I learned from this avatar can only be experienced by being in the presence of Sathya Sai Baba, humble and compassionate, with his eyes overflowing with love. There were about eight people who were chosen for an interview on this morning, and I was lucky enough to be among them. We sat in a modest room filled with some couches and a chair, far away from the masses of people. Oddly enough, we all sat on the floor in front of the chair he was sitting in, like children waiting for the teacher to read a story. He welcomed us and then stood and asked us to hold out our hands, palms up. Sai Baba held his arm out, pulling up his sleeve with his other hand, and began to sprinkle a gray powder from his fingertips. It was Vibuti, the Holy Ash of the Divine, which carried vibrational healing powers.

This Holy Ash is a substance originally made from burning cow dung (with or without addition of rice husks, sandalwood, etc.). It is a kind of talisman, believed by many to heal almost any physical or mental illness. Sai Baba has given it to people every day for most of his life. He gives away many small bags of it at interviews, grasping a large handful of them for each interviewee from a plastic basket in which they are invariably kept. After my own research, I learned the ash came from a cow's holy ass! Real or placebo, its healing powers have worked for thousands upon thousands of followers. I still have a small tin container of the stuff and it never seems to run out, no matter how much I use.

Within an hour, Sathya Sai Baba interviewed a few of the people who were chosen. When my turn came, he looked at me puzzled, and asked, "How is your husband?" I was taken aback, as here I was, exhausted after traveling across the world on a whim to see this avatar, and the first question out of his mouth was about my husband. I thought to myself, "Well, if he is the Great and Powerful Oz, then why didn't he know I did not have a husband?" I was deflated. So, I played his little game back and laughed, "Oh, he's at home watching TV."

He looked around with a confused look on his face because he did not understand my sense of humor. He asked the question again, and I simply stated, "I don't have a husband." This was disappointing and confusing for me as my sexuality was not yet as fluid as it is now. My experience in relationships growing up, even during my college years, was challenging because I experienced much sexual wounding from males, so to this point I had primarily been with women. With this, he used both of his hands to show me two fists rotating back and forth and resisting up against each other. He said, "The left is pushing too hard against the right." I did not understand what he was saying to me, but that was it; that's all I got. He then placed his hands on my head, gave me a blessing, and said, "You have plenty of time."

Later, I asked another devotee who was in the interview what he meant by husband. She explained to me the term *husband* is an analogy for the left side of you, or the inner masculine part of you. He asked me this question because he knew there was an imbalance between the inner man and inner woman within me. I was an initiator, a doer, a leader, pushing on to be better, higher, and stronger as an Olympic athlete would strive for. I had been neglecting my inner woman, who was screaming for attention. Surrendering, being more receptive, creative, and allowing more pleasure in my life, instead of working to "succeed."

I thanked her quietly and continued my stay in Kodaikanal, India, pondering this new information. It would be several years before I realized what Sathya Sai Baba's message was about, when I went to my first tantra workshop in early 2000 and learned how to heal past sexual wounds and embody my Divine Feminine.

A Colorful Expedition

I was still reflecting on the meaning of the message Sai Baba had given me during the interview the day before, when a woman from the bungalow approached me and invited me on a secret outing with some of the other women. Of course, I said yes, as I always love an adventure. A beautiful young woman in a pink sari pulled up in a new Jeep. Apparently, she was a princess of the Taj Mahal and offered to take all of us for a ride into Bangalore to shop for saris. The city is known as a high-tech hub, sprinkled with parks and offering an array of eateries and night-life options. I relished this escape from my primitive village accommodations to enjoy a glimpse of modern Indian civilization.

The roads were narrow and tightly squeezed as we made our way to the fabric store. It was small, but it was packed from wall to wall with many bright colors and textures of yards and yards of material. In fact, 10 yards of material are used to make one sari to wrap around a woman. I chose two fabrics: one was soft in stunning aqua blue with a black paisley print; the other was a stiffer linen type in a temple orange hue with golden double-striped trim along the edges. It also had splashes of golden teardrops throughout the drapery. It was to be worn on Sunday, the holy day. I picked out lovely Puja pants and a long shirt set in a cream color with stenciled green leaves. I matched a beautiful pine green and black scarf with golden sprinkles to accent the outfit. What a special surprise it was to shop in the city with the princess and purchase such authentic Indian clothing at a wholesale cost. Aqua to darshan, orange to temple. Wear sari over skirt. Wear a scarf or a sarong over the shoulders. I was into it.

We stopped for brunch at a high-end hotel and paid seven rupees for a large all-you-can-eat buffet. In American currency, it may have been $3 at the most. I don't believe the currency exchange is that good in India anymore.

Golf in the Clouds

My most treasured and precious experience beyond meeting Sathya Sai Baba was visiting Kodaikanal Golf Club, nestled 7,000 feet above sea level. The mountaintop course is populated with dense forests, verdant rolling grassland, gurgling streams, and wooded hills. The fairways were brown, and the greens were green with old wooden flagsticks stuck in the putting holes.

It was about a two-hour jaunt from the ashram, such a lovely trip through the forests, filled with precocious monkeys. When we arrived at the course, it was very foggy. The golf shop was a small wooden building with a small front porch and a tin roof. There were some boys getting ready to tee off, so I took a moment to watch. What struck me was their equipment—very old, steel-shafted clubs, maybe Wilson or some brand like that. The clubs and balls were used and had seen better days. Later, I learned that all the clubs and balls were donated to this golf course. I told the golf course manager that I was a golf professional and I would like to send some new golf balls for the kids when I returned to the United States. He thought it was a kind gesture, but the chances of this gift ever reaching them would be quite slim, citing theft of packages as the main reason.

He suggested I catch up with the boys, who had just teed off, if I wanted to play the course. I hurried and joined the boys on the third hole, a par 3, 183 yards to the green. Their enthusiasm to see me coming up the hill was precious, their almond-colored eyes in wonderment with big, wide grins. Interestingly, the name of the hole was Hope. I told them I was a golf professional from America and immediately asked them what "sticks" they were using. They were old sets of forged steel Wilson staffs, many with ripped or loose grips. The golf balls were various brands, yellowed and dimpled. It didn't seem to bother the boys what they were playing with, as they were more interested in making shots atop the mountain.

We talked a little bit about the course, and they hoped I could play along to at least the sixth hole, named "Tiger Hole" because tigers used to be sighted in the vicinity. They all spoke broken English with an East Indian accent. Their love for the Palani Hills, with cool breezes blowing off the cliff face and misty fairways, showed me how much the boys appreciated and respected the natural world.

The high school boys were simply playing for the love of the sport, keeping no score and communing with nature.

I stepped up to take my shot after all the boys hit. I jiggled the Indian coins in my pocket in search of my wooden tee, grabbed my 3-iron and teed my ball up. I took a smooth swing and hit the ball crisply down the middle of the fairway before it disappeared. In the descending mist, we had to listen carefully to know where my ball landed. "On the green," I said with a smile. Then, I asked one of the boys to putt out for me as I had to head back to catch my cab. I shook their hands and watched the silhouette of the backs of four boys walking down the fairway with canvas golf bags slung over their shoulders until they disappeared in the afternoon mist. I chuckled as I heard the youngest boy yell out with his East Indian accent, "We're playing in the clouds!"

What I learned from my trip to India humbled me, and I have a greater appreciation for the simple and ordinary things in life. Hot running water is a luxury. Driving a car is a privilege. And interacting with other people, whether from this country or any other, will always be an act of love and kindness to me. A moment to be shared and cherished. For if there is no other, to whom do we relate? We can sit in the lotus position in the mountains for a while, but physically interacting and communicating with other people are a lot more fun. (I experienced this personally in the isolation that a traumatic brain injury can bring.)

I was a bit emotional when I left India and returned to the United States. I thought about staying longer—months longer—because the culture had such a great impact on me. I was pondering this when my taxi dropped me off at the Madurai Airport in India. Then, a rude reality set in. The security officers were unfriendly and threatening, and they wore black berets on their heads and machine guns slung over the shoulders. They appeared to be part of the military and were quite aggressive in their actions at the security checkpoints, shouting and shuffling people along. Somehow, I made it through the checkpoints, and I walked up the rolling steps outside to board the plane. I began to stow one bag in front of my seat on the floor and then put the other suitcase up above my seat. Apparently, one of the security guards had followed me onto the plane. He pointed his machine gun at me and firmly stated, "One bag per passenger."

I was shocked as I turned around to see his stern face and large gun pointing directly at me. Nervously, I said, "No, they told me two bags were fine at the checkpoint." Pointing his gun closer, he reiterated, "One bag per passenger." With that, a young Caucasian man sitting in front of me stood up and grabbed my bag, congenially saying, "We're together. This is my bag." Then, he quietly placed it on the floor in front of his seat. The security officer was satisfied with this solution and turned to leave the plane. Terrified, I profusely thanked the young man for his quick thinking to help me in such a scary situation. I honestly felt that I would be detained for having two bags instead of one. I was Divinely protected once again in my pilgrimage to India.

Upon landing at LAX, I walked down the steps, kneeled, placed both hands on the ground, and kissed the pavement. I was elated to be home again, even though I had just burned my lips on the hot asphalt. My spiritual journey, however, did not end there. I continued to study the Eastern philosophies, specifically the teachings of Indian yogi and guru Paramahansa Yogananda and self-realization fellowship, the religion of Hinduism, and the Tantric techniques of the ancient yoginis. The practices I learned during my spiritual journey tremendously enhanced by personal and professional growth, making me strong, empowered, loving, and grateful.

CHAPTER 7

FROM GURU TO GODDESS

Ever evolving in my adventurous spirit, I decided to expand my horizons while escaping the dreadfully hot, smoldering summer in Palm Springs. I picked up and moved to Sebastopol, California, where I could cool off. I conducted clinics and gave golf lessons in this charming, politically liberal small town in Sonoma County.

Sebastapol is known as the "Gravenstein Apple Capital of the World." I used to meander through an apple orchard near a small house I rented while living and working in Sebastopol. During apple season, this distinct fermentation smell came from the apple factory near the end of town. The Apple Festival and "everything apples" each autumn were delicious consolations for the vinegar smell.

This was an ideal place to start my golf business. In fact, it only took writing one article, "Feel the Fear and Swing Anyway," which was published in the local paper, to attract attention. My women's golf clientele exploded, and I received 85 calls in one weekend. I was hot on the teaching track once again.

One afternoon, after my golf clinic, I stopped at a gas station right in town to fill my tank. As I pumped gas, two lovely women were filling their tank and they struck up a conversation with me. A mother and daughter, they lived in Sebastopol and were part of the "goddess community." By the end of our conversation, I was invited to attend a goddess celebration in honor of the summer solstice on private land near the Pacific Ocean. I knew I would passionately participate in this weekend because it was in sharp contrast from being a golf professional, who always wears the proper uniform and conforms to proper etiquette.

Your Birthright: Be a Wave of Ecstasy

I had no idea how large the event would be, but as I stood on the hillside overlooking the land, I saw hundreds of women of all shapes and sizes, colors, and ages: mothers, sisters, daughters, girlfriends, aunts, grandmothers, straight and gay. They had all come together in sisterhood for an ecstatic weekend of deep connection with the energies of Mother Nature to honor the Goddess, ourselves, and one another. There was a large pond, where a few children and women were swimming, to the right of the land.

Several tents had already been put up nestled among trees and bushes around the perimeter by the women participants. There was a large fire ring, with a circle in the middle, and toward the back was the kitchen tent, with large pots and pans and a giant oven to help feed over a thousand women. There were already women in the open tent chopping and preparing food for the evening meal. I strolled to the left of the property where there was a "Red Tent," constructed as a plush, velvety temple with pillows for those women in need of rest or for those who were bleeding (menstruating) to honor this special time of the month. There was another tent beyond that was called "Crone," for women of wisdom to gather and rekindle stories to share and delight in. There also was a wellness tent, which housed massage tables, an apothecary, herbal and healing books, and several sitting chairs. The whole property, nestled in the forest, had been transformed into a magical village of women for the next few days.

During these days, there were powerful workshops to partake in, like learning how to drum, sing, or dance with the elements. There was empowerment through studying sacred archetypes of women and developing ritual skills. There was learning to identify and use herbs for medicinal purposes and for healthy nutrition. These powerful workshops were guided by world-renowned priestesses and leaders, including Starhawk, a writer, teacher, and theorist of feminist Neopaganism and ecofeminism, and Carol T. Christ (who was named the 11th Chancellor of the University of California at Berkeley in 2017—the first woman to fill this position). I found Carol's last name interesting, as she had written several books and gave keynote speeches, including "Why Women Need the Goddess." Here is an excerpt from that keynote.

> The simplest and most basic meaning of the symbol of Goddess is the acknowledgment of the legitimacy of female power as a beneficent and independent power. A woman who echoes Ntozake Shange's dramatic statement, 'I found God in myself and I loved her fiercely,' is saying, 'Female power is strong and creative.' She is saying that the Divine principle, the saving and sustaining power, is in herself, that she will no longer look to men or male figures as saviors. The strength and independence of female power can be intuited by contemplating ancient and modern images of the Goddess. This meaning of the symbol of Goddess is simple and obvious, and yet it is difficult for many to comprehend. It stands in sharp contrast to the paradigms of female dependence on males that have been predominant in Western religion and culture.[1]

---

[1] Carol T. Christ, "Why Women Need the Goddess" (keynote address at the Great Goddess Re-emerging conference, University of Santa Cruz, CA, spring 1978), 3, http://www.iupui.edu/~womrel/Rel433%20Readings/Christ_WhyWomenNeedGoddess pdf

This new information astounded me because it opened another arena to embrace. I loved being a woman, yet I was constantly compared to a man's standards. The priestesses said it's all right to step into your own power as a woman, which has nothing to do with men, and that it is a woman's right because she is a woman. Unfortunately, I, too, experienced the male ego threatened by my charismatic personality and inner strength growing up. Many times, I would play down, stand back, and even dress down to avoid the uncomfortable feeling of being better than some of my male friends or colleagues. The backlash was just too much growing up in a white male–dominated system, with a white authoritative savior.

I noticed this while playing sports in my childhood years. I loved playing basketball, baseball, and football with the neighborhood boys, and usually was much better at the games because I was gifted in eye–hand coordination. Many of the boys became jealous and didn't like to play with me because I was so good. Despite my passion, I learned to play down my abilities, often assisting them in making the score or making them look good just so they would like me. If I built them up, I could hang out and play sports with them. I loved sports so much that I played along with this lopsided game.

This also happened in working at the stock exchange when I was in my 20s, where I would assist my male counterparts in looking good on special projects, allowing them to take the credit, receive pay raises, and advance their careers within the corporate ladder. In this way, I could still be a part of the team, yet I could only go so far before I hit the glass ceiling, acquiescing to the built-in good-old-boy network. The golf industry was no exception.

Hearing and seeing how beautiful and confident the priestesses were out in the world was exhilarating. Here was another piece of my long spiritual journey, and now it was my turn to be in a new direction as a woman. Perhaps this was part of the message that Sathya Sai Baba eluded to when he said, "The left is working too hard against the right." It was time to let go of the stereotypical way of a woman's role and begin to give more attention to my feminine side as its own entity: a real woman whole unto herself!

The Goddess Is Alive

The last evening was extraordinary, with the coming together of all women in a large circle around a fire. Within this sacred ritual space, a priestess honored the elements, directions, and invoked our foremothers, as the moon rose in the night sky. We sang and raised energy with goddess performance and drumming, singing our prayers for ourselves and the Earth. The ceremony ended with a grapevine type dance where I embraced arms and shoulders with other women. We circled rhythmically around and around the fire, with moonbeams catching bare breasts, flowing skirts and sarongs, sparkling eyes, and smiles of all the passing women in the dance.

It was uplifting and invigorating to be dancing with all these goddesses whom I did not know at first but who all came together in perfect love and trust. The celebration continued through the night, as I lay my head upon my pillow of my screened penthouse bed in my Volkswagen Westfalia camper. I could still see the women dancing around the fire in my mind as I drifted into slumber, their melodic voices echoing in the night air. I was filled with rejuvenation and a renewed purpose of being a woman and of having a new sisterhood I could count on. I made several friends that weekend, all who were inspired by the Gathering of the Goddesses. I continued the sisterhood by circling with women weekly, learning about many aspects and traditions of the Goddess.

Circling with Women

I circled with about a dozen women in Northern California, with a boisterous curvy priestess named Stella. I called her the "Big Booby, Belly Bottom Goddess" who had much wisdom . . . an older woman who had lived. With large green eyes; a big, toothy smile; and long, curly red hair, this woman took up space. Vibrant and dynamic in expression, I easily absorbed every word she spoke.

In our first meeting, Stella shared each aspect of the Goddess. The trinity in the Goddess tradition is the Maiden, Mother, and Crone. The Maiden represents the "wisdom of innocence," where she is all about enchantment and new beginnings, youthful ideas, and enthusiasm. As Stella described the Maiden, she skipped across the room with one long-stem white daisy while batting her long lashes and whipping the daisy across the cheeks of my sisters. She is the color white, the clear space. The Maiden is associated with the waxing phase of the lunar cycle, as the moon grows from dark to full.

Stella stopped in the middle of the circle of women with her hands on her round hips, head arched to the sky, and puckered her mouth. She let out a howl and we all joined in! I love the Maiden quality of being youthful and enthusiastic in life. Stella invited us to all lie down as she played soft, lilting music and guided us through a Maiden meditation. The Maiden's flowery message to me was to be playful as a child, frolicking and tossing rose petals wherever I go in life.

The Mother represents the "wisdom of being," and she is about creative ideas and contributions. Stella sat regally on an antique high-back stuffed chair and, with reverence, stated, "The Mother is queen of her life." She lifted both hands up to the air, "Repeat after me, please: I know who I am, I know what I am here to do." I responded with an English accent, imitating the Queen, waving to the crowd with one hand, with the rest of my sisters in perfect unison. This was a nervous response, as I did not fully understand the full realm of the Mother.

Stella continued in a dynamic fashion, with waving hands and widening eyeballs, as if performing on stage to an eager audience. The Mother is fertility, fecundity, abundance, growth, and gaining knowledge. She is fulfillment, whether sexual, social, or emotional, and is represented by the full moon. Her color is blood red, the color of birth. Spring and early summer are her domain; just as the Earth becomes green and fertile, so does the Mother. A woman does not have to have biological children to embrace the role of the mother. Ah, now I was beginning to understand, as I had not experienced the painful exhilaration of having a baby or mothering a child. For me, "children" were all the creative aspects of being an entrepreneur in my golfing career.

The Crone represents the "wisdom of retrospect," a woman who has lived and acquired wisdom that comes with age. Stella whirled a long, navy blue cloak around herself, and then, in a swoop, slipped her arms in the holes and around her body, still twirling in the center, around and around, representing the length of her life span. Then, she stopped and slipped the hood over her head and softly said, "The Crone is about the darkness of night, her ultimate destiny and death. She is the color black, the void." She proceeded to walk slowly around the circle of sisters as she continued. The Crone is the waning moon, that dims to dark, the Earth dying. The Crone is a reflection of all that has gone before her. Stella sat down and asked us to sit quietly for a moment with eyes closed to reflect on our own lives with respect to mortality.

In retrospect, there were two times I had almost died, both in my 20s. The first was while I was in college at Indiana State University and working in the mental health unit of the local hospital. In 1982, I had toxic shock syndrome from using tampons during my monthly periods. The second time was in 1989, when I had a bowel obstruction from Crohn's disease. I learned from the

Crone you don't have to be old to experience her wisdom of appreciating life eternal, for the cycle always continues with birth, death, and rebirth. Thank Goddess, I would not become a "Crohny Crone."

Circling with women inspired me to write a poem in fall 1997.

Vertical Vortex

Caught in a vertical vortex spinning out of my mind.
Delusion, illusion until I stepped outside to find,
The confusion in my head was completely left behind,
When the great cosmic wind, with one breath took me in.
Twirled me and whirled me, whispering wings to soar,
This sweet honey soul, I had never known before.
Polarity, clarity, with new eyes memorized,
No longer hypnotized, the great comic voice had given me a choice.
Nature's soulful playmate had cast my fate,
In a new direction without reflection.
Vortex of knowing
Vortex of growing
I giggled and laughed and started to sway,
with dancing leaves in magical play.
Sweet vertical vortex, my breath of inspiration,
My continuous creation . . .

The Wheel Keeps Turning

Women have been oppressed for 5,000 years. It was time to undo and dismantle the past, create healthy boundaries with men, make healthy choices, and come home to myself. I was circling with women as a witness, not to try to fix them. I was circling with women with integrity and compassion. It was time to share the power and live in harmony with women, and not contribute to the cutthroat environment of a male-dominated corporation. It is a natural traditional for women to gather. It was and never has been a reaction to the male patriarchy. It is about living, according to our values in relation to Mother Earth. "Is it good for the Earth?" and "Is it good for my body?" became the themes during this period.

I was mesmerized by Dae, a gorgeous brunette in the circle of women who was about my age. Her body radiated a fragrance of pure love and beauty. Her silky soft skin was a smooth honey color. She always had a glow about her, with a bit of makeup that was bright but very natural-looking: coral lipstick, light sage-green eyeshadow, with a hint of dark-brown eyeliner, and soft, rosy cheeks. When I hugged her to greet her at the circle, she was a bundle of flowering fragrance, with a melting sensation throughout my body the longer I held her in my arms. The essence of her exuded the Goddess Aphrodite, the Goddess of love and sensuality.

I discovered she was the creator of a line of sensuous beauty products. She spent years concocting enriching lotions and potions and delicious syrups to delight in, nourishing the mind, body, and soul. Another holistic teacher, we hit it off beautifully. She taught me to love myself more by nurturing and primping more. Now, this was the life!

When I would visit her at her house, we always went straight to the outdoor clawfoot bathtub, filled with warm water and rose petals, to indulge in a long chat. There she had set up an array of her body cleanses, facial masks, and seaweed wraps for the hair. After we lathered up in the bathtub, we would drink a divine sweet herbal nectar drink she had whipped up before I arrived and chat about all things healthy and happy. Dae had a way of speaking very eloquently, with words and phrases dripping off her lips like the morning dew, so cool and refreshing.

After the full nourishing body cleanse and hydration, we towel-dried ourselves and lay on a soft blanket in the grass to enrich our skin with blossoming lotions, continuing the heavenly ritual of physically caring and pampering our bodies. The effects were all encompassing, as I felt lighter, fresher, and more invigorated after my visit. Was it good for my body? Oh, yeah! And for the Earth as well, because Dae used all-natural ingredients in her products.

On one occasion, her daughter, Rosie, and I were relaxing in the bathtub when Dae appeared with a light snack. She served up steaming quinoa with roasted sea palm for me and a plate of mashed potatoes and cut-up turkey dogs arranged like a giant smiley face for Rosie. Dae walked back into the house to get her plate, but before she returned, Rosie had eaten all the hot dog chunks and then promptly pressed the plate to her face, smashing the mashed potatoes all about! Then, she yelled, "Mom, I have a new facial recipe for you!" With that, Dae returned to see Rosie with mashed potatoes dropping from her face. We all laughed and knew who inspired this spontaneous creative act.

I delighted in my visits with Dae because it was purely an act of sacred sisters honoring the goddess, within ourselves and with each other. I loved the sensual practice of caring for my body in such a delicious way. We became very good friends for years to come. Eventually, I assisted her in some of her special slather gatherings with women, sharing in the pleasure of the temple of our bodies. Even more fulfilling was the joy in working with a woman I did not have to compete with. I could totally be myself and be a part of this beautiful unfolding of women helping women in a most unconditional loving way.

By circling with women for a few years, the pendulum had finally swung the other way. I had immersed myself completely into embracing the Goddess in her many forms and being empowered as a woman through this new connection. I lived intimately with my sisters in the goddess community, sharing the poetry of wisdom, compassion, struggle, and joy. I became more aware and in direct contact with the elements that support my life, in fact, all our lives: the air, water, sun, earth, animals, and plants. I had come to know a more deeply expanded and cooperative way of life, than the white male–dominated system to which I had become accustomed.

I literally cannot share in words many of the experiences I had with my sacred sisters. How to explain magic and insightful moments, some from altered states of consciousness, in a spiritual tradition based on the Goddess religion? The average or brilliant mind could not possibly conceive or even understand the mystery of the Goddess, for it must be conveyed by experience. Felt. Evoked. In the magical, mystical summer of 1997, I was inspired to write more poetry, which flowed out of me effortlessly.

Woman of Mother Earth

Oh, what is this I'm feeling, Mother Earth beneath my feet . . .
Endless roots journey, through fresh rich soil, grounded and strong.
Forever reaching, forever pulsing out the beat.
A voice of a thousand mothers in synchronicity.
Let yourself be seeded in the womb, belly of heart and soul,
And all that is grown, the richest gift ever known.
Wisdom of the land, nurtured by hand,
Are the women who give birth, to the children of the Earth.
Plants and trees and flowers and seeds
Breathe life with energy from the sun and rain.
As in me, I remain, a woman of the Earth.
That is this feeling . . . I am woman of Mother Earth.

My weekly classes continued. A favorite class topic was learning about some of the feminine archetypes. Stella described several Goddesses, including Brigid, the Celtic fire Goddess; Isis, the Goddess of power and strength and, especially, of the spoken word; Hestia, the Goddess of the hearth (the center of self, home, planet); Yemaya, an African Goddess of life and the ocean; and Hecate, the queen of darkness and wisdom (the Crone), to name a few.

Stella invoked each Goddess with such beauty and strength, again in performance art style. I reveled in her passion as she became each Goddess. Stella asked us to sit with our eyes closed while she played some ancient soft music. She asked us to listen and then wait and allow a Goddess or Goddesses to come to us. A visit, perhaps a message, or a chance, to live more in touch with this specific Goddess. Three Goddesses came to me in that mediation: Bast, the Muse, and Artemis.

Bast is the Egyptian cat Goddess who moves from instinct and sees well in the dark. I embraced her qualities as I wanted to trust myself and experience life through my body. I had already learned volumes of the Science of Mind; now it was time to move from my belly, my womb. The cat Goddess inspired me to get back to the basics and to develop my senses as keen as a cat: fierce, fast, loving, and always in the present moment.

Seeing in the Dark

There was a naturalist in my circle of woman, a tall, stocky woman with a soft smile named Sandy, who loved to venture out and hike at night in the Point Reyes National Park in Marin County. I was delighted when she invited me at the circle to join her on her next night hike. We started at the entrance of the trail at dusk, with flashlights, water, snacks, and a sense of curiosity and adventure. The field trip was peaceful through the meadow, though with a nonstop frenzy of looking, touching, and sniffing. Plenty of birds and fowl shifted and soared in the distant trees, as Sandy attempted to identify every rock, tree, wildflower, and bug along the trail. It was all very educational and interesting until the sun dipped below the horizon and a cool breezy haze descended on us.

There would be no moon glow that night, and I was starting to feel a bit uneasy as we entered the forest. We walked a few hundred feet toward a cluster of downed logs and sat down for a moment to have water and snacks. She said it was a good time for us to stop as to let our eyes adjust to the changing of light to dark. I grabbed my sweatshirt from my pack as the cool moisture came up from the forest floor. Sandy began to talk about the night sounds, such as the hoot of an owl, distant voices of another group hiking, and the occasional settling of the land and forest, such as squeaky branches swaying in the breeze, or falling to the Earth. Once completely dark, we started out again on the tree-lined path.

When I grabbed my flashlight and lit the trail, Sandy asked me to turn the flashlight off. It was so dark. Nervously, I asked, "Why?" She whispered, "Be like Bast and use your keen senses to maneuver through the terrain."

"Whoa, OK," I said and inhaled a few deep breaths. I stood and listened first, hearing only the sound of my breath moving in and out from my mouth. I looked up through the parting trees and relaxed my straining eyes. The trail was illuminated ever so slightly, and there was just enough to begin putting one foot in front of the other. I slowly shuffled my feet forward, feeling the Earth beneath my feet, noticing the small subtle textures. Pebbles, twigs, and rocks all gave way to the weight of my feet, my body gliding now down a winding dirt path like the silence and stealth of a hungry cat.

I was moving along well, "seeing in the dark," and experiencing the nightlife through my body, trusting every step. Then, I heard a stirring ahead of me. I stopped and tilted my head to the right to put an ear to the strange sounds. Sandy had been several steps behind me to allow me space, though now she caught up to me as I stood there frozen. My heart pounded as the stirring commenced again, and deep sounds of munching, snorting, and shuffling lingered on in the darkness.

I reached for Sandy's hand trying to compose myself when she turned the flashlight on straight above us and then slowly to the ground. There, just a few feet to our left, was a pasture filled with cows leisurely strolling for fresh grass. In a sigh of relief, I chuckled and said, "Another cow," remembering my adventures with the cows in India. Sandy and I had a good laugh before we headed through the fence and out to the parking lot where our cars were parked.

Such a different evening, such a new sense of wonderment in the moments of the night. I remember this hike vividly, and the emotions I went through as I traversed the dark forest. Most of all, how I embodied the Goddess Bast and her instinctual prowess. I knew I had to share this experience with my women golf clients to help them move out of their fears. I immediately set up a night hike with the ladies' travelling league group, with walking sticks instead of golf clubs and with Sandy as our guide. It became another fun and unusual method for teaching my holistic approach to golf performance.

The Muse Goddess is filled with originality. She knows there is hidden art in everything, and she flourishes with new and entertaining creations. She is the Divine spark and revels as actor, dancer, artist, singer, writer, and performer. I often wrote in my journal about my experiences of the Goddess, including poems. I would sing and chant by the fires and under the moon by myself or with my sisters. "The earth, the water, the air, the fire!" and "We all come from the Goddess, and to her we shall return, like a drop of water, flowing to the ocean."

The Beat Goes On

Inspired by the Muse, I learned Afro-Brazilian dance, bringing out the tribal woman in me. The bouncing drum beat each week brought me closer to the Earth and my ecstatic sisters. I also learned Middle Eastern dance (belly dancing) and wore coined scarves over long skirts or pants, to accentuate my fluid movements, with rising hips and exposing my belly. Performing these dances was a positive and fun way to help heal and tone the past wounds of abdominal surgery. I practiced my devotion to the Goddess through freedom of expressions that came to me in quiet moments, especially at night. My imagination ignited to higher goals, such as vowing to complete a women's holistic golf book.

The third Goddess who came to me in Stella's guided meditation was the archer, Artemis. She is protectress of the forest and is so empowered that she deserves a chapter of her own. You will read about her in upcoming chapters.

CHAPTER 8

A HOLLOW AWARENESS

Upon my release from the emergency room, I spent the next four months at the two-story guesthouse that I was renting about one mile from downtown Sebastopol. It was my haven and only a mile to my favorite hangouts. Before my accident, I often walked into town for breakfast at a bagel shop, The Grateful Bagel. Posters of Jerry Garcia, of The Grateful Dead, and hippie busses dotted the walls. I ordered lox and cream cheese with capers on an "everything bagel" on a regular basis. I also strolled down the main street and patronized grocery and health food stores or browsed the gift shops. Sometimes I would drop in at the used bookstore for a cup of coffee and a pastry. Occasionally, local artists would show up for open mic night, which was always a real treat.

After savoring the local color and flavor, I would return to the cedar-sided guesthouse, which sat behind a large main house occupied by my landlord, a single mother and schoolteacher who needed the rental income to offset her monthly expenses. I took great pleasure in admiring the views of the well-manicured grounds from my windows. A round stone umbrella table hugged by curved stone benches always caught my eye. It took center stage on a redbrick patio, surrounded by a colorful floral garden that separated the main house from the guest unit.

The first floor of the guesthouse was covered with Mexican pavers. I purchased a brightly colored futon for the living room to serve as seating or a bed for out-of-town visitors. In the kitchen area, a country-style table and four chairs with green-checked cushions welcomed guests for coffee or a hearty meal. I always planted a vase of fresh wildflowers in the center of the table, which was draped with a matching green-checked gingham tablecloth. My grandmother taught me as a teenager how to make pies, from picking apples off the tree to making buttery crusts. I started baking fruit pies on a weekly basis in my small, but adequate, oven and placed them next to the flowers on the table, creating a homey vignette you'd see in a decorating magazine. My favorite part was placing a clean cotton towel over the pie to allow for the aroma to fill the air while keeping it fresh for a few days.

The kitchen had white-painted wooden cupboards, a two-burner stove, and a window that looked out on a vegetable garden. Through the kitchen to the right was a rose-colored bathroom with a sink, a toilet, and a shower stall. Going upstairs was tricky in inclement weather because the wooden staircase to the second floor was outside and vulnerable to the elements, rain or shine. My upstairs bedroom had a double bed, a nightstand, and a small desk for the phone and a fax machine. I hung my clothes in full view in an open closet—which was basically a pole that spanned the length of the room. French doors opened to a covered balcony, my favorite spot in the guesthouse. I placed a comfortable chair and a padded stool for resting my feet in the corner of the balcony. I often sat there to read or simply reflect while gazing at the backyard.

The wonderful pre-accident time at the guesthouse haven was short-lived. The traumatic brain injury rendered me incapable of fully appreciating my charming abode. Often, I didn't have a clue what was going on. Thank goodness for Tina, a golf friend who lived upstairs in the main house.

One night, I stood in the middle of the driveway, clad in my pajamas, staring blankly at the street. From her window, she observed my bizarre behavior and was very concerned. She approached me outside and asked, "What are you doing out here? It's after midnight." Of course, I had no idea what I was doing or how I got there. She escorted me back to the guesthouse and tucked me into my bed.

Within a week, a couple of friends packed up belongings from the Sebastopol apartment and put them in a nearby storage unit.

Before heading to Ventura, I stayed with my cousin Lori, who lived near the San Francisco Bay Area in Walnut Creek, for a few days. Lori and I had very similar characteristics and could have passed as sisters. We even emanated the same free spirit vibe, but she had endless brain power. I knew Lori since she was 5 years old, as we used to play when our families got together. She was always on an adventure or a mission. Whenever she visited my family's house, we had to hide the candy dishes because she had such a sweet tooth. Little did we know there was a grand plan at work. She was training for her future career as the owner of a Belgian chocolate shop with her husband, Kurt.

Lori was on the leading edge of life. She travelled the world, rode a motorcycle, and ran marathons. A natural leader and initiator, she thrived in researching and creating more sustainable and healthy ways to live. Oh, how I wished I could live at her house permanently, but there was simply no room for me and my two orange cats, Maple Leaf and Jack. Plus, I needed a head injury support team, which was completely set up and available in Southern California. Lori drove me down to Ventura in my new white Ford 150 truck with an extended cab to help me get settled at her friend's house.

The 350-mile drive seemed never ending. My head hurt, I had double vision, and I was very confused. Time passed slowly, and conversation was scarce. If there was any talking, I don't remember it. About eight hours later, we turned into a cul de sac and pulled up to a wide flower-lined driveway. The house was huge, like a mansion, compared to the Sebastopol guesthouse. Upon arrival, we were greeted by Robin, who was one of Lori's Yoga buddies. An only child, she had inherited her parents' extravagant home.

Robin was in her forties, short and slender, with long, silky black hair looped with a colorful scarf and gold ring. Her soft almond complexion complemented her hazel eyes. I remember her smile the most with her white teeth and bright red lipstick. She reached out her arms and took me in for an awkward hug. I really needed to skip the introductions and lie down, but she insisted on taking Lori and me on a tour of her home. A proud single parent, she introduced her 8-year old twins, Carlo and Louise, both with shoulder-length black hair and huge cocoa eyes. They wore matching soccer jerseys and were openly friendly with happy smiles and curious hellos. They immediately ran to the truck to pet my calling cats.

Lori was delighted to see Robin again, as the last time they had connected was at her mother's funeral over a year ago. Lori had been instrumental in supporting her friend through her grieving process, well before her mother passed of cancer. Robin was happy to return the favor by watching over me for a few months. Plus, she was delighted to have some adult company and fill her large home with the hustle and bustle of the head injury rehab team when they came for my scheduled appointments.

Robin's home was an impressive two-story with cathedral ceilings and a loft, four bedrooms, two-and-a-half baths, an eight-person dining room set, and an enormous kitchen area. A playroom was off to the side of the house and had a large pool table, stocked bar, bar stools, and a dartboard on the wall. The living room was large and fully furnished, complete with a huge entertainment set up. She had a three-car garage that housed a Mercedes Sedan, a Jeep Wrangler, and a funky old red golf cart.

Robin escorted me to a guest bedroom at the back of the house, adjacent to the garage. It had its own rear entrance with an orange grove directly behind it. The room was neatly furnished with an old Victorian dresser, a nightstand, a headboard, and a queen-size bed draped with a floral bedspread and matching window curtains. Disoriented, I proceeded to place a large litter box in the double closet with the shuttered door slightly ajar, so my cats could freely roam in and out as needed.

Lori spent the first night with me at Robin's house, which was very comforting as I was in unfamiliar territory. The next morning, she helped put my clothes away. She took out a pad of sticky notes and wrote down the contents of each dresser drawer and tagged it onto the outside the matching drawer. She helped me mark everything so that I would remember what I had and wrote a contact sheet with important names and phone numbers and placed it by the nightstand.

When Lori was satisfied that I was all settled in, Robin took her to the Ventura Amtrak station, where she hopped a train back up to Walnut Creek. Lori called her later that night to assure me she had arrived home safely. Robin then relayed Lori's message to me. There was a landline cord phone on my nightstand, but I would just watch the flickering lights of the different lines, not knowing really what to do.

When Lori returned to Walnut Creek, she placed an ad in the newspaper to sell my new truck, as I could no longer drive. About a month later, the truck was sold, and the money went to paying off the auto loan. This left me at Robin's mercy to drive me to medical appointments, the grocery store, and wherever else I needed to go. I felt like one of her kids being dropped off for school events or soccer practice.

My parents were delighted that I was getting the help I needed, although I did not fully disclose the details of my living situation with them. While I was growing up, my projected role in the family was to always be the strong one. I was the mediator, or "Miss Perfect" as some family members would say, so I was usually clear on what I told them. With my traumatic brain injury, it was a bit different, so I didn't share much of the daily happenings with my parents, except for the therapy sessions. My parents trusted that everything was going smoothly and, for the most part, it did. My father was vulnerable, as he already had two bypasses in his life. I didn't want to put him through another one, so I kept quiet about any stressful experiences.

One stressful matter pertained to daily legal matters. As part of the litigation process, I was bombarded with copies of many legal transactions. It amounted to a vast hoard of papers that were haphazardly stored in my room and the adjacent hallway. This contributed to my already overwhelming sense of being reduced to just a name on paper.

One day, I was returning from my trip to Santa Barbara. Robin picked me up at the train station and we headed back to her house. As we came upon her street, we noticed a man sitting in a car in front of the house. As we pulled into the driveway, he got out of his car and approached us. He was a tall, heavy set man, and carried something in both hands. Not thinking, I opened my car door and started to get out of the car. Suddenly, he grabbed the door and swung it open. As I stood up, he shoved a big stack of papers into my stomach. Then, he ran to his car and sped away. She tried to get his license number, but to no avail. Shaken, I dropped the papers that were obviously a gift from the defense lawyers. I saw my name and some lawyers' names across the top. Robin helped me gather them up and escorted me to my room. Trembling, I put them in a box and added it to the heap in the hallway. Such grim reminders of a long litigation process.

To help me forget these stressful events, I enjoyed playing games with the twins, especially Louise. She was a very compassionate little girl, brimming with love. We would sit on the living room floor and play the memory game. That's where you lay all the cards out face down and take turns picking up two cards and try to match them. Then, count how many pairs you have, and whoever had the most won the game. Louise always won, but she helped me try to remember. "Here, Kathy, look here, and now try this one," she said innocently. Little did she know how much she was helping my brain to recircuit itself. Sometimes she would sit on my lap on the couch while she watched a kid cartoon movie. I'd wrap my arms around her and we'd snuggle.

Louise's favorite game was a video game called Mario. A little Italian guy with a mustache would fly down a snowy mountain with several obstacles to overcome down to the finish line. Louise was good, Carlo, her twin brother, was great, and I was the comic relief. I barely got out of the blocks before I would run into a tree or fall off the side of the cliff. Oh, how they would laugh and shout, "Do it again! C'mon, do it again!" I would laugh, too, because funny music played every time Mario fell or bumped into something. I always enjoyed Carlo's and Louise's company, as it seemed real to me and it was just pure fun.

Carlo loved to play soccer; however, at the time, it was not my forte. It was too hard to track a darting ball and run. So, we used to play catch out in the cul de sac in front of the house using a soft football. Catching was a different story. Often, I would duck out of the way for fear of getting hit in the face and head. I must have looked like I was trying to catch a falling leaf in the wind, with the sun in my face. The days passed easier with the kids.

Robin encouraged me to make myself at home, including cleaning up, especially in the kitchen. Washing dishes became my evening chore. It passed the time, but since time didn't exist for me, it just passed. It also got me out of the bedroom, which I'm sure was good for me. I realized I was staying in someone's home for free, but most of the time I was in pain or confused, so I couldn't do much about it. I tried to pitch in to the extent of my abilities.

The frontal lobe of my brain was the hardest hit from the injury and executive functioning was lax for me, so doing chores became a good way to relearn daily living activities. I also enjoyed walking a loop from Robin's house. We mapped it out on a piece of paper first, and then she drove me around the street loop in her golf cart to show the way. I would walk daily around the loop, following the white painted line on the street all the way around until I returned to the cul de sac. Occasionally, I sensed someone was following or watching me. Weird. I'd look around, but never saw anyone.

Robin's true joy was rearing her children, along with aspiring to be an actress, performing on stage. Singing show tunes was one of her favorite past times and, occasionally, I sang along. I had been in a few musicals during high school and sang in the college choir. Singing along with Robin helped me to remember words and phrasing in a fun way. She also hosted a kids music class once a week down at the local church, so the house was always filled with music. Carlo and Louise would often join in with their musical instruments, marching with flittering tambourines, rattles, and drums to keep the beat.

I truly love music, as I grew up in a household of performers. My dad and mom met in marching band, both playing the snare drums. My dad continued to play the drums the rest of his life, including his own three-brother polka band and more than 30 years in the local town community band. My mom played the harmonica and organ in their home on the lake and sang in the church choir on Sundays. I even took organ lessons as a child, and eventually, switched to playing keyboards and, occasionally, the accordion. Although the music in Robin's house was uplifting and joyous, my brain just couldn't handle all the tinkering sounds. I'd have to bow out because of the disorientation in my head, and then there was the pain that seemed to well up from deep inside my ear canals causing that long, empty tunnel feeling.

Many days and nights, I sat at the edge of my bed, staring out the window. I had no thoughts, just a hollow awareness.

Occasionally, Robin would open my bedroom door slightly and watch me just sitting and staring at the edge of the bed. "What are you thinking, Kathleen?" she asked me quite concerned one day. "I'm not thinking anything. I'm not thinking at all. My mind is just hollow," I replied, without turning toward her.

Looking back during this time, the noise in my head was debilitating, painful and made me feel numb, paralyzed and unable to function or think clearly, thrusting me into utter despair.

CHAPTER 9

THE REHABILITATION TEAM

Dr. Cheryll Smith, a prominent, California–based neuro-psychologist specializing in head injuries became instrumental in my rehabilitation and coordinated my therapy with the satellite Head Injury Rehabilitation Program through the Santa Barbara headquarters. Like clockwork, therapists arrived at Robin's home for cognitive, speech, and vision sessions four times a week. I would sit at the dining room table with each therapist for an hour or so, depending on my threshold levels. Often, I was instructed to sit on my hands to keep them under control. In the early days, apparently my tongue and eyes moved involuntarily, which I was unaware of at the time.

My cognitive/speech therapist, Carol, was an older woman with dark brown hair and wire-rimmed glasses that frequently ended up on the tip of her nose. We met weekly to work on my internal reality, such as cognitive issues, especially my slow and disorganized thinking. She would have me read short stories about a half-page long, and then I would have to answer a series of five to six questions regarding the content of the story. I read so slowly that the story sounded more like a series of separate words, which made it very difficult for me to string those words into a reliable sentence, let alone a full story. My cadence was about a word a second, with extra syllables. "This-is-a-stor-y-a-bout-a-but-ter-fly-who-live-d-in-the-rho-do-den-dron-bush."

When I became aware of this, I would feel greatly distressed, and cry because I did not understand why I could not talk normally, which only made the process of changing the thinking pattern longer. Plus, when I became distressed, my tongue would involuntarily start wiggling back and forth in my mouth. I had to overcome these emotional responses, mainly through focusing on my breath, and then go back and begin the task again. When I became too overwhelmed, Carol would instruct me to go outside on the deck and look at the hills. Robin's house was situated atop a hill and overlooked other rolling hillsides, with plenty of greenery, and long plots of farming on the flats in the distance. The scenery was calming and helped to clear my brain. After a while, we would go back into the house and begin again.

My short-term memory loss prevented me from remembering the whole story, so in the beginning, Carol instructed me to answer each question by reading the story over and over until I found the answer on the written page. This took more time to go through and flooded my brain, although it was effective in developing a new skill level through reprogramming my brain. Eventually, I could answer questions from a short story, even though I would have to reconstruct the story in my mind for the answer to be revealed. I did not automatically remember specific content, so I had to organize the story from the beginning. I still use this strategy today.

After each session, I walked down a long hallway to the back of the house where my bedroom was located. My brain would be fried and fuzzy, and I had to lie in my bed until I became less symptomatic. This usually lasted several hours, and often I would even forget to eat meals.

One day, I created a small collage to gain relief from left-brain programming because creative expression resides primarily in the right hemisphere. I glued two manila folders together and flipped through some *Home and Garden* magazines in search of photos that made me feel happy. I cut out beautiful flowers, a ruby-throated hummingbird, a glowing fireplace, a water fountain with cascading green foliage, and the words *truth, passion,* and *freedom*. I found an old black-and-white photo of a woman who resembled me. Her back was to the reader as she sat on a hillside looking out into the future. I glued her into the center of the flower garden. But was that me? I didn't know.

I received a fun package in the mail that day from my Aphrodite friend, Dae. It contained some rose facial cream and a rosewater spritzer, which I immediately delighted in. It brought back memories of our days in the bathtub together, with edifying conversation and mouthwatering treats. She also enclosed a cassette tape of "focus wheeling" by Jerry and Esther Hicks and their teachings of the law of attraction.

I loved listening to Esther's inspiring voice and even scribbled out a focus wheel of my own on a sheet of notebook paper. First, I drew a circle in the middle of the paper, and in the center, I wrote, "My body is a body of well-being." This is the general statement of what I desired. Then, I deliberately chose other statements which were soothing, and when I wrote them, I would feel a sense of relief. Some examples I used from Esther's tapes were: "I like the idea of deliberately focusing and my body responding." "This inconvenient experience will serve me well over time," and "Every cell in my body is listening, every cell in my body is rejuvenating now."

As I continued to write the positive thoughts, I experienced a cognitive combustion with more positive thoughts joining in. I held the thoughts as best as I could, as I rambled around and around the center with the phrases. I knew that if I could keep my focus, if only for a few seconds, the point of attraction would move up the vibrational ladder, setting my own tone, and the desired outcome would eventually surface. I always felt so much better just doing the exercise, even if I didn't understand how the whole process worked. I know it lifted my spirits although today I cannot tell you what was on those spirals of words and phrases. I only remember how I felt, and back then that was the most important sensation as my "thinking cap" was very fragmented and discombobulated. It would be months before I came out of the tunnel and became aware of all the issues from the traumatic brain injury.

My Day of Freedom

Dr. Smith was the highlight of my rehabilitation. For almost a year, I travelled by train to see her once or twice weekly. I enjoyed the independence of getting away from the house I always sat by the window, facing forward. I loved seeing the ocean and, occasionally, I caught a glimpse of a porpoise swimming in the surf.

Upon arriving in Santa Barbara, I walked a couple of blocks to the street trolley, plopped my quarter in the ticket machine, and off I went down State Street. Sometimes, I stepped off the trolley at the correct stop, although many times I would get lost and needed to ask someone where I was. People were always willing to point me in the right direction. I usually ended up at the office out of breath and a bit disoriented but always happy to see Dr. Smith.

Her office was in an old white stucco Spanish-style building just off upper State Street in Santa Barbara. I took the small elevator up to the third floor, turned right, and there was an ordinary wooden door, with a bronze sign emblazoned with her name. Once inside, there was a waiting room with a couch, a couple of chairs, some potted plants, and plenty of old magazines. When it was my turn, Dr. Smith came down the long hallway and introduced herself. She led me back down the hallway to a door on the left.

Upon entering, I felt like I was walking into someone's living room, with a love seat to the right by the picture window and a couple of high-back Victorian chairs across from the couch, with some handwoven blankets thrown over their tops. There was an oval maple coffee table in the middle. A long table topped with pens, pencils, paper, and an alarm clock occupied the back of the room. Floor-to-ceiling bookshelves lined the back wall, which was filled with what seemed to be hundreds of books, props, and gadgets.

It was a corner office, so the right side had another window with a small desk in front of it, and a metal file cabinet next to the desk. A few inspirational posters adorned the wall, along with a large paper calendar. The whole room was carpeted, and the windows had drapes that were open. There was a large potted fern near the window to capture sunlight. I observed the city view and caught a glimpse of the ocean in the distance. It also provided some natural lighting and relief, if necessary, from the confinement of a "processing" room, even though it was set up to be comfortable and inviting. In my mind, I knew this homey setting would be conducive to my rehabilitation.

Dr. Smith was an attractive blonde in her late 40s or early 50s. She was curvaceous and a bit shorter than my 5-foot 8-3/4-inch stature. She dressed professionally in pant suits or skirt suits, with matching scarves, pins, and earrings. Her hair was always styled with just the right amount of lift and wave. Dr. Smith reminded me of country singer Faith Hill because of her big smile and the way she talked, which was very kind and pleasing to the ear. I felt at ease with her immediately, with her soft blue eyes and a hug that was welcoming and warm, like a hundred mothers had taken me in. The more I came for office visits, the more I fell in love with her, literally.

Not only was she helping me, but we were making progress in my emotional healing process. She knew what she was doing, and many of the strategies and exercises were helping me right away. She was very positive and responded to my many questions with, "We'll get there, Kathleen." She had a way of tilting her head to the side and smiling when she said it, which felt very assuring to me.

I applied many of the strategies I learned from Dr. Smith to my daily living situations. She also recommended using earplugs, which were helpful in lengthening my threshold levels. I wore them at Robin's house, to the mall, and to the grocery store. I always popped them in when spending one-on-one time with the twins, especially while watching TV or playing board games.

I was paranoid about someone lurking in the shadows and watching me, like when I walked the loop at Robin's house. One afternoon, I was in Alice Keck Park Memorial Garden with Aphrodite Dae and her daughter, who were visiting from Northern California. We tossed a frisbee, watched turtles in the pond, and enjoyed a picnic in the grass. I noticed a man taking photos of me, but I just kept on playing. Dae saw him, too, but quickly redirected me back to having fun. Dr. Smith explained that it was very possible the defense team in my legal case would put my actions under surveillance to use the videotaping in court, and that I was not experiencing paranoia at all, but that it was really happening. Of course, this made me even more paranoid.

The Doctor–Patient Relationship

The work I was doing with Dr. Smith was very exhausting at times. She called it "brain flooding." Sometimes, I reached a point where I'd be talking with my eyes closed, and then I just slowed to a stop. That was one of the first senses to go when my brain shut down. I would rest for several minutes, and then we would pick up where we left off in our session after the short nap, or sometimes that was all I could do for that session. Dr. Smith was smart, experienced, and supported me in my head injury rehabilitation. She listened attentively to my every word, seemingly captivated by my story, humor, and wit.

I fell into the predicted path of transference, where the patient falls in love with the therapist. I remember some touching moments together, like when it was spring in Santa Barbara. All the jacaranda trees had lost some of the purple blooms down State Street, and the ground was covered like a purple carpet. It was like a Monet painting of reflection. So, I scooped up as many of the blooms as I could and slipped them into my pockets. When I entered Dr. Smith's office, I dropped them from my hands onto the chair and table where she was sitting, and the rest fell to the floor. There was the beautiful re-creation of the resplendent scene the trees and petals had created in the street. "Charming," she said in a soft voice.

Another time I walked into her office and handed her a large rock and said, "Falling rock. A gift for you. I watched it fall from the foothill cliff where I walked on my way here today. What are the odds of that happening?"

She thanked me, tilted her head, and smiled. Did she love me? Maybe, but not a romantic love, I'm sure. Dr. Smith had integrity. Love played a central role in our alliance. It kept the healing juices open and flowing. I trusted her, and she had confidence in me to keep going, despite the challenging journey. But I was romantically in love with her, so much so that I would write poetry to her in a secret journal. I never told her. I have a degree in psychology and knew about the behaviors of the heart and mind. Although I never disclosed the love journal, I did dedicate a sketch to her. She spoke of a loon on one of her vacations in Wisconsin and how it sat out on the lake and gave its mating call. So, I drew one for her on a lake, and put myself nestled right on her back. (See Figure 1: In Perfect Love and Perfect Trust.)

Dr. Smith encouraged me to meet people and eventually to try to build intimate relationships again. Then, one day she said I would fall in love and maybe get married. Although she was accepting and understanding, she never allowed me to become dependent on her. It was because she held her professional ground with integrity and respect, coupled with the fact I expressed my love for her through a love journal, that the romantic feelings simply faded into appropriate affection. The transference was complete.

At each session, we worked together for an hour, and then I would travel back to Ventura. I often stopped at Baja Sharkeez, a famous taco shack and surfers' hangout, where I would sit and eat a couple of fish tacos and all the chips and salsa I could devour before I headed back to the train station. This was my favorite part of the trip because they had large overhead TVs with professional surfers from all over the world surfing the big waves. It was a familiar feeling for me, as I had been learning to surf before I had the accident. I asked Dr. Smith if I could ever surf again, and she said maybe, although I still had to work on setting my alarm, getting up in the morning, combing my hair, brushing my teeth, getting dressed, and getting to my appointments on time. Many times, I would do all that and not be able to go anywhere because my brain was already too overloaded. So much for getting to the ocean at high tide.

Thanks to Dr. Smith's efforts, I had some spending money of my own. She helped me fill out paperwork to apply for disability. It was a very tedious process, but once approved, it was a big payoff for me. It was retroactive for nine months, so I received quite a reimbursement check from Medicare.

An occupational therapist helped me open a bank account in Santa Barbara so I could write checks. It was good practice to learn how to balance my checkbook again.

Now, when Robin dropped me off at Barnes & Noble at the mall, I could indulge in a coffee and pastry and look at magazines. Pictures were easier to look at than reading the words. The old right brain thing, right? I was unable to read books at the time. The rehab center would send books on tape to me for free, although the list of books was limited. They also sent a clunky cassette player the size of a toaster oven. The tapes looked like bulky eight-track cassettes, and I would pop them into the player until I heard a click. I also treated myself with buying books on tape.

Art Played a Part

To alleviate anxiety, I began to sketch. I grabbed a paper bag and pressed it neatly to lay flat like a canvas. I used a stubby No. 2 pencil and began to draw a woman who looked like a butterfly on the brown bag. It didn't take long to finish it; time didn't exist for me anyway. At one of my appointments with Dr. Smith, I showed her the butterfly sketch. She promptly grabbed my hand and took me to an art store where she bought me a sketchpad and pencils and sent them home with me that day.

I drew a beautiful lenten rose and another sketch became a naked woman's back with a long string of pearls. I had her sitting in her bedroom on her cosmetic bench, looking out an open window. The last sketch I drew in that home was a mailbox, titled "M. Lonlee" (as in "I'm lonely"), which surely disclosed my unhappiness. (See Figure 2: M. Lonlee.) Thoughts translated into pictures, which was a first step in addressing the emotions these images represented. When you say something, it becomes real.

Lori Takes Notice

Lori visited me again on her way back from a massage workshop in Los Angeles. She carried in a massage table and, at Robin's direction, hauled it upstairs to the meditation/yoga room, the only private room with enough space to work around a large table. The upper area of the master suite had a futon mattress on the floor adorned with an aqua blue bedspread with golden tassels and elaborate gold curtains that billowed with the outdoor breeze. There was a small altar on a long, low wooden table, with several ritual items positioned on top. A lower-level sitting area was two steps down from this sacred space and housed a huge statue of the sitting Buddha. It was an ideal spot for entertaining those higher vantage point conversations.

Lori set the massage table up in the upper area. I was unable to lie on my stomach due to head pain, so Lori instructed me to lie on my back with two pillows beneath my head and proceeded to gently massage my arms and legs over the sheet. Although she didn't say much during our session, she commented on the joy of practicing her new techniques so quickly. I felt comforted by her presence and feeling her soft touch.

I sensed Lori was observing my living situation while she was there. I watched her eyes as she talked with Robin in the kitchen after my massage. They were sipping green tea at the counter bar stools, and she was asking lots of questions, while I played a board game with the twins. Lori instinctively knew I was unhappy with this isolating living situation, despite Robin's compassion and generosity. Robin also filled her in about the stranger, who aggressively unloaded legal papers into my gut, and that I was probably being videotaped by the defense team.

Lori escorted me to my room and said she had to leave soon and get back home before dark. She mentioned that she wanted to talk with Dr. Smith and schedule an appointment in the next moon or two. We always talked by way of the moon. With that, she kissed my forehead and said she would make all the arrangements and not to even think about it right now. "Love you," she whispered, and out the door she went. I heard them at the front door in the foyer saying their good-byes, and in a moment, it was just Robin, the twins, and me again.

CHAPTER 10

THINGS AREN'T WHAT THEY SEEM

Nighttime was long at Robins' house. I kept hearing unfamiliar sounds in the house. On many nights, I would hear a man coughing in the garage adjacent to my bedroom. I thought, poor thing, he's going to get sick in the cold, damp garage. Why is he in the garage anyway? Why doesn't he wear a warm wool coat? What is he doing in there so late at night?

My thoughts were fleeting and came and went like a darting bat in the dark. The coughing mystery was solved weeks later, when I finally grabbed my all-weather coat and tiptoed down the long hallway to investigate. I opened a door that led directly into the garage. Alas, I looked around and there was no one there. I'm going crazy, I thought. I slumped down on the cold cement floor and began to cry. "Where are you?" I yelled. Was I hallucinating? After a while, I picked myself up off the floor and returned to my bedroom. I laid across the bed with my coat still on, and drift into a semi-sleep state. Dark scenes of the many depositions I took part in began to flash before my eyes. Defense lawyers' faces, cold sterile rooms, and white male hands prodding and poking.

And there he was, the coughing man with a short steel needle pricking me slowly up one leg, then down the other. "Can you feel that?" he'd ask, then cough like something was tickling his throat. He'd move a couple inches up my leg more, "Can you feel that?" he'd ask again, and then cough. Slowly up one leg from foot to the upper thigh, then slowly down the other. And then onto each arm to the arm pit, inching slowly, "Can you feel that?", cough. There I sat on a cold steel table, bare legs dangling, with only a short patient's gown on tied in the back, at the mercy of this "doctor." I was shocked that I had to take off my clothes and put this gown on. What does this have to do with a head injury anyway? What the fuck is going on here?

Apparently, no one else was allowed in the examination room for some of these tests, not even a friend. When he was done sticking me, he proceeded to look into my eyes with a thin, bright flashlight. He told me to look straight ahead as he searched inside my pupil for what seemed like minutes. It was difficult to keep steady with such a bright beam of light pointed directly into my eyes and many times I had to bow my head. I asked him to please stop as it was hurting my eyes and head, but he'd cough and say, "Are you asking me to stop the examination?" "Are you refusing to go on with this examination?" I guess I had to continue, because he'd have to schedule another appointment, and I'd be right back in the same situation. Even with a traumatic brain injury, I was lucid enough to start realizing this "doctor" may not have my best interest at heart. He seemed antagonistic at best, and I started feeling terribly shamed and trapped.

I saw colored blots that would get brighter when I blinked. He finally took the bright light away, but his questions persisted, flooding my brain well past threshold levels.

I roused from this sleep state and sat up. It all seemed so real. Pulling the coat closer for warmth, I recalled other stressful and painful experiences with the defense doctors. Unfortunately, the tests had to be conducted to confirm the extent of my disabilities.

There was another male defense doctor who gave me an examination at the top floor of an old hotel room right off the elevator. The room had a wooden table and two chairs, with papers and some pens on the table. He gave me a couple of timed written tests to do. He'd start the clock and then he would leave the room. Every so often there would be a doorbell ring sound and the elevator doors would clang open and people would look in and say, "Oh, sorry, we must have the wrong floor." I stared in disbelief. I'm trying to take a test here. The defense doctor returned and yelled at me for not doing the test correctly. "You're going too slow. You're never going to finish this test today at this rate!" I could only go as fast as I could read the question and try to figure it out. Plus, the elevator doors didn't help matters. Frustrated, he insisted on staying in the room to watch me. The hours of testing and interruptions were taking a toll on my brain. I was getting nauseous and I had that pressure type headache and my brain felt like it was going explode at any minute.

The testing continued. The doctor handed me a standard sheet of white typing paper and asked me to draw a box and put my full name in the center of the box. I placed the paper slowly onto the table and began to draw the box somewhere on the sheet of paper. The little box came out to be about the size of a quarter. I started to write my first name in tiny letters. In one sweeping motion, he snatched the paper right out from under my pencil. "Time's up," he said. Something changed in his voice as he ended the evaluation. My head dropped from the tension, and I felt I had done something wrong. The doctor walked over to the coat rack and grabbed my jacket. With one hand, he placed the crumpled jacket up under my chin so I could see it. He knew I had tunnel vision at this point, and realized that I truly had a traumatic brain injury.

I met another defense doctor at another hotel, although this time it was actually in the hotel room. There were two double beds and a small table and chairs. The very old white male doctor in a worn business suit sat in the chair with a clip board and pen, and instructed me to sit on the bed. It was so intimidating to be with this stranger, but at least I got to keep my clothes on. He only asked me to take off my shoes and socks, and sit back on the bed a bit so my feet rested comfortably at the edge. Then, he performed some kind of reflex test with fishing line. He took the piece of nylon cord and dangled near my bare feet, touching different points here and there, asking if I could feel that, and watched to see if my feet responded to touch. By the way, he didn't cough, but he did ask me some questions. He stated that cases like mine were usually decided with scientific-based evidence, like a pet scan, a colored image x-ray of the brain. Huh, why did he offer that information? I had this type of brain scan done, and it showed exactly what brain parts were injured and weaker. I will explain brain function in upcoming chapters for better understanding.

Night turned into early morning as I heard birds chirping outside. I was exhausted from replaying the demeaning examinations in my mind. I took my coat off and flung it on the floor near the closet. I slipped under the covers to get a few hours of sleep before the day's activities unfolded.

The Suicide Attempt

I awoke in the afternoon, still feeling miserable. I was in the pool room a couple of hours later hitting balls into the cups with a cue stick. My vision therapist gave me this exercise as homework. Creating shots and tracking the angles to make it in the hole helped me forge new brain pathways, especially the occipital region that caused the vision problems. I could not perform this exercise for very long because it really taxed my brain. When the therapist first taught me, I would become nauseated and have the dry heaves. After an eventful night, my brain was already overloaded, and saliva began to build up in my mouth.

After some shaky practicing, I set my cue stick down, walked over to the window, and looked out unto the hills. There was nothing calming about their existence today. An unrelenting litigation was draining me, despite my efforts to stay focused on my healing path. I was done. My heart hurt, my brain hurt, and I felt trapped. I couldn't do this anymore. With that, I walked past the pool table and up a couple of steps, preceded past the dining room through the foyer, walked down the long hallway to my bedroom, and closed the door behind me. I sat on the edge of the bed and stared out the window until dark.

It was after midnight and all was quiet, except me. I was still awake and fumbled with all the books and papers in my bed. It must have been fall because I heard a professional football game on the big-screen TV. Someone must have forgotten to turn it off. I kept hearing voices and my head hurt badly, so I got out of bed to turn the damn thing off. Oddly, the living room was dark, the TV was off, nobody was around, but I could still hear some muffled voices.

I returned to my bedroom and looked at the mirror where I had taped my handmade collage with colored pictures of nature, inspirational words, and the woman in black and white sitting on the ground, looking out into empty space. This woman was me. I was more than sad that night—I was giving up. The pain, the isolation, a stressful litigation, and the constant learning and relearning with all the therapists were overwhelming. I reached for my prescription bottle of Valium and walked into the bathroom, where I set them on the edge of the bathtub. I ran the hot and cold water in the tub to a peaceful warmth and shut the handles off at about three-quarters full. I also lit the white candle that was already on the edge of the tub, too.

I returned to my bed, slipped off my pajamas, sat for a moment, and then reached for the glass of water on the night-stand. "The plan" was to take all of the Valium, lie back and rest comfortably in the bath water with my feet up on the sides so the water came to just under my chin, and then wait for the Valium to take effect. If the Valium didn't work, I would surely slide into the water and drown. End of pain, end of lawsuit, end of life. Even now in writing this, it is very difficult to look back. I had written "the plan" instead of "my plan," which completely removed me from ownership of the suicide scheme.

Suddenly, I remembered a promise I made to Dr. Smith. When I discussed my suicidal thoughts in a therapy session, she asked me to make two phone calls before I went through with it. One call would be to her, and the other to a good friend. I looked over at my two orange cats, Jack and Maple Leaf, who were snuggled together in their sheepskin bed. They loved to spoon each other after their preening session. They looked so peaceful together.

I grabbed the phone and called Dr. Smith. After several rings, she answered in a daze, "Kathleen, Kathleen?"

"Hi, Dr. Smith," I said calmly. "You asked me to give you a call if I was going to commit suicide."

Sounding a bit annoyed, she said, "Do you know what time it is? It's one o'clock in the morning!"

"Yes, I know it's late, I'm sorry, but I can't take it anymore, and I am going to end my life," I said somberly.

Fully awake now, she asked, "How are you going to do this?" I shared my bath and Valium plan with her, and the tone in her voice softened. I felt her heart speaking directly to mine. "Kathleen, I know it's hard right now, but one day you will look back on all this fondly. And you will know how strong and courageous you really are. Where are your cats? I want you to go over and pet them right now." I began to pet my cats and felt their warm fur on my hands, and they began to purr.

She continued: "Do you know what will happen in the morning? The two children who live there are going to come in to say good morning, and they will see you floating in the bathtub." She paused. "And you won't even get to say good-bye to them. Is that what you want?" I muttered, "I don't know," and before she said good night, she reminded me of our appointment Tuesday morning and that we could talk more about this at that time. I said good night, hung up, and immediately dialed my friend Christine.

She was startled as I explained my plan to commit suicide, although she knew this call may come one day because I promised I would contact her before going through with it. I was just fulfilling my promise. We talked for several minutes about our golfing extravaganzas and how much fun we had together. She shared her plans to visit me very soon and asked if that would be all right. Sleepy-eyed, I said I didn't know and hung up the phone.

I kissed Jack and Maple Leaf on their foreheads, grabbed the glass of water, and walked slowly into the bathroom. I sat on the toilet seat, picked up the bottle of Valium, emptied two into my hand, and plopped them into my mouth, with a quick swish of water to wash them down. Surprisingly, I pulled the stopper from the tub and listened to the water begin to drain. I blew out the candle, crawled back into bed, and drifted into slumber, too tired to kill myself.

In hindsight, it was a very poignant time in my life. Dr. Smith's strategy worked. The two calls got me through the night with purpose and compassion. I met with her at our regularly scheduled session, and she strongly advised that I find a new place to live so I could move on in my healing process. Dr. Smith promised me things would get better in my life if I continued practicing the strategies faithfully, as I was reprogramming my brain every day, and that it would just take some time, if not years. That whole period was confusing to me because I didn't know if what was happening in my mind was reflected on the outside with appropriate gestures. For example, I know I was asked to smile by one of the doctors, so I did, I thought. But he asked me repeatedly to please smile. Apparently, I was not smiling at all; I had a dead pan expression, no matter how many times I tried. Later, I learned this was a symptom of PseudoBulbar Affect (PBA). It is a neurological condition noted for outbursts of uncontrolled or inappropriate laughing or crying, which I did unexpectedly at the slightest change of daily routine. Various regions along the brain pathway were likely responsible for the loss of inhibitory or regulatory control on the expression of emotions. Part of this pathway includes the cerebellum, which plays a key role in modulating or monitoring emotional responses and ensures they are appropriate to the social situation. Disruption of the neural pathways were evident from the golf ball striking my head to certain areas of the brain, such as the cerebellum that lead to a loss or lack of control over emotional expression. In the instance of the facial expression, I had lost the capability to move the muscles that controlled my mouth appropriately.

When I learned that I had PBA, I would practice the inner smile technique, smiling from within, just like I had taught my college golf team to do. I would look in the mirror and practice curling the ends of my lips upward, to help those brain circuits to fire up again. Eventually, what was happening inside my brain was transmitted to the appropriate action or gesture on the outside.

Another important distinction in my doctor's appointments to note was that every sound or action was amplified for several years after my brain injury. Did the doctor poke me with a needle all those times, or was this a figment of the injury? Was the prodding extensive or was my sensitivity to touch extreme? Did the heavyset guy thrust papers into my stomach? Was there a mountain of legal papers, or were there just a few stacks lying around? These questions will never be answered. More important, I found a way to move forward to the best of my abilities, and that is what I remember most.

Santa Barbara Calls

After receiving my call about contemplating suicide, Dr. Smith jumped into action and connected me with Linda, an occupational therapist in Ventura, who would assist me in moving to a trailer in Santa Barbara. Linda reminded me of Laura Petri on *The Dick Van Dyke Show*, long and slender, with black hair styled from the 1950s. Dr. Smith told me that Linda would help prepare me to move into my new home, a trailer in Santa Barbara.

Linda visited me at Robin's home twice a week for a month to commence the moving process. She showed me a timeline of the steps we needed to take for a smooth and easy transition. We moved through the items, step by step, starting with locating a new bank in Santa Barbara and scheduling utility start-ups in the new trailer. We looked at what I had at Robin's house, mainly clothes and my cats' stuff. We prepared new labels for all the items so that when I moved, I would know exactly where everything was. We boxed and marked everything accordingly. We transferred my books on tape addresses and set up a forwarding address for the post office.

Although my stay with Robin was timely and very supportive, it was time for me to begin integrating into a community that was not so isolating. In Santa Barbara, I would be able to become more independent. Dr. Smith also wanted me to begin classes at the Schott Center once a week to practice my writing skills, and she wanted me to attend a vision training center. These were paramount in my rehabilitation process.

Moving day finally arrived. All my items were packed in the bedroom and ready to go, including the cat dishes, bedding, and litter box. Carlo and Louise helped me haul some of the smaller things outside to the front of the garage. They played with Maple Leaf and Jack, who were securely locked in their double carrier cage, while we waited for Linda to come with her SUV. When

Linda arrived, my heart began to race. I could feel a stirring excitement. I was really going to leave this place!

Linda, Robin and I loaded the car, and then I thanked Robin for welcoming me into her home and caring for me. There are still good-hearted people in this world who are compassionate, even though they seemingly have no gain. They care just because they care, and that is a gift and a great lesson in humanity.

Robin and Linda exchanged phone numbers and my new address in Santa Barbara. With that, I hugged the kids and Robin and quickly jumped in the front seat of the SUV, closing the door behind me. Everyone waved as Linda and I drove away from the big house. Carlo and Louise ran down the driveway shouting and waving until we turned the corner. I remember looking down and softly sobbing, knowing that I was taking a huge step in my life to become independent again.

CHAPTER 11

TALES FROM MY TRAILER HAVEN

My new home was a classic white trailer with rounded ends, built in the 1950s, with three louvered bay windows with screens on all sides, making for great ventilation and fresh breezes from the outside. There was an old furnace built in right off the front side door, and I would use it to help burn off some of the moisture, especially during the June gloom, characterized by foggy mornings. Otherwise, it sometimes had an unpleasant mildew odor. The furnace warmed up the place quickly, especially in the short winter months of Santa Barbara.

The living room area had an old gray couch on one side, and my small cherrywood bookshelf on the other side. I also had room for a medium-size mother-of-pearl accordion that sat upright on the floor, which gave the place an authentic feel. Many a night, I would sit on a small wooden chair in the middle of the room with a steel music stand in front of me. I'd place my music sheets on it and practice my songs for the next weekly lesson.

One of my favorite songs, "La Vie en Rose," literally translates to "life in pink." However, it would be better translated to "life through rosy glasses." The idea is to depict a state where everything appears rosy and cheerful to you. I also enjoyed playing an Italian song called "Barcarolla," which translates to the "boat ride," or "long journey." And, of course, there was the occasional polka tune, given my Polish ancestry. Even though the lights weren't very bright in the trailer, I could see enough to play. Once I started to get the feel for the song, I would close my eyes anyway, so it didn't much matter. It gave me great joy to play, especially because no one was listening.

I remember walking back from town one day with a real find at the thrift store: a small three-legged circular table that cost one dollar. I flung a red fringed scarf over it, and it looked so beautiful next to the old gray couch. I kept my phone and a notepad and pencil on the top. I managed to create a milk crate shelf structure with a cat pillow on top for Jack and Maple Leaf to sit or lie together and peer out the front picture window. They loved looking out into the large rose garden area and up into the surrounding ridge of trees.

Many animals would come through the hollow there, including bobcat, deer (who ate the plums right off the plum tree), raccoons, and coyotes. I could hear a mother opossum and her three babies scrambling up in the persimmon tree right off the front window. I loved looking up the animals in my *Medicine Cards* book by Jamie Sams and David Carson (New York: St. Martin's Press, 1988, 1999). There, I'd discover what message of healing or life lesson they brought to me. It was a fun and personal pathway to connect with the animal kingdom; plus, I enjoyed looking at the cards.

There were some large boulders in view, scattered about up toward the ridge where the back of the property ended, which provided great spots for sitting and meditating. I also heard the crickets' song at night, although in the beginning it contributed to the unbearable "white noise" ringing radio static in my ears.

There was a small kitchen area in the middle of the trailer next to the living room, and a small two-basin sink for washing and drying dishes. My two pots and lone frying pan could be stored easily in the small oven and two-burner stove. It was no bigger than a bread box, but I could still bake brownies and even roast a chicken. The counter space was even smaller, but I didn't have many kitchen gadgets to take up space anyway. One of the first things I bought while on disability was a water purifier that hooked right up to the kitchen faucet and sat on the counter. I may not have had much, but, at least, I had the freshest water around.

The walls and trim were constructed of light-colored wood, with plenty of lacquer that caused a bright shine on the inside, making it easy to wipe off any dust. The quaint trailer had worn blue indoor/outdoor carpeting throughout the 22-foot by 8-foot cabin area. I would walk up and down the middle aisle of the trailer to get some exercise and relieve some anxiousness. My cat Jack would always follow me because I would coax him along: "Come on, Jack, take a walk with me now." We would get to the end and I would turn around, Jack would circle around, and then we'd walk the whole length again, which for me was about 15 paces. We'd walk for a long time, sometimes maybe an hour. It was easy to get lost in the sounds of nature, like crickets and frogs or the stream that ran alongside the trailer. I remember just being grateful to be able to walk and be in my own space. The wooden ceiling was quite low, and if I got a little dizzy, I just put my arms up and dragged my hands along the smooth, shiny surface.

Toward the back of the trailer was a bed that was slightly smaller than full size, with wood drawers beneath it for storage. My sheets and green comforter hung over the one side as it was a platform bed nestled between three walls. I placed my rainbow-colored chakra candle on a small shelf above the bed along with one of my first sketches—a wolf. I hung a green-leaf sarong with frilly tassels over the window as a curtain. Across from the bed was a built-in dresser, and I kept my small TV with a VCR on top. That whole side also housed a small closet for hanging clothes, and a few more cabinets for some canned food and miscellaneous items.

At the very back of the trailer was the bathroom with a yellow toilet, a small yellow sink, and a yellow half bath. It was so small that I had to soak my lower half sitting up and then lie back with my legs up the wall to enjoy a soak on my upper half. The shower worked, fortunately, so that was much easier to do. I had plenty of hot water from my own hot water heater. Whenever I wanted to use the bathtub, I had to remove the litter box, as it was a great place to store it for my two feline friends.

A large jasmine bush on the lattice fence outside the bathroom window produced a fragrant scent that hung in the air. There was a back door near the bathroom, although I never used it and always had it locked. I hung up another colorful sarong over the door and placed two long wrought-iron candle holders I found at a yard sale in front of it. Defused lighting was always helpful to my eyes, although the flickering flame would sometimes stimulate my brain too much.

On the long wooden deck near the front of the trailer, I placed a small white round table and two wooden chairs. The paint was chipping, but I just threw one of those plastic red-and-white-checked tablecloths over it to give the feel of being in Paris. Jack would frequently jump up onto the chair, then the table, and then onto the roof of the trailer where he'd sit for the day. I frequently had to spray the water hose on him toward the evening to get him down from there. Maple Leaf was always off and running the full length of the lot, with plenty of foliage and trees to hunt for rodents and snakes. Often, he would present me with a fresh kill, laying it on the deck for all to see. I also had a colorful Mexican hammock that fit perfectly between the two large oak trees. I could only lie in it if I had one foot on the ground; otherwise, I felt like I was falling into an abyss.

Toward the middle of the property was a built-in swimming pool at the main house. It was very refreshing to take dips to cool off from the summer heat. Lori was the first to visit me at my trailer home and partake in the refreshing waters. "Divine order in order," she boasted with a smile. It was a phrase I learned when I first heard Esther Hicks speak on the law of attraction. Lori and I used the phrase often however our day was going. We sunned ourselves poolside, elated with my new surroundings, and talked of how different my life would be now; it was still challenging but in a more adventurous, independent way. I was grateful for her perseverance in helping me finally move out of Robin's house and looked forward to many more visits.

That day, we played with the Motherpeace Tarot deck by co-creators Vicki Noble and Karen Vogel, derived from matriarchal consciousness. Matriarchies are mother-centered societies that are based on maternal values: caregiving, nurturing, motherliness, which holds for everybody: for mothers and those who are not mothers, for women and men alike. Their precepts aim to meet everyone's needs with the greatest benefit. Drawing cards and pondering the visual images was one of Lori's favorite activities to do with me and offered insight into the situation or question at hand. During my stay at the trailer, I frequently drew the Strength card, which showed a naked redheaded woman in a green meadow surrounded by her animal friend helpers. (*I* was that woman.)

This card represented matriarchal consciousness instead of patriarchal dominance, which conveyed to me to stay on my healing journey and allow the litigation to take its course. I also loved the "no thinking" aspect of the cards, as my creative intuitive mind would open. I had been using the tarot deck since 1996, when I first learned of this powerful, playful approach to understanding my life as a woman at the goddess gatherings. My heart opened fully to the messages of Motherpeace, and I related to the Goddess images and magical helpers, which enriched my life immensely.

The main house was concealed quite well on the hillside with plenty of trees and a very long driveway to the street below. The garden was down in this area with rows of chard and tomatoes and lots of large zucchini. The placement of the trailer was ideal because I could walk a mile down the mountain drive to the bus stop in front of the old mission. I could be in the center of town in a matter of minutes. I could hop on the street trolley from there for a quarter and be down at the marina and stroll the beach or just look at the vast ocean. There would be free water shows as schools of jumping dolphins coming through, and sometimes they would ride the waves. You could see them in the sunlight as the wave reached its peak and curled over. In the migrating season, you could see whales heading to northern waters, slapping their tails on the ocean surface and spouting fountains of joy, which made me giggle with delight.

I would stop at the surf shack for a couple of lobster tacos before heading back to the house in the foothills. Walking uphill was a bit exhausting, but before long I was in decent physical condition. My cat Jack would somehow always be waiting at the top of the driveway when I returned from town. He was a welcoming sight with his loving eyes and playful purr.

Staying in Tune

I played soothing, healing music in the trailer, like Enya, which carried the vibrational frequency of 432 Hz. It filled me with a sense of peace and well-being and brought me into altered states in the unified field of love and bliss. To understand the healing power behind 432-Hz frequency, you must first learn about another frequency, 8 Hz. It is said that between 7.86 Hz and 8 Hz is the fundamental "beat" of the planet. The heartbeat of the Earth is better known as Schumann resonance and is named after physicist Winfried Otto Schumann, who documented it mathematically in 1952.

The frequency of 8 Hz seems to be the key to the full activetion potential of the brain, and it is why I spent much of my time lying on the Earth. If the two hemispheres of the brain are synchronized with each other at 8 Hz, they work more harmoniously and with a maximum flow of information, according to information on AttunedVibrations.com. This, I am certain, contributed to the quality of my life and a transformed state of wellbeing.

As I continued to practice and research this phenomenon, I learned this tuning was unanimously approved at the Congress of Italian musicians in 1881 and recommended by the physicists Joseph Sauveur and Felix Savart, as well as by the Italian scientist Bartolomeo Grassi Landi. Interestingly, in contrast, the frequency chosen as the worldwide reference frequency in London in 1953 — and to which all music today is tuned, is defined as "disharmonic" because it has no scientific relationship to the physical laws that govern our Universe.

I also listened to the sacred worldly music of Jennifer Berezan, especially her *Returning* CD, recorded in the resonant oracle chamber in the Hypogeum at Hal Saflieni, Malta. I listened to this healing chant continuously during my rehabilitation. It gave me a deep sense of tranquility and connection to the ancient priestesses and the Great Mother, who embodied me in her loving Divine womb. When I met Jennifer at a celebration of renewal retreat in Northern California, I shared my passion for being alive with music and told her about my father's polka band and how the accordion music was in my blood.

A woman overheard our conversation and offered a little red accordion to me that had been collecting dust in her home. She said it belonged to her son, but it needed to be played, and she knew I would appreciate this gift. Again, it was music which activated and lifted me. Eventually, I learned to play this magnificent instrument one variable at a time, through Ross, a very patient and proficient Italian accordion instructor in Santa Barbara. It took several lessons over the course of several years to be able to play some songs with sheet music. In the evenings, I would play the accordion in my dimly lit trailer as if no one were listening. I could stand up for a while or even try to stroll while playing it, which was very comical. I'm sure people in the vicinity could hear the accordion music echoing in the foothills.

How Long Is a Day in the Dark?

When day slipped into night, my home became a mysterious void and as dark as a blue-black raven. As I fumbled around in the long dark tunnel of the trailer, I reached with outstretched arms to embrace the wooden closet. I held on until the spinning stopped. In the darkness, I spied a small light: a lamp on the table. My pencil friend was waiting for me to scoop her up. I whittled her sides with the knife set beside her and tested the sharpness on my finger. I wanted to write words, yet I could not. My fears were hidden in this deafening echo chamber. Where was my muse to walk and dance with?

I kept my pencil moving in the darkness on a large blank slate, eyes closed or open. They must be open, for how could I stay focused? The scarecrow body came into form, the face distant as blank space between stars in a night sky. My vision began to blur, and I had to stop because the pain had thickened between my brows.

My coin scarf was draped across the bed. I wrapped it around my hips with a secure knot and began to sway to the Middle Eastern music I created in my mind, complete with tiny symbols and tabla drums. I glided up and down the narrow center of the trailer in lilting synchronicity, holding my hands up and out to the sides to touch anything that could guide me. My hips rose and fell to a melodic beat as I gently shimmed to shake the coins. I laughed and returned to my sketch board, adding strokes and shades to the scarecrow's eyes.

Suddenly, an image of Elizabeth Taylor as Cleopatra popped into my head. We gazed intently at each other. I transposed the deepness of her violet eyes onto the face of the scarecrow, feeling death. "If I only had a brain," I hummed. Standing back with the end of the pencil resting on my lips, I began to see my sadness.

How long is a day in the dark? I could no longer track time. I sketched in the heart of the Tin Man with brisk, brushing pencil strokes and then formed the numbers on the face of the heart-shaped clock. There it is again . . . the same sequencing of numbers never quite matched up. During my therapy sessions, my neuropsychologist would ask me to draw a clock and then insert the numbers. Each time, I came up short, because I started with the number 1 instead of the number 12. It seems so simple now, but then, with a short-term memory deficit, the first number never got anchored. My head fell back in frustration. If only I could find my thinking cap.

My pencil picked up the staccato pace as I drew the scarecrow's tall black hat that was whisked away by the wind. There must be a way out of this empty dark space. An image of the wizard in *The Wizard of Oz* flashed. Maybe his hot-air balloon could take me back home. I scanned the sketch board with tunnel vision and, in a fury, began to draw flames of fury in the upper-right corner. Round and round, I created a large balloon with a basket tethered by ropes, although the basket seemed very small. How could I ever crawl into this basket and fly home to myself?

I heard sacred women's voices in the distance softly chanting, "Spirit of the wind, carry me; spirit of the wind, carry me home; spirit of the wind, carry me home to myself." Humming along with the words, I laid down in the bed, pencil still in hand, as coins gently settled amid the fluffy covers. How long is a day in the dark? Or is it night?

135

I woke with a high-pressure headache. I felt as though I were upside down, like the Great Houdini in the famous Chinese Water Torture Cell of 1912. Houdini's feet would be locked in stocks, and he would be lowered upside down into a tank filled with water. The mahogany-and-metal cell featured a glass front, through which audiences could clearly see Houdini. The stocks would be locked to the top of the cell, and a curtain would conceal his escape. The mystery clung to me as I crawled on the floor to the bathroom, which was only four feet away in this trailer. I clutched my head with my hands as I sat down to relieve my bladder. How did the Great Houdini ever get out?

I rested my forearms on the bedside, knees on the floor, and gazed up at the sketch board in wonderment. Did I do this in some numinous state? The phone rang, and I fumbled to answer it. A man with an interrogative tone on the other end was asking questions. I had been in litigation for more than a year since the accident. I hung up confused and looked at my sketch. I saw a hand with a white glove popping out of the sketch paper in the bottom right corner; then it quickly disappeared. I scrambled for the pencil in the bed covers, then picked up that staccato pace, and drew the looming hand of authority. I wanted to move on with my life, but I was in a vicious circle of pomp and circumstance ... the music kept playing. I am smarter than this. I am a fox who will bide its time in camouflage. Patience will prevail. I confidently sketched the fox with fine, feather-stroked precision.

I stood back to look at my sketch and noticed something was blatantly missing. All the pieces were there, but all the pieces needed to be pieces, as if I had taken a ceramic mug and thrown it on the floor. I grabbed some scissors and cut the whole sketch into pieces with swift, sharp cuts, the numbing pain stabbing me with every *clip-clip* of the steel scissors. Thin, pointed spears penetrated my tunnel vision. Jagged triangles of varying sizes flashed into my mind and body, and settled on soulful memories of my newspaper headline, "Golf Instructor in a League of Her Own."

Tears streamed down my cheeks as shards of shadowed paper clippings fell onto my bed. Shattered dreams complete. My hands trembled when I glued each piece of paper back onto the poster board. One by one, I dripped the white goop onto the backs of the clippings, careful to smear the glue to all edges. Methodically, I placed them with unwavering focus in their resting spots. Time disappeared as I continued to place each strip of paper. I was transfixed as the scarecrow's head reappeared with his braided rope choker and crooked stupor eyes. The lost time-heart was complete, with a pointed shard protruding the right ventricle. The hand of authority seemed even larger now as impending black clouds signaled a storm.

The sly fox was very much intact and was lying low, camouflaged and resting deeply. This was the fragmentation of my mind and my life. The sketch depicted it completely now. (See Figure 3: Illusions—misspelled as "Illiusions" on the sketch.) I placed my pencil back on the lamp table and sat contently on the couch. Gazing out the window, I viewed a blurred rose garden and a shimmer of light.

CHAPTER 12

BECOMING ARTEMIS, THE ARCHER

I identified strongly with the Goddess Artemis, a woman whole unto herself—untouched, untamed, unsubdued, and wild like a virgin forest. She is the sacredness of female autonomy worshipping her own identity and uniqueness, not what society or past oppressive conditioning would suggest. She defines her own path and honors the very core of herself with integrity. Artemis is an archer, drawing back her arrow with a curved bow, and the protectress of the forest and its creatures.

I became Artemis to protect myself during my recovery. I had to be strong. I was struggling to get back to the core of my being through this feminine archetype. Artemis is the she-bear warrior who uses her bow and arrow for one pointed vision of her ethereal target. The arrow is her focus, intention, and will. This vision pierces through fear and guides her heart through to her Divine path. My living affirmation became "My will is sacred. I worship my own."

Artemis is the healthy predator who keeps the balance of nature. She understands the rooting power of trees and sits with them to ground deeply. I also learned to exchange breath with the trees. (These are the standing people, as the Native American Indians say.) This intimate act of appreciation brought tears of joy and uplifted my soul. Artemis lives by the phases of the moon, with the purest magnification of her light beams. She seeks hidden answers in these waves of consciousness to deepen her experiences of wisdom, understanding, and instinct. Often, I would sit in my stone circle and gaze up at the moon for guidance and comfort. I could always count on Artemis.

I made a moon journal and followed the phases, carefully drawing and shadowing in her different aspects. I learned from the moon calendar what each of these phases meant. They were like mini cycles with a beginning, middle, and end in a short span, which was important for my self-esteem and laying a track of confidence. This corresponded with my goal setting. For instance, knowing to start a simple project on a new moon, which represents the planting stage, and then following it through to completion to the full moon, the amplification or ripening, of the project.

It was tremendously helpful to utilize the right brain to distinguish the phases of time moving forward in a positive way and to not to have to figure it out with the left brain, where I kept losing time. I was still in the early stages of my rehabilitation, and the constant strain of charting new pathways in the left brain was sometimes overloading and overwhelming. I followed the moon cycles closely, and it was a source of great fun during my days in my cozy respite in the hills of Santa Barbara. Plus, in the coming years of menopause, even though my blood cycle stopped, I still felt my daily biorhythms with the phases of the moon, and this comforted me greatly.

Artemis also showed me how to be vulnerable and safe. I danced naked in the rain among rose bushes, plants, and trees, feeling alive with unbridled passion. To this day, I let out a "Yaaaaahooooooooo!" when it begins to rain or thunder. I am the sounding one, using my voice to release and express wildly. I am at home with the forest and the waters. Apparently, I splashed naked in an old steel tub as a baby and danced in the rain as a small child. And, yes, I still run out in the rain to dance and appreciate refreshing drops that fall from the sky.

The Sacred Stone Circle

I created a stone circle outside the rear deck of my trailer. I enjoyed walking the property, which was like a large hollow on a half-acre, with a rose garden and large boulders on the grassy hillside. I picked up medium-sized stones one by one, and placed them in a circle, about 30 feet off the deck, beneath a towering oak and a couple of elms. This provided a protective sacred space within the original sacred space of the natural world. I would lie on Mother Earth in this circle, or under the nearby oak tree, and feel her heartbeat and the pulsing energy that flowed through the circuit of the soil, plants, and critters that passed through the land. Instantly, I was comforted by this tuning and became content as my brain matched this free-flowing energy. It was a sustained stream for me, like a slowly augmented circulating escrow of life force, ensuring my well-being.

As a lunar lover, one of Artemis's favorite rituals was called "Catching Moonbeams."

Pleased with the stone circle she had created, Artemis stood in the middle slowly sipping chilled apple cider from a champagne glass. The cool drink was always refreshing after a hot soak in the bathtub. In ritualistic fashion, she turned to the east, and proclaimed, "Here's to the air, the very breath of life"; to the south, "Here's to the fire, spirit of the sun"; and to the west, "Here's to the water, the ooooooocean of emoooooootion!" as she did a twist-like dance. She then turned to the north and called, "Here's to the Mother Earth, keeper of the land."

It was the evening of the autumn equinox and yet another celebration of the full moon. Artemis took her place in the sacred stone circle, surrounded by oak trees, big boulders, and a huge rose garden. She chanted, "I invoke the Goddess of Love, Beauty, and Abundance through the clear light of the full moon."

Suddenly, headlights flashed from the driveway across the yard and, within seconds, a door slammed, and a familiar voice sounded, "Who-who-who-whooooo." Artemis's newly acquired friend, Sara, approached the trailer with her usual owl-call greeting. "Artemis, are you home?" she called, squinting at a silhouette in the circle. "Artemis, is that you?"

"Shhhhhhhh, yes it is I, protectress of the forest," she said, standing tall with outstretched arms.

"What the hell are you doing out here?"

"Oh, I am blessing the Earth and giving thanks to all of nature and all of her critters," Artemis replied.

As Sara moved onto the trailer porch, she realized the only thing Artemis was wearing was a pair of black wooden clogs and a knitted wool hat.

"Your ass is as bright as the moon!" she smiled.

"Thank you," Artemis replied, shaking her big white bootie.

Sara quickly followed suit and stripped off her clothes, strewing them on the deck. "It's freezing out here!" she proclaimed as she tiptoed in exaggerated style, knees high, wearing only her furry boots. Well, boots and a sporty headband with a lamp attached to it.

Sara is a slender, well-toned rock climber and never leaves home without her headlamp. One night she wore it to grill chicken. It shines like a flashlight, so you always had to be looking at exactly what you want to see. It made Artemis dizzy just watching her head and that beam of light moving while turning every piece of chicken on the grill, then talking to her, and so and so on.

"I'm so glad you stopped by, Sara," Artemis said softly, turning off the beam of light.

"It's almost 10 o'clock. What are we gonna do out here?" whispered Sara.

"Catch moonbeams," Artemis said, rejoicing and clapping her hands. Sara rolled her eyes. "Yes, of course, we're gonna catch moonbeams."

"We bask in moonbeams to feel her vibrational waves of consciousness," Artemis explained while walking with her friend inside the stone circle. "You give yourself to the darkness so you can emerge into the light." Sara listened intently as Artemis continued. "In this place, there is truly nothing to fear, except fear itself. So, you choose to be courageous, strong, and receptive." Artemis placed her hands on Sara's shoulder and looked her straight in the eyes. "You learn to be open to receiving all of the gifts the twilight of the full moon offers."

"That is beautiful," Sara said, leaning forward to hug her friend.

Still embraced in their hug, Artemis and Sara started jumping up and down in ecstatic jubilation. They broke away and danced to the pounding of their hearts, chanting, "Spirit of the wind, carry me home to myself."

Maple Leaf and Jack peered through the trailer window with heightened curiosity at the two women, butt-ass naked, wearing only hats and shoes, and dancing in the moonlight. Exhilarated by their frolicking, Artemis and Sara collapsed to the ground and crawled onto a Mexican blanket spread inside the circle. Together, they sat and pondered the fullness of the moon.

"Look there, inside, can't you see the Energizer Bunny?" Artemis said confidently, waving her hands in the air.

"There's no bunny. No, no bunny. It's actually a beautiful woman singing to me," Sara said.

"So much for the man in the moon!" Artemis joked. They both chuckled quietly.

Awestruck by their surroundings, they sat speechless for a few minutes with only the sound of their breath drifting in and out of the crisp night air, accompanied by the rhythmic sound of crickets. Ah, yes, the perfect balance of life is the very essence of the fall equinox.

Suddenly, the piercing cry of a lone coyote penetrated the darkness with a resounding shrill. The coyote was joined by the rest of the pack, and the howling grew louder.

"What do we do now?" Sara screamed.

"Run for your life!" Artemis shouted as she jumped over a bush.

Sara bolted from the stone circle and ran through the rose garden. Artemis clip-clopped up the hill and onto some rocks, her head hung low. Sara circled back and, breathing heavily, squatted next to her. Artemis looked at Sara's face in the luminous light and smiled sheepishly, covering her mouth with her hands.

"You're such a luuuunatic!" Sara gasped. "Yeah, there's nothing to fear, except fear itself."

They laughed hysterically, holding their bellies, until the cries of the coyotes commenced again. Their frantic yapping echoed through the trees of a distant hillside. Apparently safe, Artemis and Sara meandered back down into the stone circle, where Artemis pulled a dish towel off a loaf of homemade cornbread, still warm from the oven. Munching on a piece of cornbread, Sara wondered exactly how long Artemis had been practicing these nightly rituals. Fascinated by her friend's innocence and unbridled passion, she smiled and said, "This has been one crazy night, girlfriend."

Artemis brushed crumbs off Sara's face and said, "You could say it was a little crazy, but don't you just love the wonderment and thrill of the night?"

Sara walked down to the deck and put her clothes back on. "You're just a moon worshipper, Artemis. That's what you are, a moon worshipper." They both giggled.

Then, Sara blew her friend a kiss good-bye and headed for her car. "See you next month!"

Day and night, I continued to embody Artemis's fierce wilderness prowess as I walked the property. Tuning into my keen sense of touch and trust, I synchronized with the vibration of the land underneath me. I worked on feeling steady on my feet, though at a deeper octave, and the ground would come up to greet my every step, profoundly supporting me. Often, I walked with my eyes half closed because of brain fatigue or double vision. It's amazing how when my sense of sight was weak, more energy and processing power in my brain shifted to the senses of hearing, touch, and even smell, heightening and improving my ability to move through the land and my world efficiently. Listening to the sounds of nature became another magical blessing of the moment.

I eventually wore prism glasses to correct the double vision—they looked like Coke bottles—until a spontaneous healing occurred. I knew it because I started getting headaches from the glasses after a year, so I took them off, and voilà! I could see again, but I had to remain under threshold levels of visual stimulus or the problem would recur.

Saluting the Moon

The catching moonbeams ritual inspired me to start doing a series of cooling yoga moves called the "Moon Salutation" by Laura Cornell, PhD, founder of Divine Feminine Yoga. I had already learned and practiced the sun salutation in traditional hathya yoga classes years before my traumatic brain injury. The sun salutation is a sequence that awakens the energy of the inner sun, heating and energizing the body. This was no longer appropriate for me, with its series of deep backward and forward bends done at a sweeping clip. I needed something that was gentler and more comfortable for me to do. Plus, this would help awaken and nourish the lower energy centers of my body, stimulating the Earth element and providing a more sense of stability.

The moon salutation is formed from nine basic standing poses, including side bending, forward bending, lunging, and squatting. (See Figure 4: Moon Salutation.) I worked on one pose at a time, fully reading and understanding its description first and then mimicking the pose. Once I overlearned that pose, I would add another and then another. Learning in this modified way was easy because my brain could take in the pose and it would be anchored by doing the previous moves first, like the phases of the moon, in a continuous circle of movement. Completing the sequence of moves was beneficial for my nervous system, especially my brain, which needed much soothing and grounding, and it helped me to expand into a fuller sense of self. I felt like a poised superheroine, embodying strength and beauty with every pose. I especially loved the goddess pose because I honored my own feminine power and felt deeply connected to Mother Earth. The star pose followed, and this amplified my power, energizing every cell in my body and radiating it outward to the cosmos.

Finally, the full squat pose is right in the middle of the sequence of the moon salutation. I used to love hanging out in this pose while talking with people who were picnicking or at parties with people sitting around in the living room. It had always been a comfortable pose for me because I am as close to the Earth as I could get without sitting. Plus, it was just a great pose to do to stretch out my lower back muscles. The squat pose also complemented the other hip- and pelvis-opening poses of the sequence, which massaged my entire pelvic area. During my trip to India, it had proved invaluable in squatting over the ground toilet and remembering to "eat with the right; wipe with the left."

The moon salutation was a daily practice I enjoyed that was nourishing and healing to my body. Later, I added a light drum trance beat mix during the sequence for another dimension of imagery and mystery of my inherent Goddess within. According to moon salutation creator Dr. Cornell, in her book *The Moon Salutation: Expression of the Feminine in Body, Psyche, Spirit* (Ann Arbor, MI: UMI Dissertations Publishing), "The moon salutation represents the spiritual path of accepting things as they are, of reaching out to embrace the beauty of the dark as well as the light."

Artemis knows and understands that what we do to the Earth, we directly do to our body. Poison the Earth and we poison our body. It is the reptilian brain, the one that responds instinctually, that receives and stores this information. Unfortunately, with today's fast-moving technology and the assault on the planet with radio frequencies and other toxic tactics, many have been cut off from this connection or ignore its subtle signal, moving more from an analytical, rational, or insane approach instead of the experiential or body-based mode. The intelligence of our magnificent body is linked to the Earth itself, and we respond to these movements and currents. I had unwittingly benefited from the direct hit of the golf ball to my head as it took out my thinking brain—for a while anyway, long enough to understand the balance of both and to recircuit my left-brain function.

Birds and Bees

Artemis taught me to be more in nature, reconnecting to my instinctual self, and to watch and listen to life. Many animals wandered through the property, including bobcat, possum, deer, skunk, coyote, and raccoon. There were several bird species, and

147

one day, even a swarm of bees circled way above the trailer and the trees. This was truly a holy and joyous event. I placed my trembling hands on my heart with this vibrational show. The humming buzzing sound was wildly crazy, yet mesmerizing, because they were doing a wavy figure-eight movement.

Later, I learned this movement is replicated inside the beehive by one bee and is called the magical "Waggle Dance." One bee dances on a honey comb and all the other bee's watch. The bee is not just doing a fancy dance, it is actually showing and transmitting to the other bee's the exact location where the most potent flowers are blooming. This bee has already calculated this location by using the sun. These bees are very intelligent and intuitive.

Bees swarm once a year to move their hive, usually at the invitation of the old mother queen bee. She gets to dance in the sun for one day, gracing the land and other bees with her hormonal scent and a mating dance in the air. Then, half of the bees follow her like one big, superorganism (or orgasm!) and begin the magical swarm to their next location (like a tree branch). They leave their old home, which contains young bees, a new virgin queen, and stores of honey and honeycomb. This is how the beehive reproduces itself. I have always enjoyed watching the bees in the backyard garden, swooning from one flower to another, sipping nectar, and bathing in the yellow powdery pollen. But witnessing the deeper mystery of the bee swarm was truly a blessing from the Goddess Artemis. To think, every flower needs the kiss of a bee to seed the next generation of beautiful flowers and our food!

Another day, I was walking toward the back of the trailer where there was the most fragrant blossoming jasmine bush. The long vines of jasmine stretched across the lattice fence, the pink and white blooms showing their faces to the morning sun. I stood tall, slightly arching my back as my nostrils filled with the sweet scent of their fresh and potent nectar. I opened my eyes in delight filled with the essence of joy, when I realized I was looking straight into the eyes of a tiny hummingbird, his pink-and-green velvet feathers suspended by the translucent motion of his wings. I smiled, and my body shimmied with its vibration.

The joyous moment was ours, like the timelessness just before a snapshot is taken. The little hummer slowly did three to four reverse turns, with wings to the sides spiraling about two feet down landing gently atop the lattice arch. I had to contain my laughter. The hummer tucked his wings back in, satisfied and content. It was a wondrous sight, an amazing moment with this hummingbird showing off to me. Perhaps he was showing me how easy it was to rewind and begin again, especially with the strength and courage of Artemis.

CHAPTER 13

A HARSH REALITY IS REVEALED

Living in Santa Barbara was beneficial in many ways. My rehabilitation process was moving right along as I took on new learning programs, classes, and even a job. Walking everywhere was becoming a problem, however, with the new schedule load. I couldn't make it on time to appointments by walking and trying to catch buses.

My landlady had a dear friend, Gladys, a thin elderly woman with short, curly gray hair. When she donned her big, black sunglasses to block the sun, she reminded me of a little bug. Gladys was a retired town clerk and very involved as a community volunteer. She offered to pick me up and take me wherever I needed to go. This was such a relief, so I took her up on the offer. She was always punctual, and she drove slowly and carefully to my appointments in her light blue Chevy Impala, her "stretch limo" as she called it.

Her services were working out well, although I started to feel guilty about her driving me around and receiving nothing in return except light conversation from point A to point B and a gracious thank-you. I wanted to do more, so I suggested a small payment system. I would give her a quarter for each ride. In this way, I felt I was giving something back in exchange for her services, and I wouldn't go broke doing it.

Reluctantly, Gladys agreed to my plan, and she used a chipped coffee mug in a plastic cup holder between the front seats to hold the coins. The new payment plan boosted my self-worth. More than this, there was a cycle of give-and-take happening that kept a natural flow of energy in my body. I didn't feel "blocked" from not giving this kind woman something in return for her generous services. A free flow of energy is important in maintaining a healthy body and mind, like a pool filter that keeps running to ensure clean flowing water for the swimming pool. I was nourishing my body and mind while I continued to expand my quality of life. More than this, it was like an overflowing cup that kept me going. Never underestimate the power of a simple, kind gesture.

My Supportive Family

After I settled into my trailer, my sister Kim visited me occasionally. She stayed with me one time at the trailer; however, she booked a room at a nearby hotel for subsequent visits. Apparently, I was high maintenance, and she needed to rest before spending the day with me. We had good conversations about my brain injury, and she made several new observations about my behavior since the accident, such as my excessive notetaking and adherence to a rigid schedule. Scribbled pieces of paper were scattered everywhere in the "tiny trailer," as she called it. I explained it was a way for me to stay aware of my most important thoughts.

I enjoyed Kim's visits as she drove me to the grocery store and took me on special outings to the Santa Barbara pier shops and restaurants, where we would stroll the beach or go to the park and lie in the grass. We played with the animal medicine cards and chatted, although we did more laughing than talking. (I truly believe my sister missed her calling to be a stand-up comedian.) We also relaxed in the back yard, but I often had to retire to bed.

Kim spent time walking the property or resting in the hammock while petting Jack.

Kim confided how angry she was when she found out about my tragic accident. During one visit, she lamented, "I was heartbroken this fluke accident happened to you while you were doing something you loved to do: teaching golf and inspiring people. It seemed things were starting to really happen for you and your career."

She expressed many feelings about the accident's impact on my life, such as sorrow in seeing how my life completely changed in an instant; fear that I would not recover sufficiently enough to enjoy life; happiness to see my many successes along the way, such as playing the accordion, drawing, and writing; and pride in watching me overcome so much and having such great accomplishments. My whole family shared these sentiments and supported me to the best of their ability.

My parents continued their love and caring from afar with many prayers, candle flames, and phone conversations. My mom, an accomplished painter, was especially gifted in sending handmade cards of encouragement, along with fun care packages. And, of course, the Klawitter sense of humor always helped us through tough times.

My parents visited me for Mother's Day weekend on their return trip from visiting friends in Seattle. To celebrate, I baked a cake for my mom using two separate heart-shaped cake pans. I wrote "Happy" on one and "Mother" on the other. I ran out of room to write "Day." She loved it all the same, and we spent the day together in the Santa Barbara Botanical Gardens. My parents also met Dr. Smith one afternoon and had a separate meeting with her to understand my traumatic brain injury and how to effectively support me. These family visits were encouraging and uplifted my spirits.

The Flood Gates Open

For several years, my rehabilitation ran concurrent with my litigations with the golf course and the golfer who hit the ball that injured me. It was taking a tremendous toll on my well-being. The surveillance also continued, and the guys who were filming me became more obvious. On one occasion, I was spending some time near the built-in swimming pool by the main house. I was meandering around the pool with some pruners and clipping off brown dead heads from the many flowers in the gardens. I was butt-naked and enjoying the tranquility of this caring gesture, then stood up to stretch my back. Something from across the driveway and over in the neighbor's yard caught my eye. It was a fair distance, but there was definite movement of sorts. I arched and stretched a little more, then went back down to snip at the roses, and again I saw something move. I shifted my eyes to the movement and there was a man standing halfway behind a tree with a camera in his hands taking shots of me. Shit! This is fucked up. I grabbed my towel, frantically wrapping it around my body, and darted through the pool gate, walking through the back yard and jumped into my trailer from the back entrance. I called the authorities, but it seemed useless. These creepy guys were quick and disappeared before anything could be done. I wondered how many pictures they took of Artemis frolicking in the woods.

There was another time when I enjoyed the company of my friends down at the beach. With our blanket and cooler laid in the sand, we romped in the refreshing saltwater for a while. I had to get marks even while being in the ocean currents, as to not get vertigo, such as a huge rock on shore, or a boat that was anchored. It was quite challenging, but worth the practice, as I enjoyed being able to have some fun with my friends. Plus, my vision therapist had shown me a beneficial way to work on my equilibrium while standing or walking in the shifting sands. At Robin's house, I stood and balanced on one of those half squish balls for as long as

I could. I was grateful for the indoor practice, but being out in nature was much more fun.

We were just getting ready to stroll the beach when my friend noticed some creepy guys with videotaping equipment hiding behind huge rocks. "I'm not cutting my beach time short to escape the lens of these assholes." I said in frustration. Let's just walk and forget about them. "I don't care anymore. Well, I care, but it is what it is."

The dam of my emotional healing finally burst during a nightmare I had. The psychological trauma of the perpetual litigation had reached a crescendo. I was crying and confused about the many depositions and doctors' examinations I had to go through. The process seemed shaming and unhealthy for me. The creeps who were shadowing my every move seemed to keep popping out from behind tree's and buildings. I was going on and on in my "dream state," trying to wake myself up, but my mouth seemed clenched closed. Something deeper might be happening because I could not articulate the pain and disgust I was displaying. Suddenly a phone rang in the dream and I awoke with a gasp of breath trying to pick up the receiver. Instead I flipped on the light, and quickly reached for a piece of sketch paper.

I was breathing heavily as I grabbed a pencil and immediately hit the paper with bold marks and jarring scribbles. Moments later, I rested my pencil, sitting back in my bed to view the sketch I had drawn as I wiped tears from my eyes. There it surfaced: a horrific, dark phallic symbol only a rape victim could draw . . . the representation of this legal case amplified the underlying wounding from all men during my life, including the softball coach who had molested me and the man I had tutored and trusted in college who'd date-raped me.

It was a disturbing uprooting of my shadow side, now exposed to the light of day. I was exhausted from this horrible nightmare, but I sighed with a sense of relief. It was out in the open now, no longer hidden in the depths of my being, and in my next session with Dr. Smith and I would be able to sort through the pain and confusion of the episodes with the present-day occurrence for several months.

Much later, I designed another vision board, where I played in the realm of creativity, not the analytical mind. The poster board was covered with bright pictures of many male/female couples enjoying different aspects of life: kayaking, dancing, hiking, relaxing at the beach, and traveling together. I cut out positive phrases like "bring on the sunshine," "a new you," "I can see clearly now," and "all for love." which was framed in an open lotus flower in full bloom. I was adding positive phrases to the pictures now, and this was certainly progress.

In the right corner of the poster was a beautiful little fawn. I did not consciously think about this. In the "Illusions" sketch, I drew a sly fox that would bide her time, lie low, and now, years later, she had become a graceful baby fawn. And above the fawn was a beautiful colorful garden photo with the words *artful living*. I had not embarked on the physical/cellular journey yet; this was just the beginning, a vision board of what would come. This vision would pull me through difficult times until I started dating again, and until I participated in the realm of tantra.

CHAPTER 14

BACK IN THE DRIVER'S SEAT

To fill time and keep my brain active, I accepted a volunteer job at the planetarium just a mile and a half from my trailer. Walking down was easy, but trudging back up the hill was exhausting, especially after working a few hours. I'd ask Gladys to pick me up, happily plopping a quarter into the coffee cup. My volunteer job was to hold the flashlight and collect tickets at the door for the children's night sky program. I loved this job because I also got to watch the night sky show over and over and eventually learned many of the constellations.

After the program one day, I strolled into the other night sky exhibits. In one exhibit, I noticed lights suspended at different heights in a dark glass box and suddenly realized it was the Big Dipper. This was a revelation to me because I thought all the stars were on one plane, like someone had pasted sticky stars up on a bedroom ceiling, but this was different. I was amazed that the stars of the Big Dipper were each on different planes. This was a new dimensional perspective firing back up in my brain.

Viewing stars in the real night sky was a trip, but sometimes I would get very dizzy, and the constant strain on my neck from looking up was a love–hate relationship. I enjoyed connecting the dots to form constellations like the big "W" of the Seven Sisters, Delphinus (the dolphin), Draco (the dragon), the Big Dipper, and the Little Dipper and identifying some of the planets, like Mars,

Venus, and Jupiter. This whole learning curve started when Dr. Smith suggested an activity of high interest to help me break through the brain fog in the beginning stages of my head injury. I started with an eighth-grade star book with connect-the-dot exercises. Now, just two years later, I was adjusting to the real night sky, which would be critical when I started driving again.

Visual Strategies: Seeing Progress

I had already gone through "tracking," the toughest part of the visual strategies with Ginger, my vision therapist, by playing pool at Robin's house. Now, she drove from Los Angeles up to my Santa Barbara trailer once a week to help me with some exercises I could do in the indoors or in the yard. I remember watching a glow worm dangling from its long silk string from the oak tree, a soft breeze making it swing back and forth. I watched intently, careful not to move my head. It was a fun way to track as my eyes would roll all around with the worm.

I practiced my near and far exercises, called "thumb pursuits" with the trees in the distance. I held my arm out at full length and made a "thumbs-up" gesture. I looked at my thumb with both eyes to see one thumb and then look beyond my thumb out to a distant tree, which produced an illusion of two thumbs side by side. I would repeat the action near to far several times, which strengthened the eye muscles. I still do this exercise today after working on the computer or reading too long. It helps to relieve the tension headache between the eyes and forehead. Apparently, the computer throws off a quick vibrational frequency that transfers to the optical part of the brain, which hastened the headache pain and caused my double vision. This also happened with fluorescent lighting and after watching flames dancing in a campfire or fireplace.

I also did the internal clock and diagonal vision exercises just before I went to sleep. Now that I can see the clock numbers easily in my mind, I began the diagonal exercises. It's like drawing a diagonal line with my eyes being the pen. I would start at 12 o'clock, then take my eye pen and go straight down to the number 6, and back up to 12. Then, I would go to 3 o'clock with my eye pen and go straight back to the number 9 and back to 3. Next, I went to 10 o'clock with my eye pen and then diagonally to 4 and back. And finally, I went to 2 o'clock and down to the 8 and back. Sometimes it would get confusing, but if I did it slowly and concentrated on each step separately, I could make it through.

The exercises helped tremendously in maintaining and even improving my eyesight. Both Ginger and Dr. Smith thought I was ready to take the next step in my vision strategy journey. The local hospital facilitated an adaptive driver training program, which provided a pre-driving evaluation, behind-the-wheel evaluation, driver training and evaluation, and training on adaptive equipment for those concerned about their ability to drive due to health-related conditions. This was the next logical step for me because I managed some of the cognitive and visual issues much better now.

I was thrilled to enroll in this program. All my hard work with Ginger was paying off. I was no longer dizzy and nauseated from the exercises, so I was ready and excited to start the adaptive training program to prepare to drive again. Unbeknownst to me, it would take three years to relearn how to drive efficiently again. Video games played a major role in my progress.

I enjoyed the simulation games at the center. In one of them, I would get into a video game box called a simulator, complete with a seat and steering wheel. The video game would come on and present different driving situations and conditions. Every time I would come up to a stop sign, I would hit the brake pedal with my foot, apparently in slow motion, and the car would stop five to seven seconds later. This was a huge delayed response time when pressing either the accelerator or the brake. I spent lots of time in the driving simulator. It was a real trip! Although I could not quite get the hang of it, I was fascinated with the process.

One time the screen was quite dark and dribbling like a waterfall. I realized it was raining, so I had to locate and turn on the windshield wiper switch. "Ah, there we go," I said calmly. "I can see again," I said, feeling confident. "But, what's this? Oh, a light way in the distance. Wait, it's two lights. Oh! It's another car coming toward me in the other lane!" It was fun to play in the simulator, but I realize now the severity of my visual and cognitive abilities—unseen but deadly if I had been in the streets.

I was making continued progress with my adaptive training exercises for several months, until I was introduced to a new scanning game. Right after my injury, I remembered having tremendous difficulty driving to a few scheduled golf lessons and, of course, there was the episode when I tried to drive to the voting center. Each time I looked left or right, I would get dizzy and nauseated. It was like a badly focused movie where the scene I just saw tried to catch up with me in a wavy motion. I felt like one of those bobblehead toy dogs that people placed on the rear dashboard. This exercise made my brain feel disconnected from its brain stem.

There was a long corridor, flanked by walls covered with posters, pictures of people, road and street signs, buildings, and houses. It was a maze of environmental stimuli that I would encounter out in the real driving world, and I was already getting confused with the explanation of the game. I had to walk slowly down the corridor, looking left and right, and then report to the trainer how many items I could remember. The first time, I stopped halfway because my brain had already flooded. I became disoriented and dry-heaved for a few seconds. The trainer told me to sit down, handed me a tissue to wipe my mouth, and gave me a glass of water to sip. Tears came to my eyes as I could do no more and was finished for the day.

We tried to do the exercise later in the week, but the trainer stopped the game altogether. "We'll have to try a new approach, Kathleen," she said. "We'll back up and start with some vision exercises you can do at home and go from there." I had no choice but to stop the adaptive training sessions at the center. They said they would keep my name on file for my return, so I got to work.

I added a left–right head exercise to my daily activity sheet and marked it for five days a week. I would sit in a chair, or just lie on my bed, and start by looking at an object to my left, then slowly turn my head to the center and look at a mark there, and then slowly look to my right and look at an object there. The idea was to be able to scan in one full motion, but I had to divide it into three or four moves, stopping at each mark before moving to the next.

The symptoms would return each time, though not as extreme. If I started to reach my threshold level and sensed the dizziness or nausea, I stopped and walked in the garden or lie on the Earth. Then, I began again the next day and marked it off on my daily sheet taped to the refrigerator. I practiced faithfully, according to my daily activity sheets. It took months to slowly retrain this part of my brain without getting sick. For days on end, I practiced when I walked in the backyard, marking different trees and bushes and flowers. I practiced when someone drove me in the car. I even practiced in the grocery store aisles, scanning the different canned items.

The day finally came, and I called the training center and announced I was ready to come back to try the corridor game again. Two days later, I stood in front of the long corridor, ready for my first run in six months. I started to walk down the carpet, slowly looking left and right, breathing with an open mouth and a wiggly tongue. I saw a big stop sign on my left, then a child with a ball on the right, a tree on the left, a street sign on the right. Slowly, I continued down the hallway looking at objects on either side of the walls until I made it to the finish line. "I did it!" I exclaimed, placing my hands on my face. "Yes, you did it!" the trainer echoed, "Now, tell me what you saw as you walked down the hallway." I listed all the objects I recalled. It was a good first attempt.

We repeated the game at the same speed for a couple of weeks, then I had to walk faster and faster on subsequent practice rounds, without getting flooded or sick. Sometimes, she would roll a bouncing ball in my path or walk alongside to help with the filtering process. The big test was what I could remember in the moment. This would eventually translate to driving down a road and knowing where I was, who was around, and if I had to navigate any potential problems.

The game was set up to systematically recircuit my brain in a manner I could tolerate and reach my goal of driving down a street. I compared it to working out at the gym. You could never do a bicep curl using 20-pound weights on your first try. You would start with two pounds once or twice a week, then move up to five pounds for a few weeks, then 10 pounds, and so on until you reached your goal of 20 pounds and a well-toned bicep. It just takes patience, perseverance, and a willingness to give it a go.

Putting It to the Test

Now that the long litigation was over and my rehabilitation was moving along, I thought about visiting my folks in Indiana. I had one more obstacle to overcome: taking the driver's test. To my surprise, I did very well on the written test, only missing a couple of questions. I did, however, complete several practice sessions with old written driver's tests, making sure to circle the appropriate answers with my No. 2 pencil. Ginger provided me with some sample tests and questions.

The real-time driving test was like driving two friends around town. I drove a four-door Nissan sedan, accompanied by a male-and-female test team. They gave me obstacles to navigate, like talking to me while I tried to drive or switching on the radio to try and distract me. I apologized sweetly, but firmly, and said I must turn it off so I can fully concentrate on the road. They gave me plenty of time to turn on certain roads or pull in to park somewhere.

I failed to parallel park correctly on the first try. It took several attempts to park between a tree and a telephone pole. Easy, right? I breathed heavier and grew more anxious with each attempt. The testers were patient and encouraged me to take a moment to compose myself and start again. I finally settled down, although I felt like Austin Powers in the movie *Goldmember*, where the title character drove a small yellow forklift and got stuck in a hallway. The only way out was to turn around, so he went back and forth turning the wheel slightly each time as he bumps into the wall in front of him and behind him. Hilarious! I finally got the car parallel, heaving a sigh of relief. The driver's test lasted one hour. I was victorious and passed it with flying colors.

Indiana Wants Me

With license in hand, I made plans to visit my family in Indiana. My parents lived on Lake Wawasee, the largest natural lake in the middle of the state. It was in the town of Syracuse where I practiced my driving skills in my dad's new van. He purchased a new vehicle every two years because he wanted my mother, family members, and friends to ride in a safe new vehicle. I would chuckle because I thought he just liked driving a brand new car. The van was easy to drive because I was elevated in the driver's seat and had a wider field of vision. I enjoyed driving to the local grocery store just four miles away in town. I drove several short distances and practiced parallel parking and backing out of the garage until I was satisfied with my accomplished skill level.

My parents were elated by how far I had come in my rehabilitation process, although the first time I visited them after the accident was shocking. My dad and sister picked me up at the airport and saw me sitting in a wheelchair at the gate. My head was down, and I was disoriented and drooling, with a name tag secured around my neck with a long nylon cord. Kim said I was almost unrecognizable.

The two-hour car ride to my parents' house was silent. Despite being ill, I still had to mark from the moving car so that I would not get dizzy and dry heave. When we arrived, my mom was in disbelief, as they carefully helped me into the guest room bed. My dad placed the headboard legs up on blocks so my head would be elevated. I rested in that bed for three days before I recovered enough to get up and visit. They witnessed firsthand all the issues I was living with: always having to wear earplugs; only having one-on-one conversations where the person sat directly in front of me with focused eye contact, no overhead fan movement, or TV background sound; and how much I had to sleep, to name a few.

My dad and I had a very touching conversation one day down at the "Point," just a short walk from their house to the edge of Lake Wawasee. We sat on a wooden bench with a full view of the lake and spoke of how rich our lives had been and how happy we were, despite our various health issues through the years. I confided that my head hurt a lot and that the rehab work was so hard that I didn't know if I could go on this way. If I died tomorrow, I would be quite content with all I had done in my life.

My dad understood and heartfully replied, "If I died tomorrow, I will have lived a good life with a beautiful family." In that moment, we sat quietly listening to the sounds of the water, boats, and birds. Interestingly, he lived another hardy 12 years before he passed from cancer.

My parents accommodated me well during my stay, loving me every minute. Thank goodness, those painful first visits were over and our time together became more pleasant, like this one. I even drove my parents down to the mini putt-putt for a fun activity together, and we had pizza down by the lake. With all my driving practice with my parents, I realized I was ready and able to start driving again full-time.

When I returned to Santa Barbara, I purchased a new Honda Odyssey van, compliments of part of the structured settlement funds from my lawsuit. I immediately had both the captain chairs in the cargo space removed and utilized the extra space for transporting my cats. The extra space came in handy if I needed to stop, pull over, and lie down to rest. The rear bench seat folded down, which revealed a full eight feet of resting and stretching area.

I realized how valuable the adaptive training driver's test was because when I really drove a friend or two around town, I had to insist on silence so I could concentrate on the road. I forbade talking or turning on the radio. It left us a bit quiet and awkward, but they understood. I was just delighted and appreciated that I could take a turn and even offer to drive. After two years, I learned to filter out the noise from the radio and talking and still drive a car safely and effectively.

The most difficult roads to navigate were winding roads full of twists and quick turns. I had to use marks, just like I did when walking in a mall or down a crowded street. Instead of following someone's jeans back pocket, I would follow the red tailgate light on the back of the car in front of me. Or, in some instances, I followed the white line off the right side of the road for as long as I could before it again curved. I followed the best I could, but sometimes it was necessary to glance up at the trees and get marks that way.

I found glancing from the speedometer out to the road or mark for long periods was not a good practice for me. I would go over my threshold levels and become symptomatic. Even if the road wasn't winding, the near and far sightings would produce headaches and sometimes double vision if I didn't stop and pull off the road. Seeing double street signs and road signs was frustrating, as it made them that much harder to read and decipher. I was happy to be able to drive short distances to alleviate this potential problem.

I drove at non-peak hours to run my errands in and around town when roads were less crowded, which made focusing that much easier. Fewer variables equated to less confusion. I also mapped out my route ahead of time, so I knew exactly where I was going. I wrote down each place to go in the order I would drive it and pasted the paper on the dashboard for easy viewing. I avoided night driving completely for the first five years.

CHAPTER 15

CREATIVE EXPRESSIONS

I continued to focus on activities that were of high interest to me, including taking classes in pottery and colored-pencil sketching that were offered at the community center. Dr. Smith suggested these types of activities were more fun than a therapy-type exercise because they used my creative right brain. I immediately realized the benefits of these "hands on" experiences.

Upon entering the pottery barn for my first class, my heart skipped a couple of beats when I saw the teacher, Ryan. He resembled the Academy Award–nominated guitarist and singer-songwriter Kenny Loggins, a crush I had during my college years. Ryan was hot and muscular, standing six feet tall, with a sweet smile and a short beard. He motivated me even more to come to class each week. The connection between us was flirtatious fun.

On our third meeting, Ryan introduced the process of raku pottery making, which we learned over three sessions. It emerged in Japan as a quick method for making roofing tiles in an emergency and later became the primary way to make ceremonial tea bowls. Raku is an exciting ceramic firing technique because the students are so involved with the firing process. Many people are attracted to raku because of the bright metallic colors you can get from firing copper glazes by using a clay designed for raku firing. "This type of clay is an open body with good thermal shock characteristics," Ryan said in a sultry voice. He made me blush.

He plopped a big blob of tan clay into the middle of the oblong table where eight of us were sitting and unwrapped the plastic covering. He encouraged us to take a big handful and start massaging it into a ball. "The next step is to take a smaller bit and roll the clay down to the size of a grape between your hands." He demonstrated this process slowly and seductively. At least, I thought so. As we continued to roll our clay into a bunch of grapes, Ryan handed out different sized plastic bowls, brushing quietly up against my arm as he gave me mine. "We're making brain bowls tonight."

I looked at him quizzically and thought he was making some sort of bad joke at my expense. "Please explain," I said, tilting my head to the side and widened my eyes.

"You take the grape-size clay and, one by one, start pressing them against the backside of the bowl, connecting each of them by dipping your hand in a little dish of water, then smearing them all together. The back side will be smooth when you're finished. Then, flip the dish over and carefully slip the whole clay bowl out of the plastic dish."

"There, you see," he said, as he held up his clay bowl, "it looks like a brain on the inside of the bowl where the clay grapes were undisturbed from their roundness but still joined together."

He was right. It did look like a brain. I was so proud of my brain bowl so far that I flipped it over and marked it with my initial K and the arrow going through part of it—my signature.

The class ended with students placing their brain bowls on the wooden shelves in the back room where several kilns were located. They would be bisque-fired the next morning by another assistant. A bisque fire is a low fire. In a low fire, the bisque temperature is usually hotter than the firing temperature. For example, most commercial glazes recommend bisque firing to cone 04 and glaze firing to cone 06 (which is cooler).

The second class was about glazing. Ryan brought out a few different types of glaze and explained each one. Next, you can apply slip, glaze, or just leave the pot bare. The surfaces of the pot that are not covered with a glaze will turn black from carbon from the post–firing reduction process. Slip is applied to the pot before it is placed in the Raku kiln. The slip cracks and breaks apart during the firing and is chipped off after to reveal a blackened crackle pattern.

With all the choices Ryan described, I covered my whole bowl with the raku glaze and let the magical firing process create the color of the bowl. I set my brain bowl back on the wooden shelf to dry until next week. We were asked to wear are dirtiest duds for our next class. The next session was exciting because we were going to fire the clay bowls outside in the back of the community center, where an outdoor pottery section was all set up. It consisted of a cylinder kiln, a metal garbage can resting on cement blocks, a station of newspapers, wood chips and sawdust, leather fire gloves, goggles, and long tongs. A bucket of water and a garden hose were off to the side in case of any drifting flames. There were several stools and benches already set up at the different sections.

The more Ryan explained the raku firing process, the more deflated I became. There was already so much environmental stimulation with the new outdoor setup, coupled with a host of instructions that depended on speed and accuracy, not to mention working with intense heat, that I realized I was not going to be a part of this magical team. There was just too much overload for my brain; it would be a dangerous endeavor.

As soon as Ryan finished, he asked if there were any questions, and I quickly raised my hand and told him the bad news. He came over and put his hands on my shoulders. He said he understood, but he wanted me to stay to remain with the group so I could unveil my brain bowl when it cooled. I obliged and sat out on one of the perimeter benches of the small garden area.

I watched intently as the students listened to Ryan's direction as they loaded some of the brain bowls into the kiln. While the bowls were heating, they prepared the reduction chamber (garbage can) by adding the combustibles, such as the newspaper and wooden ships.

"Wearing protective gear, grab the hot pieces from the kiln with your tongs," he said, sweat forming on his brow from the heat of the kiln. Ryan's tattered, skintight T-shirt revealed his muscular arms and chest. He continued, "Then, you place the piece in the reduction chamber, and you put the lid on the can for about 20 minutes."

While they waited for the bowls to reduce, some students loaded more bowls into the raku kiln. "In about the time it takes you to remove your bowls from the reduction chamber and prepare them for the next usage, your bowls will be hot in the Raku kiln," Ryan explained with a decisive tone. "We'll be finished here in about 30 minutes, Kathleen," he said as he smiled at me and wiped the sweat off his brow with the back of his hand. It was a long glance, and I stayed engaged with his eyes until someone dropped a bowl while transferring it with their tongs. It made everyone jump, but my heart was on fire. I was really getting into watching Ryan work, and now this long gaze made me want him.

It took more than 30 minutes before we could check out the colors of our brain bowls. I was a bit brain fogged by the time Ryan handed mine to me, wrapped in newspaper. He had marked and handled it separately for me. The bowl was completely cooled, and I slowly unwrapped the newspaper from the bowl and used a bit of Ajax cleanser to clean off the carbon to reveal a beautiful blue-green metallic color. It shined up like a magic lamp, and I wished I could be alone with Ryan.

After the last pottery class, Ryan invited me to dinner and show. I was surprised but didn't question him as I thought he may be dating someone else. I merely asked where and when. I was just excited to be on the dating scene again. I remember Dr. Smith encouraging me to be more social in this way, and months later, I finally began.

I was nervous when Ryan picked me up. I heard the car coming up the long driveway of the main house and ran out the trailer door because I didn't want him to see my living conditions tucked in the back. I was wearing loose, flowing bohemian clothing with sandals and no makeup. It was the best I could do being on disability. I had worn these clothes back in the goddess days of Northern California. He was wearing jeans and a blue button-down shirt.

We ate at a Japanese sushi bar in downtown Santa Barbara, in honor of our raku brain bowls. I love sushi but could never afford it after my accident, so this was a real treat. Plus, it is just so sensual to eat. We talked and then slowly reached across the table and placed bits of sushi roll into each other's mouths with chopsticks. It was erotic.

Alas, something not so delightful was happening as we continued to feed each other. I was becoming distracted by half-masticated raw fish and green seaweed rolling around in Ryan's wide-open mouth. I mentioned it to him when I could no longer take it without bursting out laughing from the green slime in his teeth and a few bits on his beard.

We finished our meal with warm sake and walked over to the theater just a few blocks away. Before we entered the theater, Ryan steered me to an outdoor garden area and pulled me in close to his firm, toned body. Oh, it felt so good to wrapped in his warmth. Our heads touched, then a synchronized slide of our cheeks, where mouths and moist lips found common ground. I pulled away with a wincing smile. Ryan's breath wreaked so badly I could not go any further with a lingering kiss. It was nasty!

Ryan reacted by saying, "I was hoping you wouldn't notice that." "Argggh! It's really foul, Ryan," as I backed away. "You need to brush your teeth or chew on a mint," I said. He guided us closer to the theater and mumbled something about a dentist. My mind drifted because the moment was ruined. I had been forthright about my disability, yet he said nothing to warn me about his gum disease. We watched the movie without saying much, and he drove me home in near silence. As I closed the car door and said good night, he said he'd call me in a couple of days and we'd go out again sometime. I waved and ran around the fence gate to the back of my trailer with a bad taste in my mouth, not from sushi but from what I learned that evening. Ryan never called, but I didn't care. I had fun, but I wanted to date someone I could trust. It was a good thing the pottery classes were over, as this first impression was enough for me. We never saw each other again.

Sketching in Color

After the pottery class ended, I continued my creative expression through a six-week colored-pencil sketch class at the Schott Center. I was already sketching with my No. 2 pencil, with each rendering in black-and-white. Now it was time to bring some color back into my life! My teacher, Helen, was a tall, older woman with long, silky gray hair. She dressed neatly and had lots of style. She introduced several color wheels to the class and taught us how to layer colors to add depth to a scene. Even black was not just black. We would start with blue or green strokes, and sometimes even red or orange, and then color over with shades of black. It was a beautiful black with a hint of color.

Aphrodite Dae, from the goddess days, knew the color palate specific to my skin and hair tones and always told me never to wear jet black. I should enhance my coloring with black that had threads of green or gold running through it. "It will make your eyes and skin pop!" she'd say with her coral-lipped smile. Now I understand what she meant.

I was practicing several color wheels in class, using the colored-pencil set the rehabilitation center had given me. They also gave me a credit at the Santa Barbara bookstore to pick up a new book bag, pens, and pencils with a sharpener, too.

One day, I made a little seahorse in the underworld ocean. In another class, Helen created a still-life out of some fruit and vegetables cut in precarious ways and arranged on plates. I sketched the strawberries on one sheet of paper and the sliced green pepper on another. I worked on them for over an hour, while the other students labored over their own artistic creations. As I stood back, I noticed how erotic the pictures looked. I was surprised at the amount of focus required to draw the fruit and vegetables with such detail and in such mesmerizing colors. I wanted to eat them! (See Figure 5: Strawberries, and Figure 6: Green Peppers.)

In the last class, I sketched myself riding a horse in a beautiful green meadow that had hundreds of flowers and pine trees. I created a stone circle in the middle of the picture, like Stonehenge in England, and topped it with a glowing full moon. History buffs know that Stonehenge is an ancient megalithic monument that was erected in the Neolithic Age on the Salisbury plain in southern England. The people there consider this the spiritual heart of Britain. This complex consists of a ring of standing stones, each towering up to 13 feet high and almost 7 feet wide and weighing about 25 tons. There are horizontal stones atop these stones, forming a window or doorway on the landscape. The mystical site was noted for being aligned with the summer solstice sunrise, which inspired me to sketch it in color.

Something sacred was happening while I drew this sketch, because now I used colored pencils instead of my usual No. 2 pencil. I was no longer living in black-and-white, as in the collage I made in the back bedroom of Robin's home. I wasn't the lonely woman living in isolation from a traumatic brain injury. I was beginning to live my life in color, and the unveiling of this scene was depicting this experience. I finished the colorful sketch by signing it with my usual arrow signature, and then titled it "Freedom Rider." This would be one of the last sketches I would ever draw during this healing period.

Let's Talk about Sex

I was thrilled when my friend, Sara, invited me to a goddess gathering in Santa Barbara, although the event was quite different from the days I spent in Sebastopol with women who studied the archetypal Goddesses. It was more a festive party of like-minded women coming together for feasting, chatting, and camaraderie.

I met an adorable woman named Maile, who had long, sun-kissed brown hair and crystalline eyes. Her essence exuded pure joy, like a mermaid or dolphin frolicking in the ocean. Maile and I shared the same exuberant qualities of love, joy, and happiness, so we quickly got to know each other that night and started hanging out.

One day, we were in my trailer talking about her latest boyfriend and my stint with Ryan. It was easy to talk to her about sex because she had already gone to a tantra event, and I had read some tantra books before my accident. The desire for sexual expression is inborn and natural. I discovered how to give this sexual energy an outlet through forms of expression which enrich the body, mind, and spirit. I shared some techniques with Maile that I was already doing by myself to keep my juices flowing, especially with sexual breathing. And how sometimes I would simply fall asleep just holding my heart and my "mound of

Venus," to keep my sexual connection alive, even though I was single and not sexually active in a relationship. The human mind responds to constructive stimuli, especially with sex, love, and music. It boosts up the vibrational frequency in your brain to fire up the physical action, or especially creative imagination, which is the sixth sense.

Oh, I did pleasure myself, as the saying goes, "An orgasm a day . . ." or, at least, I had an orgasmic response, where I spread the potent sexual energy throughout my body with my breath, instead of climaxing. This is a powerful therapy for the maintenance of health. Many women find their *yoni* (Sanskrit for "vagina") becomes weak and nonresponsive and, in some cases, it simply goes dormant, especially in their later years when hormonal levels fluctuate. By doing these exercises, including the sexual muscle squeezes, I kept this hot spot nourished and fit. I would later join Maile and her boyfriend in my first workshop with Margot Anand to expand into my Divine Feminine.

I also cultivated a different kind of companionship . . . an imaginary tantric partner who bridged the gap beautifully and erotically through creative expression.

The Arrow-Making Yogini

In the goddess days, I loved roaming a bookstore called Milk and Honey in Sebastopol. I could smell sandalwood incense wafting from the open door and, once inside, I was mesmerized by all the lotions and potions for the feminine desire, along with a CD of women's voices caressing my ears with ancient songs. There was an inviting sitting area with a velvet love seat and matching chair, an Oriental rug, and an elegant tasseled lamp to enhance the posh setting.

One day, I was drawn to a book titled *Passionate Enlightenment: Women in Tantric Buddhism* by Miranda Shaw, one of the leading authorities on the subject. She maintains that, although men were historically credited with transforming erotic ecstasy into spiritual enlightenment, women were major contributors to shaping this movement. I was delighted to find this book, as I felt a kinship with Eastern ways and the beloved Goddess.

I had been practicing devotional union with an imaginary partner in my trailer in Santa Barbara. I would sit cross-legged on my bed facing the headboard where my altar rested above on a wooden shelf. In sacred space, I would breathe into deep meditation, allowing for my imaginary partner to come forth. It was always a woman with long, black hair, cocoa eyes, and a closed mouth smile. A white light shone behind her as we slipped into melodic bliss. I immersed myself in these exhilarating experiences, which took me far beyond the mental realms of brain training and into the spacious world of the Dakini, the women who dance in the skies. Was she really a product of my mind, an imaginary partner? Or was I truly connecting with this Dakini on the level of Infinite Intelligence?

As I read more about the founding mothers of "the founding fathers" of tantra, I noticed the arrow-making yogini strongly resembled my tantric partner. Her provocative essence inspired me to sketch her with incandescent strokes, based on the artistry of Tibetan woodblock prints by Emily Martindale in Shaw's book. I was wholly focused on pencil to paper as I drew her face, breasts, and those delicate hands that poised her hand-made arrow of perfection. Streams of long, black hair grazed her shoulders, and jewels on strings to a medallion graced her round belly. (See Figure 7: My Arrow-Making Yogini.)

My connection with this Yogini helped strengthen my capacity to focus in a more enlightened way with the precision of a finely crafted arrow that, when pointed at its target, knows no other determination, yet it is not attached to this target. Thus, the grander theme may be attained. This faculty within me became more developed and cultivated through use, and I learned to rely and trust that "still small voice." The journey of any person has many twists and turns and dealing with a head injury compounds this journey. Embodying this thread of tantra helped me birth many more enlightening capabilities from this higher vibrational plane.

On another occasion, Maile and I were chatting on my bed. I was lying on my back with feet up on the wall to help with circulation in my legs, when a postal truck delivered a large box to the porch deck. I sprang to the door and opened the package. It was from Aphrodite Dae and was filled with several jars of lotions and potions. We had a slathering good time opening the jars and pampering ourselves. I really loved those acts of kindness and instant uplifting.

I often went to Maile's stone jewelry parties, even though it was a walk, a bus ride, and another walk to get there. She had become one of my best friends in Santa Barbara, so it was worth it. As a stone diva, she coined the phrase "Adorn the Body, Nourish the Soul," and was gifted in making outrageously beautiful hand-carved stone jewelry. Her jewelry reminded me of the jewels that rest upon the Arrow-Making Yogini's décolleté and belly. I enjoyed going to Maile's parties because I met the most interesting people, and she always had plenty of hors d'oeuvres and wine, a real plus for someone on disability.

I could only afford to buy a couple of beads at a time at each stone show, but over a two-year period, I finally had strung a most beautiful beaded necklace on a brown leather string. A great lesson in patience, the tale of the tortoise and the hare, my forte. It reminded me of Dr. Smith's words: "You'll get there, Kathleen."

CHAPTER 16

ALL ABOARD THE BRAIN TRAIN

I enjoyed the creative surges immensely as it gave my analytical brain a break; however, I was itching to go back to school, especially to see if I could finish a master's degree and then go on to a PhD. Dr. Smith suggested I try the Santa Barbara City College first, because of its Disabled Student Programs and Services (DSPS) Department. In my office interview, the professional support staff suggested I enroll in the assistive technology class before any other class.

This was a new and interesting process for me. My vision and occupational therapist had turned me loose, so I was on my own to initiate a plan to take this class. Interestingly, I never made it on time to register for the class in the spring semester. I made practice runs from my trailer to the college to familiarize myself with the driving route. Then, I scanned the catalog for the date and time of my classes and practiced walking from the parking lot to the designated building and classroom on campus several times.

I was experiencing déjà vu with the delayed processing of the simulator driving game. I would set off with book bag in hand, purse, water, and car keys and drive to the college, a mere 12 minutes away. I timed myself to see when I would get to the classroom door. Unexplainably, I failed to get there on time, being off by 20 to 30 minutes. Where did the time go? Where did I go?

Who knows, but I kept practicing until I overlearned the whole process, which took several months and the next semester.

I was relieved to see the class filled with people like me who had suffered a traumatic brain injury. The professor described the challenges for disabled people and shared the dynamics of the class progression and how we would reach our goals and navigate with alternative methods to function better in the classroom. It was a good learning curve and, with the help of my professor, I wrote an article about recovering from a traumatic brain injury. It was the cumulative "test" that we could understand and use the methods we learned in class over the past two months.

My professor submitted my article to the campus newspaper. The editor contacted me and said she wanted to publish it in the next issue; however, I felt uneasy because of being in a litigation. I declined publication of my article, which follows in its entirety, for fear of being reprimanded. This is something I regret to this day.

I Have Half a Mind to Tell You the Truth:
Recovering from Head Injury
(Assisted by Laurie Vasquez, PhD, April 21, 2004)

When I was asked to do this writing assignment in class, a couple of bells went off in my head, literally! First, I'm hesitant to do this paper because it reminds me of my injury and the cognitive issues I deal with daily. Moreover, if I describe in detail what I go through in a day, it may change the way family and friends interact with me.

Over the years, there have been many changes in my level of functioning. They are slow and deliberate, but progressive. I do not want to alter the appearance of that in any way. This paper is written purely for educational purposes, and to help me improve upon my weaknesses with real tools and services to ensure forward movement. We all choose to move through our lives the best way we can. As for me, I must follow three to five steps before I can get something done. It is not automatic, as I will explain later in this paper.

There is also resistance in doing this paper because I occasionally question if I am head injured. If I act "normal" and don't use any strategies, will I be "normal" again? I know this isn't true, but perhaps I still do not accept the label of a "head injured person." This is mainly because of my background before I was injured. I have a very strong philosophy about life, the power of thoughts and intuition, the will to live life to its fullest, and the enormous gift of love, goodness, and spirituality.

Finally, I hesitate to publicly display my experiences and personal conclusions because I do not want the responsibility of being an "authority" and all that goes with it, including more variables and questions than I could handle, added confusion, and being on the frontline again, but in a much dimmer light. (I was the dynamic motivational speaker with a flair for humor, who thrived on audience participation.) I don't want to be the flake who cannot intelligently respond to a question, or even a friendly comment. My brain doesn't access information the same way as before, so something like that could easily send me into a tumbling babble and right off the stage.

Upon disclosing this information, there are distinct advantages in completing this research paper. I am taking an account of all my strengths and weaknesses from the initial onset of my injury to the present day. This is invaluable because I can use newly acquired assistive technology to bring awareness and attention to my weaknesses. Then, I can improve on them, make better choices in my daily routine, and recapture a newer sense of self. Thus, the quality of my life will be greatly enhanced. I will become more efficient, and the real possibility of entering back into a satisfying, competitive, and purposeful career is possible. In addition, this would boost my confidence not only in my career, but in my personal relationships as well. Most of all, I will truly know who I am in body, mind, and soul once again.

I am not alone. According to the Centers of Disease Control report (2003) to Congress, 1.5 million Americans sustain a TBI. Each year 80,000 to 90,000 Americans experience the onset of a long-term disability following a TBI and more than 50,000 people die from a TBI. Additionally, the CDC estimates that 5.3 million Americans currently live with disabilities resulting from TBI. Individuals who sustain TBI can display a wide variety of functional impairments. In this paper, I will only discuss my impairments and how I compensate for them by using strategies and assistive technology.

In July 1998, I was struck on the top of my head by a speeding golf ball. A few months later, I was diagnosed with traumatic brain injury (TBI). The Brain Injury Association defines TBI as "an insult to the brain, not of degenerative or congenital nature, caused by an external physical force that may produce a diminished or altered state of consciousness, which results in an impairment of cognitive abilities or physical functioning." TBI can result in a myriad of disturbances other than cognitive or physical: the problems can be communicative, perceptual, psycho-social, behavioral, and/or emotional.

182

To understand the characteristics of a head injury, please view the brain map on page 314. It shows the brain's various sections or lobes: frontal, temporal, parietal, occipital, and the brain stem. (See Figure 8: Brain Anatomy.) The brain is encased with fluid. When I was hit, the brain torqued and bounced against the skeletal walls. The sections of the brain that were injured were frontal, occipital, temporal, and brain stem.

The frontal lobe houses initiation, judgment, problem solving, behavior inhibition, planning and anticipation, self-monitoring, motor planning, personality, emotions, awareness of abilities and limitations, organization, attention and organization, attention and concentration, mental flexibility, speaking expressively.

The temporal lobe affects language, memory, understanding, hearing, organization and sequencing.

The parietal lobe affects sense of touch, differentiation of sizes, shapes and colors, and spatial and visual perception.

The occipital lobe controls vision.

The cerebellum rules balance, skilled motor activity and coordination.

The brain stem dictates breathing, heart rate, arousal and consciousness, sleep and wake cycles, and attention and concentration.

When neurons and nerve tracts are affected, they can be unable or have difficulty carrying the messages that tell the brain what to do. This can result in thinking changes, physical changes, and personality and behavioral changes. Immediately after being struck in the head, I experienced short-term memory loss, delayed thought processing, difficulties in reading, writing, understanding language, and speaking. I also suffered fatigue, balance issues, dizziness, vertigo and nausea, and vision problems. My behavioral changes included inappropriate behavior, self-centeredness, reduced self-esteem, depression, anxiety, frustration, irritability, denial, and agitation. I was a hot mess!

As you process this information, you will begin to understand the complexity of sustaining a head injury. The brain is a control center containing a zillion pieces of information. When I was struck in the head, all the information was fragmented and short-circuited. Just locating the right word or phrase was like being a mouse in a maze, trying desperately to find food. If someone asked me a simple question, like "How are you feeling?" my brain would search for an answer, but it could not find one. My typical response was: "Could you please be more specific?" This was an effective strategy for gaining more information. I compensate so well for my deficits that the average person would not even know I have a disability. This proves to be emotionally challenging and difficult to explain when someone asks why I'm on disability.

I want to move into real-world settings here, on issues I deal with daily as a student in the classroom. My day begins the night before. I keep an appointment book with daily log sheets that list exactly what I would like to accomplish. These tasks include home responsibilities (meal planning, laundry, bills, phone calls, and other correspondence), school assignments, and scheduled breaks or rest times.

The next morning, I use my checklist to move through my day. It is usually best to stick to the plan. Being spontaneous sometimes leads to confusion and over-stimulation. Over time, with much rehearsal, *"overlearning" a task kicks into the memory bank. I now do some daily tasks without having to write them down.*

Five years ago, I was relearning how to get up, shower and get dressed, without being able to then go out and do something. It was an enormous task just getting ready. To go back to college, I had to plan months before the actual registration dates. The plan included practice runs from my home to campus, then mapping out direct walking routes to and from classes. (I missed the registration period the first time around because of all these steps). I also schedule quiet rest breaks of 45 to 60 minutes to help maneuver through the class day.

Meeting deadlines is still a difficult task, as I described in the example above. I have three to five steps to do before the actual step is taken. If I allot enough time and adequately pace myself, then I usually have a good result. Although adding another variable, such as going to school, has created several more challenges. My daily living tasks have suffered tremendously, including preparing adequate meals and cleaning my apartment. This provides the possibility, however, for new compensations and perhaps expanding in ways not known before.

In the classroom setting, I experience a variety of difficulties, such as taking notes, being distracted by external noise, light sensitivity, trouble seeing the blackboard, losing track of the lecture topic, inability to process information fast enough to express my opinions, not seeing the big picture, procrastinating on completing assignments, and fading or shutting down from too much stimuli.

Assistive technology is the alternative path to traditional methods of functioning in the classroom, at home or in the office. This new technology aids the person with special needs, or in over-coming limitations, making them more productive in the classroom as well as in their daily life. Fortunately, there are support services available to help in my learning, such as tutoring, computers, calculators, possible alternative assignments, note takers, or a copy of students' notes, detailed syllabus, preference in seating arrangements (I usually sit up front toward the far right or left), taped texts and tape recordings of lectures, readers, extended time on tests, different tests formats, developmental and/or organizational classes.

Other technology-based strategies to compensate for my limitations are: books on tape, adjusting software to support visual processing, isolating text in manageable chunks by high-lighting and enlarging, programs that allow you to practice learned strategies or remember cues, concept map-ping to organize ideas, using head-phones or ear plugs to block out noise, easy-to-read screens, screen diffusers, concept mapping to organize ideas, and software that provides frequent feedback. With advances in technology, it is easy to see just how helpful these tools and support services are. They enable me to become more efficient in the classroom and in some areas of my life.

The Brain Train

If I could create a piece of technology that would help someone who is brain injured, it would be the "brain train." The brain train is a device that would look like a hearing aid. It fits into both ears, and the wires would attach to the different sections of the brain that were injured (like the wires or electrodes that are used in an EKG (electrocardiogram). That's the physical hook-up. This device would then connect via satellite to your home computer, where a software package specific

186

to your head injury is stored. The software would assist the person in thought processing, such as sequencing, organizing, phrasing, and words.

The amazing part of this product is that it is immediate! There is no more delayed response time or scattered tangential thinking. The brain train routes ideas, concepts, and thoughts in an efficient and real-time way. The cost of the brain train is the same price as any other software package and much less than the cost of a hearing aid. A product such as this would especially be available through Medicare. (Note: In years to follow, I learned how to create my own manual brain train. No device necessary, just a willingness to practice. Neurons that fire together wire together. All aboard!)

In conclusion, what I have learned about myself in writing this paper is pleasantly surprising. It's OK to be vulnerable. It's OK to talk from a place of personal experience because it may help other people with TBI and their own recovery. It certainly has been very therapeutic and helpful to me. I am very fortunate my injury is mild to moderate, not severe. There was also physical injury — a nerve impingement in my cervical — that was taken care of with surgery. So, I no longer have any physical disability. This opens more options for me. I continue to progress slowly and steadily with strategies and assistive technology. Moreover, I have great discipline in using these support services and strategies. I can go to school and learn the necessary tools and skills at a pace I can understand and handle. Eventually, I hope to reenter the employment world. If I am not for myself, who will be for me?

For me, the DSPS office at Santa Barbara City College and its professional support staff and affordable programs of assistive technology opened a new avenue of hope and possibility. Surely, I could step up to the plate on an equal playing field for which I am set up to succeed. Taking this class—and finishing it—was a real confidence booster for me, although I realized it would be too hard to try to get my master's degree or a doctorate on the college level. Too much information, too much reading, and at a pace that zoomed along like a speed boat in a period of three or four months would be insurmountable and unhealthy.

The Write Stuff

I loved having the classroom experience and wanted to continue in some way. Dr. Smith suggested I take an adult writing course at the Schott Center off upper State Street in Santa Barbara. The class was only eight weeks long, with a small number of students in the program. This class was a bit easier to get to and closer to my trailer haven. I could even walk if I chose to. The center was in one building with several classrooms, so it was easy to locate my writing class marked by a room number, instead of searching aimlessly for a building on campus and then a classroom.

My professor, Cork Milner, was a handsome and debonair older man who lived life with gusto and expressed it fully. He always wore crisp, pressed pants and shirt; a colorful scarf; and a cashmere sweater or finely woven bone jacket. Cork wrote several articles on travel and wine, and a popular book, *Write from the Start* (New York: Simon & Schuster, 1992). I loved listening to him talk or read prose from his book or literature. I learned so many writing tips in this class, and it inspired me to write seriously again. Cork would give a writing assignment each week, and I would handwrite mine in the little trailer. I had several handwritten drafts, and then I would take my time and write the final paper in cursive. After I finished taking the first set of eight classes, I took the whole class again to anchor what I was learning.

The second time around, Cork suggested I write about the golfing accident, which I did. I remember him asking me to read it aloud to the class the following week. I was honored and felt up to the task, but once I began reading, the words became an emotional journey. By the second paragraph, I was crying, and Cork, who was seated near me, suggested I sit in the chair as he read the rest of the story. It was quite touching, and all the students were very engaged and compassionate. Cork knew what he was doing and explained how writing and reading aloud can be very therapeutic. I would take a third round of the eight classes and rewrite the prologue and read it aloud again, this time with some tears, though being able to compose myself to finish it.

I used this piece for a speech I delivered at the Kathleen Klawitter Golf Classic in April 2004. Jodi House, a home for people recovering from head injuries, hosted its fourth annual golf tournament in my honor at the Sandpiper Country Club, just north of Santa Barbara, to raise funds to support its programs for adults with acquired brain injuries. More than 100 people attended.

Golf Digest rated this championship golf course as one of top 25 public golf courses in the country, featuring rolling fairways and challenging greens on a spectacular seaside links-style layout. In 1938, ARCO used the Sandpiper site for crude oil production after oil was discovered in 1927. At the peak of production, the site had 25 oil wells. In 1965, oil production officially ended, though some infrastructure remains both above and below ground. In 1972, the property was purchased and developed for what is now called Sandpiper Golf Club.

My older brother and younger sister flew out two days before the event to visit with me and then stayed to play in the tournament. They are avid golfers, just like my father was, and shared the great Klawitter humor. Christine, now a dear friend of many years, drove up from Palm Springs, and my new friend, Maile, also played in the 18-hole golf tournament, which was organized with foursomes playing in a scramble format, allowing each player to play his or her strengths and help in the overall scoring.

Kat's Naps

The golfing event was fun for me as I got to high jinks a bit with the four of them on the putting green before they plopped in their carts to play their round of golf. While everyone was out playing the course for four to five hours, I slipped into the ladies' locker room for a long cat nap on a plush leather couch. I needed some rest before delivering my speech to the attendees after the tournament. The essential cat nap started with the onset of my traumatic brain injury, where I would nap three to five times a day for about 60 minutes each session. It was part of the process, and I learned to accept it. Being at the golf outing was no exception.

I lay on the couch and flopped my lavender-filled eye pillow over my eyeballs. This blocked out any light in the locker room, especially the fluorescent lights. This was an important aspect of taking my cat nap because it allowed my brain to shut down completely. Seeing any light would be a distraction and keep my brain active. I began some deep belly breathing and then focused on my breath for about 10 minutes. This proved to help my nap time be more restful and rejuvenating.

My own inner alarm gently prompted me to awaken after about an hour, so I got up and meandered around the country club. From the balcony, I could see some of the golfers out on the course. I reviewed my speech a couple of times and then sneaked a few pieces of cheese and crackers off the long reception table. I took a one-hour nap before appearing in front of the audience that afternoon. Sleep experts have found that daytime naps can improve many things: increase alertness, boost creativity, reduce stress, improve perception, stamina, motor skills and accuracy, reduce the risk of heart attack, brighten your mood, and boost memory. I felt refreshed and ready to give my speech after my two cat naps.

As the players came in off the course, they indulged in wine and cheese at the festive outdoor party, where my former accordion instructor, Ross, and his longtime band partner, Bob, played background music from around the world. When it was time for my speech, I walked up to the front of the patio, my typewritten speech pages grasped in my hand. I was a bit nervous as this was to be a "speech read," not to be done from memory. Plus, I could swear I smelled the faint stench of the oil production from days gone by.

The Jodi House Speech
1. Step up to the podium.
2. Place speech papers on top of the podium.
3. Adjust the microphone.
4 Take a deep breath and blow it out.
5. Look at audience and smile, then look back down on your papers and begin reading. Use fingers to help mark place.

Hello, my name is Kathleen Klawitter. I am a former LPGA golf professional in the teaching division. I had a dream to play on the LPGA tour; however, after a couple of years of hitting 1,000 golf balls a day, I realized it was not my passion. I realized I was more gifted in teaching and inspiring people who wanted to play better golf and that is what I really loved to do. Inevitably, someone would always come up and say,

'How do you do that?' and then we would get to talking, and the next thing I knew I was helping them with their golf swing. Now that was fulfilling.

To inspire someone or to see them really get it was true gratification. There's nothing like the feeling of that effortless swing that sends the ball farther than you can see . . .

(Kathleen, tip your glasses and look over them; slide them back and look back down on your paper.)

. . . or at least down the middle of the fairway. I am sure you all agree, it's what keeps you coming back. That one great shot on the 7th hole. You know you have found your niche in life when your work becomes play and it doesn't matter how long your day is. I remember many a day that stretched into the twilight because "just one more person" wanted a lesson or golf tip. I always obliged then went home and plopped onto my bed and slept until morning. Remember when you were a child, you played hard all day, ate supper, and then fell blissfully asleep in anticipation for the next play day?

Golf is probably one of the most challenging sports there is, yet it remains a lifetime sport. And an expensive sport. How much did you pay for your round of golf today? Certainly, money well spent, not only for the aesthetic beauty of Sandpiper but, more importantly, to provide the funds necessary to continue the services at Jodi House. An organization dedicated in helping head injured persons, like me.

We were certainly blessed with great weather to play golf, so no excuses there, huh? On behalf of Jodi House, I'd like to welcome you and thank you for coming out today to help fund the many services Jodi House provides for head injured persons, like me.

It has been almost six years since my injury, and I am progressing well. And there are many reasons for this. Over the years, there have been many changes in my level of functioning. This is due to being disciplined in using strategies to compensate for my deficits. So much that many people would not even know I was head injured. I also have a great passion for life itself, and the people with who I come into contact. My family has also been very supportive and encouraging. My brother, Ken, and my sister, Kim, have traveled from Indiana to be with me this weekend and there are, of course, many friends who have helped along the way.

I am recovering from a traumatic brain injury. I am unable to work and play in the golf arena that I so dearly loved. I am unable to drive a car or ride a bike. I have gone from an independent entrepreneur to a dependent woman on disability. I have relearned to think and speak, sometimes which I do very fluidly. I continue to diligently work on my writing. I also can walk, and I do so every day. My sense of smell has come back and when I walk past Alice Keck Park Memorial Garden, or the rose garden in front of the Old Mission, my nostrils fill with that sweet aroma of freshly cut grass and my heart fills with the passion I once embraced.

Even tonight, as I am giving this speech, I realize how far I have progressed. I never imagined I'd be speaking in front of an audience again. Being head injured has changed my life dramatically, and it has become my greatest challenge. Although, if I were in a line-up with a dozen other people, you probably would not guess I was the one who is permanently injured.

In the last years, I have worked very hard in my rehabilitation program. I use strategies and props to help me through each day. One of the most noticeable deficits is my pace; it is much slower than normal, and my life has become very structured. What I can accomplish in a day is much less than what I normally could do. Where I once could juggle several tasks in a day, I now can only do one or two. And the preparation for each task is highly structured with moment-to-moment scheduling. Each moment is a conscious step-by-step effort; mechanical not automatic. I can be easily distracted and then my schedule becomes disrupted and I go off in another direction undetected. The use of a timer/alarms or constant reference to my appointment book helps me stay on course. I almost feel I've been handed a key to a better and higher quality life. Let me give you an example of how this works with the game of golf.

Wake up! This is your golf tip for tonight. Stay in the moment and use increments to reach a simple goal. For instance, what is the most common golf question asked? Anyone?

"How do I lower my score?"

Let's break it down to one variable and focus on that completely:

1. *By practicing the short game.*
2. *The short game consists of putting, chipping, and pitching.*
3. *Let's choose putting.*
4. *Putting consists of two parts: distance and accuracy.*
5. *Let's choose accuracy.*

6. *Now, we practice putting accuracy with one easy exercise three to four times a week, such as the "yardstick drill."* (I explained the last point in detail to the audience.)

Place a yardstick on the ground, and take your usual putting stance, putter in hand. Go back and forth on top of the yardstick making sure to keep the sweet spot of the putter in the middle of the yardstick. Do this for less than a minute each session, say just before you retire to bed for the night. Be deliberate with your stroke. Be deliberate with your focus. Stay in the moment. In about two to three weeks, watch what happens. Start to keep track of your putts. On your scorecard, mark putts per hole in the bottom right corner. Your eventual goal is one to two putts per hole. Ultimately, you will lower your score by several strokes.

We took very broad questions and narrowed it down to one variable, one goal to work with in that moment, which ultimately has a very big outcome, a lower score. When you focus on one variable for two to three weeks, you anchor it completely to your memory bank and it becomes the new familiar. Watch what happens in your golf score. This is how I taught golf, never realizing how important it would become in my personal life.

Remember, slow down and simplify, not only to improve your golf performance, but also to enhance your daily life. You can do this without the pain, frustration, and dependence that's associated with a traumatic brain injury.

The use of your brain is a gift. Choose to turn your multi-tasking life into a simple set of little steps and see how much more you learn, how much more you live and how much more you get done. More importantly, how much better you feel on the inside. That's what it's really all about and where the real change comes in. Feeling good inside; when your heart is open, your mind is clear, and you are having fun in this moment when it all comes together.

There are other organizations like Jodi house, and people who dedicate their time and energy to help us live a better quality of life. Like John Tomiozi, the director of Jodi House, and especially Bob and Nanse Chapman, who publish the Santa Barbara Family Magazine. And to Dr. Cheryll Smith, my neuropsychologist, for her extraordinary patience in repeating strategies, dedication, and commitment to my recovery, and her head injury expertise. Without her, I would not be standing here today. I thank all of you who have chosen to make a difference.

How wonderful to know at this very moment there is someone running on the other side of the world, carrying the Olympic Torch. Do we have any Olympic fans in the house? This torch flame was ceremonially lit by the rays of the sun, on an altar in the Temple of Hera, in the city of ancient Olympia, Greece. And Hera is the Goddess of courage. Her blessing is the fullness of power, as in being empowered from within. In the Goddess tradition, the month of June received its name from the Goddess Juno/Hera. I was born in the month of June!

How wonderful to know that all of you here tonight, in taking part in this fundraiser, are carrying the torch, for those who cannot.

John Michael, come up here. (Holding candle torch). This is my friend, John Michael. He has been a member of Jodi House for many years. We've been working on behalf of this golf tournament for a couple of months now. We'd like to thank you all for coming, and we appreciate your support. May that same flame of passion burn deep within your heart and soul and continue to light the way. Thank you for coming out today and supporting Jodi House.

I kept the original speech papers stapled and pieced together as a reminder of that evening and how far I have come in my rehabilitation. The sacredness of the Olympic Torch has deeper implications; it is the gesture of passing the torch from person to person, from city to city, in the race against time and how will we pass what we have learned to our children and our children's children. For persons with head injuries or other disabilities, how the willingness to live and connect with God/Source, despite any physical disability, become our greatest strengths. The heartfelt actions of all those who attended the golfing fundraiser that day is a testament to the symbol of the torch itself: "The ceremonial act of passing the torch symbolizes the ideal of international brotherhood and sisterhood and reminds us of the unity of nations." We all came together that day with love and compassion, for a common goal, to advance and uplift the human spirit in a fun and meaningful way.

Upon completion of my speech, I received a resounding applause and a standing ovation. A gentleman approached me with his team's first-place trophy for winning the golf tournament. I don't remember his actual words, but when he placed the trophy in my hands, I felt I had won that day, even though I hadn't played. The simple transfer of this prize, the Olympic Torch in my mind, lit me up inside, and tears fell from my cheeks. Courage, kindness, and inspiration sparked between us, and the glowing example of the human spirit shone brightly in that eternal moment. *As in Olympia, the athletes, coaches, and fans are "filled with the Gods," so, too, we transcend and are filled with the true Divine Spirit in us all. The sacred flame burns from generation to generation,* as written by Phil Cousineau in his book, *The Olympic Odyssey: Rekindling the True Spirit of the Great Games* (First Quest Edition 2003, Theosophical Publishing House).

My former accordion instructor, Ross, and his band partner, Bob, began playing music again. At the end of the evening, when most everyone had left, Ross had a crazy idea while he was packing up. "Kathleen, let's play a song together." I'm sure my face turned red as I flung Bob's accordion over my shoulders and secured the front strap.

Ross pulled out the two-page sheet music for "The River Seine," a lilting French melody, and placed it on the music stand. We began to play together just like at the trailer when he came to give me an accordion lesson. There were several starts and stops, nothing like a waltz, so I fondly renamed that song "The River Insane" after that stint. My friends and family didn't care. They were just happy to see me having fun with the accordion and living life.

I don't know how much money was raised that day, but I do know it was successful for Jodi House. The sponsorship levels started at $250. A foursome from businesses or organizations ranged from $1,000 to $5,000, depending on their donation ability. There were 18 foursomes that day, and organizations could make a flat donation of their choosing. At the very least, the center could have made a substantial amount to help support their programs cultivating independence, fostering community and social skills, and building self-esteem and a sense of belonging.

This was my first public-speaking appearance since before my accident. My five- to seven-minute speech required a lot of prep time, including taking a shower, getting dressed, and combing my hair. Finally, I was able to go out and do something. The light of hope shone through. But, more than this, I had regained some confidence, not only through speaking and playing the accordion in front of people, but I also felt a sense of belonging with family, friends, and strangers who applauded my efforts.

It's in the Cards

I continued to see Dr. Smith once a week to work on my progress in many ways. One day she showed me a simple card game that she devised especially for me, to help filter out distractions and narrow my focus to one variable. It's called "Smith's Red and Black Stack" card game. One single playing card has several variables in it. When I first looked at a card and studied it, I would get dizzy and nauseated from all the different colors, symbols, and numbers. This is how I viewed life as well, with so many variables and stimuli wherever I was. It was hard to stay focused, and I would constantly get confused and feel overwhelmed.

The card game went like this: Shuffle the deck of cards; then flip over one card at a time. Ask yourself, "Is it black or red?" Then, place it face-up on the table. Continue through the rest of the deck asking this question and splitting the cards into a red or black pile. Then, pick up the red pile only and ask yourself, "Is it hearts or diamonds?" Go through the rest of the cards in your hand, splitting the cards into two piles of hearts and diamonds. Then, pick up the diamond pile and ask, "Is it numbers or faces?" Go through the rest of the cards in your hand and split them into two piles of numbers and faces. Then, pick up the numbers pile, and ask yourself, "Is it odd or even?" Go through the rest of the cards in your hand. Then, pick up the face cards, and ask yourself is it male or female. Now sequence all of the diamond cards, starting with the ace, then 2, 3, 4, and so on until you've reached the king. This pile is now complete. Next, pick up the heart pile and do the same routine as you did, from the beginning, with the diamond cards. Now, pick up the black pile of cards, and ask yourself, "Is it spades or clubs?" Follow the same routine as with the hearts/diamonds. This is not a game to see how quickly you can go, but to identify the variable of the card correctly until the whole card game is finished. It's not a one-time deal; it requires daily practice to benefit from the results.

The first few days and weeks I performed this exercise, I could not finish going through the deck because my brain would get overloaded and I'd have to stop. I did the best I could every morning, taking breaks as needed. The process was slow, but through daily practice for many months, I was able to complete the whole cycle without getting overloaded and ill. With the outcome of this new card strategy, I began looking at life in the same way. I could break down a seemingly enormous situation into chunks of variables and handle each one separately with all my focused attention.

By taking a couple of minutes to do the card sorting game every morning, my brain slowly began to recircuit itself. I no longer got dizzy from all the external stimuli, if I stayed under my threshold levels, which are much higher now. It only took a willingness to begin to do this. I can do it willpower! In his book, *Autobiography of a Yogi* (Los Angeles: Self-Realization Fellowship, 1998), Paramahansa Yogananda wrote, "Willpower is energy in motion." This is very helpful in this fast-paced world of multitasking and high-tech hand devices. I still practice this card game today to solidify my strategic way of thinking.

CHAPTER 17

UNUSUAL HEALING METHODS

In 2004, I attended an extraordinary, life-changing tantra workshop, "The Yin and Yang of Sexual Ecstasy," facilitated by Margot Anand, who is an international best-selling author and one of the world's leading authorities on tantra. This alternative method marked the beginning of my journey to awaken and understand what happened after my traumatic brain injury. I needed to transform and expand myself and learn to forgive everyone and everything for my accident and the traumatic brain injury. I also had to open my heart to trust again, especially men.

The workshop was held in Stargazer Hot Springs, one of the oldest hot springs in California, with thousands of private acres of sacred woodlands and waters. Guests travel from around the world to experience the healing waters, historic grounds, natural setting, lively community, and the spirit-centered focus that Stargazer offers.

The historic communal soaking pools are filled with fresh spring waters—super hot, soothingly warm, or sassy cold. These cement spring pools are nestled one after the other, up the hill, and past the dorm-like buildings to the left, and small enchanting cabins to the right. There also was a large Olympic-sized swimming pool with a small bungalow outdoor cafe that offered salads, veggies, and smoothies.

Before my accident, I took weekly jaunts up the mountain from my guesthouse in Sebastopol when I was a golf instructor. I would leave on Wednesday afternoon after I taught my last private golf lesson, plodding along in my Volkswagen Westfalia camper. A few hours later, I passed through the gates of Stargazer, stopped to pay my $25 for overnight camping, and then selected a spot near the trail that led to the pools. I enjoyed popping up the vented canvas to create a homey feel for the next 24 hours. Clothing was optional there, so I indulged in plenty of sunning, soaking, and swimming sans swimsuit.

I'd put on a sarong, slip on my sandals, and head to the trail for a brisk walk through the woods and camping tents until I reached the large pool. Once there, I grabbed a smoothie and sat down to take in the evening, watching the sun set against the trees and mountains, before I lowered myself into the warm pool for a long soak. After surrendering to the tranquil waters, I trekked back on the dirt trail that led to my Vanagon for a cozy sleep in the bunk-bed canopy. I could almost touch the endless spray of stars because it was so dark.

My favorite part of my short visit was the hot and cold pools. I started in the covered hot pool for a couple of minutes, or for as long as I could stand it. I had to carefully walk down the steps into the hot spring waters, continually saying, "Yes, yes, yes," before I could submerge to my neck, and then slowly back up the steps of the hot pool and outside where there were more wooden steps to the cold pool. I held onto the metal rail, slowly walking down three cement steps into the cold waters. Yikes! It was freezing, but only for the first round. I stayed submerged for a couple of minutes, feeling the tingling sensations within my body, and went back to the hot pool to repeat the process. By the third round, I was not feeling a thing. All stress had left my body. I was completely relaxed and in an altered state of pure bliss.

A ceramic statue of Kwan Yin, the Japanese Goddess of compassion, mercy, and kindness, rested in a flower garden next to the cold pool. I sat on the bench in front of her to pray, to be, and to breathe with her. I appreciated my weekly trips to enjoy the sacred waters and rejuvenate my body, mind, and soul. Every time I left Stargazer, I secretly desired to live and work there someday. I always arrived on time in my rambling Vanagon, refreshed for my women's golf league on Thursday evenings down in the valley.

Dancing with the Stars

Tantra is a unique path that utilizes the energy map of the chakras. In my studies of Eastern philosophy in the 1990s, I learned this energy system and taught some of my golf students how to utilize rejuvenating energy to enhance their performance on the links. The workshop facilitator, Margot Anand, was dedicated to bringing the teachings of tantra beyond the bedroom and into everyday life. She called her unique method SkyDancing® Tantra. In her book, *The Art of Everyday Ecstasy* (New York: Broadway Books, 1999), Anand wrote, "SkyDancing Tantra teaches you to choose with awareness what brings you pleasure and joy—which opens the door to a deeper connection with spirit and a greater sense of aliveness and well-being. It is also the art of weaving the contradictory aspects of your personality into a unified whole for the purpose of expanding your consciousness"

The process seemed deeper and quicker than traditional therapy, like an accelerated transformational healing that was facilitated with the utmost of integrity. I didn't get stuck in the intellectual mind, but bypassed it with higher ecstatic states, utilizing breath, movement, sound techniques, and streaming this energy in a positive direction within my body.

Achieving Ecstasy

Ecstasy, from the Greek *ex stasis*, means "to move beyond stasis." It denotes "being in a Divine state of grace." Some athletes refer to it as being "in the zone" or "in the flow." As an athlete, learning how to compete and train for a sport was important because I learned how to deal with adversity effectively. I learned "how to rise above" and exceed my abilities far more than I thought I could. This mindset was tremendously beneficial in helping my brain to recalibrate. I had attained those peak performances of ecstasy before, and I knew and believed I could do it repeatedly. The seemingly impossible golf shot—over the tree and onto the green with two short hops into the cup, the unbelievable horizontal softball catch while playing shortstop— from bat to glove in a split second—and singing "A Whole New World" in the Unity Church with a standing ovation at the end. Not to mention the joy I felt when I held my cousin Lori's newborn son for the first time!

I learned sometimes I didn't have to do anything but be open to the moment of possibility to reach these ecstatic states, such as in listening to the operatic "Flower Duet," making love, or smelling the freshly mowed grass on the golf links. It's a real test of the spirit and, if played with dedication and all your heart, leads to a place far better than you could ever imagine. And you don't necessarily need the recreational drug to get there. I tried a clean cut of "ecstasy" one time and know the organic experience is far better than the untethered, false euphoric sense of freedom from an illicit drug. Spiritual strength is more important than physical strength and, when combined with the practice of vital sexual energy, brought me to infinite states of true ecstasy.

Contrary to the popular Western belief of tantra, where sex is secret and a "verboten" subject, the practice of streaming this vital energy released emotional blockages and rejuvenated my body through amplified inner sensations and circulation, especially in my brain. This blew my mind, because the hardest part of my brain functioning was trying to figure things out, which flooded my brain circuits, and caused me to withdraw emotionally and physically. With this method, I was revitalizing my brain and body. And even more profound, I realized it was an energy event where I didn't even have to take my clothes off or have sex. Being orgasmic in every moment brought on a whole new meaning. I was having brain orgasms!

In her book, Anand explains, "Originally, the sky dancers were wild, free ecstatic 'dakinis,' also called feminine buddhas or female awakeners. The word *dakini* means 'woman who dances in space,' or 'woman who revels in the freedom of emptiness.'"

Sky dancers were, and are, women of passion who are profoundly devoted to spiritual awakening.'"

Other notable feminine teachers elaborated on the tantric teachings in their own books. Author Miranda Shaw wrote in her book, *Passionate Enlightenment*,

> The *ḍākinīs* leap and fly, unfettered by clothing, encircled by billowing hair, their bodies curved in sinuous dance poses. Their eyes blaze with passion, ecstasy, and ferocious intensity. One can almost hear the soft clacking of their intricate bone jewelry and feel the wind stirred by their rainbow-colored scarves as they soar through the Tantric Buddhist landscape. These unrestrained damsels appear to revel in freedom of every kind. Expressions of this motif in Tantric literature describe yoginis with magical powers, powerful enchantresses with the ability to change shape at will, and enlightened women who can spark a direct experience of reality with a precisely aimed word or gesture. These female figures, with their

exuberant air of passion and freedom, com-
municate a sense of mastery and spiritual power.[2]

Elaborating even more, author Vicki Noble wrote in her book,
Shakti Woman (New York: HarperCollins, 1991), "The dakini is an
icon of liberated energy, spiritual freedom, and the untamed
spiritual nature. She is the feminine in a much larger sense than
any archetypes carried by Western culture for at least the last two
thousand years . . . she awakens in us through the avenue of
spontaneous sacred play. Her teachings may not be easy for us,
since we are conditioned to need and expect rigid definitions of
reality, but the process, once begun, leads to freedom from those
very rigidities that make us so uncomfortable."[3]

I related to these descriptions and escaped into the sacred
play of the dakini by grabbing my sketch pad and drawing them
in the sky with their scarves and clacking bones. Then, I used
colored pencils to make one red, one blue, and one yellow-gold,
and taped them to my wall, where I could see them dancing above
me.

Chakra: The Wheel Deal

Chakra is a Sanskrit word meaning "wheel" or "vortex" and
refers to energy centers of the body that receive and process life
force. We have a vertical column of seven energy centers which
align from the base of our pelvic floor to the top of our head, that
include our sex, belly, solar plexus, heart, throat, third eye (center
of the forehead), the top of the head, and beyond. This is
sometimes referred to as *Kundalini*, a Sanskrit term from ancient
India, that describes the subtle flow of energy that circulates from
the base of the spine (and sometimes the feet) to the top of the

---

[2] Miranda Shaw, *Passionate Enlightenment* (Princeton, NJ: Princeton University
Press, 1994), 3.

[3] Vicki Noble, *Shakti Woman* (New York: HarperCollins, 1991), 200.

head. Anand simply calls it the "streaming process." I believe one of the potent qualities essential to each of us is the use of this vital energy, which extends far beyond the feet and head. It is critical for staying grounded and centered in this fast-paced, shifting world, where the single most effective ingredient in empowering the self is the value of staying vertically connected to Spirit, Source, God, Life Force, and it's absolutely free." (Now, that's a quote.) It's exactly what I taught my women's college golf team, that lead to many victories.

By learning to breathe into each chakra, I activated the energy in specific organs in my body, creating more vitality. I learned several ways to consciously breathe through different exercises in the workshop, sometimes alone, sometimes with a partner. By breathing up and down this central column on a regular basis, I created a pathway in my body that flowed more easily and more efficiently, providing great benefits, mainly more oxygen, and more oxygen creates better circulation. This added surplus of oxygen rejuvenated the cells in my body, keeping my organs moist and moving, and it replenished my brain cells. This column of energy connects directly with the endocrine system, which regulates bodily functions. The breath work also helped me through the emotional trauma, including depression, anger, and even suicidal thoughts.

After several years of this daily practice, I had greater stamina, more clarity, and more vitality and moved through stressful situations simply by focusing on my breath. It continues to keep me in the reverie of the present moment and in an expanded state of awareness.

The Chakra Wave: From Shadow to Ali

The workshop week continued like a marathon, moving from a schedule that was well organized and set up to progress the tantra students in a purposeful order, with plenty of time for rest and integration. We started at 7 a.m. and ended at 11 p.m., with a couple of showers and meals in between. On the fifth day, we were guided through a couple of tantra exercises, one performed individually, and then one with a partner the next day. These exercises changed the direction of my healing process, specifically my brain, for good.

The evening session in the convention center started with a warm-up dance and fun, sexy salsa music, which got my heart pumping and boosted my stamina. I love to dance, so it really opened my heart chakra and I felt free to dance with many of the participants. It also prepared me for the next exercise. When the music stopped, I had just enough time to drink some water and take a seat on my *zafu* (buckwheat pillow) on the floor. We were going on a journey tonight, by ourselves with eyes closed, to an unknown destination.

Our facilitator began by having us do some breathing cycles, then put on some soothing peaceful music, and took us on a guided meditation. I drifted with the music and her words, and then imagery began to appear. A golf ball floated before my eyes suspended in the cool air. I could see the dimples and even the brand name. In a curious stupor, I sat Indian style, my hands resting in my lap, my eyes transfixed. This was an odd encounter, after all these years, to have a golf ball show its white face. The audacity! How do you describe fear, peace, and exhilaration in unwavering concentration? Mesmerized by its appearance, my entire body was flooded with emotions.

The sound of the instructor's voice interrupted my concentration. It was soft and distant but firm: "It is time to forgive."

"It is time to forgive, hmmm," I contemplated quietly. "I forgive you with all my heart. I forgive you." The oddity of forgiving a ball for hitting me was outrageous, but authentic. Instantly, the ball whizzed out of sight, like the speeding snitch in

Harry Potter and the Sorcerer's Stone. I blinked a couple times and looked around the room. Had anyone else seen this golf ball zip out of the convention center? Apparently, not.

As I closed my eyes and listened to the music, something wondrous happened. I felt Golden light spouting out the top of my head, like a whale spouting water, yet it was in slow motion and transparent. The golden light fell in all directions like fireworks in the night sky. I breathed deeper, and the pulse of my heart beat stronger. How incredible to have opened this blockage at the point where the ball had struck me with such intense velocity nearly six years ago. The power and depth of the blow left me with a traumatic brain injury. The destruction of the impact was once described as reverse kundalini by an alternative medicine healer. Now, the pathways were flowing again in an upward spiraling motion.

I reveled in this new sensation as all the workshop attendees lay on their backs on the floor, with hands to their sides, palms facing up. I recognized this yoga position, called a "corpse pose." How interesting, I thought, and I contemplated the forgiving session and how letting go of one thing may bring in something new: birth, death, and rebirth.

With only two days left in the workshop, I found my mind drifting with great anticipation. A sense of great relief and excitement came over me, and I slept well that night, in the comfort of my dorm-room bed. The next morning, we were to go back into more chakra work. This exercise was to be even more in-depth and physically draining than I would know. Again, we started with some energizing music, but this time, everyone had to choose a partner by the time the music ended. I was immediately drawn to Madison, an experienced spiritual healer who was participating in the workshop, not assisting. He was a slightly older hippie guy with a tanned body and a silver-haired ponytail.

We were like two magnets coming together from across the room. We danced closely as we both confirmed our choice. Next, we set up our sacred space with pillows, a sarong set like a picnic blanket, some sacred objects, and plenty of water and Kleenex. With complete trust and commitment to the process, we entered our experience with a heart connection wherever it took us. We sat facing each other on the sarong in silence and gazed into each other's eyes until Madison said with complete assurance, "This is your time." The words struck a chord in me. It was all I needed to engage freely with him. It was like I was given permission to just let it all out. Whatever came up and however it came up was absolutely OK. The space was safe and well contained for anything.

Madison moved his pillow behind me and sat close against me, his legs wrapped around me like a shell and his hands holding me around my waist. There was music playing in the background, but it had definite melodies which invoked different moods, as we moved through each chakra slowly, every 4 to 5 minutes. Madison's hands rested on different parts of my body as we tuned into each chakra. Margot Anand guided all of us along the way.

Chakra one is the pelvic floor. I froze, still settling into the reality of a man holding my sex with one cupped hand while placing his other hand flat against my heart. Listening to the music and desiring for his position to change soon, I did not quite drop into the feeling place of this energy center. Then it was onto chakra two, the belly. Madison moved his hand from my sex to my belly, keeping his other hand on my heart, and I moaned. Then, I yelled, like a lion's roar in the forest. I moaned again against a backdrop of wild rhythmic music, and I cried aloud deeply from my belly — so much pain, so many surgeries. It felt good to just yell without any attention to why or any analytical thoughts behind it. Me, Jane of the jungle!

When the music shifted, we moved to chakra three, the solar plexus. I laughed, firmly supported by Madison's arms and hands. I laughed for a few more minutes without a care of what I was laughing about. As the music shifted again, we moved to chakra four, the heart. I felt full of love and goodness, getting lost in the sweet sounds of the lilting melody. "Life is beautiful, and I am life." I swayed with unbridled passion until the music changed again for the fifth chakra, the throat. Suddenly, my mouth clenched shut. I could not speak. I felt like the Tin Man in *The Wizard of Oz*, waiting for Dorothy to oil my jaw. I wiggled my chin back and forth until a low hum resounded.

An old Indian shaman appeared in my mind, and I began chanting, "Hey na-na, ho na-na, hey na-na, ho." The song was barely audible before it started to build. Drums pounded out the beat in sync with my growing chant. In a loud and deliberate ritualistic voice, the old shaman stood directly before me, his face wrinkled with wisdom and his eyes shimmering in the firelight. Confidence consumed me and our voices rose in a crescendo with an intense "Hey na-na, ho!" The shaman disappeared and only the crackling of the fire could be heard. I began a singsong chant that drifted among the stars. I had no idea what I was singing, but I was exuberant to use and hear my own voice.

I heard the music shift and Margot said, "OK, we're moving to the next chakra centered in the third eye, the point between your eyes." I felt Madison's finger softly touch my forehead, the sixth chakra, and I began to feel lightheaded. I started moaning with pain, and I felt the saliva increase in my mouth. I became nauseated. I recognized it was the point where the golf ball struck me in the head. I was reliving the symptoms. My head was spinning, and I lost track of time.

"We're moving to the seventh chakra, the crown chakra." The music was celestial, from the golden gates of heaven above, but tears dripped from my cheeks, and I was doubled over and disoriented. Madison supported me with his left arm around my waist. I barely felt his right palm on the back of my head when I felt the point of impact. *Crunch.* It felt like a bowling ball had been dropped on my head, not a speeding golf ball. The asphalt and green grass were spinning, forcing me to dry heave. Tears and snot dribbled down my face.

Margot's firm voice grabbed my attention. "Stay with your chi."

I sat up and felt the pressure of Madison's arms and hands supporting my body posture from behind. A surge of intense energy unfurled from my ass up through my belly, my heart, my throat, and out through the top of my head with great velocity. My body vibrated with the thrust, and I screamed, "Yes!" as if to say, "Out forever!"

The emotional outburst was intense but never out of control. Collapsing against Madison, I knew I was free from the burden of that traumatic experience. The golf ball had come down through my skull with such speed and force, like lightning. The electrifying painful energy shot down through my spine. The chakra wave process reversed the vibrational sensation, and I felt a slow current of positive energy—flowing, alive, and rising—circling from my toes to my head. I was relieved and content. We listened to the music until it faded to silence. I was at peace and exhausted as we lay together in a spooning fashion.

I had never taken such a journey into the depths of my being like this. The invisible dark cloud that hung over my head like an umbrella no longer shadowed my identity. I was reawakened by this experience. I felt a deep appreciation for Margot, the master teacher who skillfully orchestrated such a delicate process, and my partner Madison, who remained calm and present throughout my whole ordeal. I did not know what would surface during the tantra session, but I was grateful for being supported with the raw and real energy that surfaced and for the gifts that unfolded.

The Role of Forgiveness

Forgiveness was the only way to free the resentment the golf ball caused within my body and psyche. Until this point, I was bound by this emotional trauma link that was stronger than the imaginary steel stake that penetrated my skull and jutted out my left eye socket. The chakra wave release exercise helped dissolve that link. I felt free and regained a sense of peace and harmony again. To forgive means to "give up" what you should not have held onto in the first place.

The negative impact of the golf ball had been replaced with a forgiving state of mind, a magnetic power for now attracting good in my life. My daily affirmation became "All that has offended me, whatever has made me bitter, resentful, unhappy, I forgive within and without. I lose you and let you go. It is finished forever."

Eventually, I was able to forgive everyone involved in the lengthy litigation, including myself. Anyone who has ever been involved in a legal case, whether you win or lose, knows the stress and frustrations of the process. A nightly affirmation became "I now let go everything and everybody of the past or present that who has caused discomfort in me, through me, and around me. We all go free to our greater wholeness, our greatest good."

I referenced Catherine Ponder's book, *The Dynamic Laws of Healing* (West Nyack, NY: Parker Publishing Company, 1966), over and over, to find even more understanding of all the people concerned in this drama saga. Another nightly affirmation I used was "Divine love brings into my life the right people who can help me and make me happy, and whom I can help and make happy. Those people who are not for my highest good now fade out of my life and find their good elsewhere. I walk in the charmed circle of God's love. I am Divinely irresistible to my greatest good now."

CHAPTER 18

RECLAIMING MY IDENTITY

My tantric path continued like a series of moving plates of the Earth, each level feeding the next, just like my body. The journey was experiential, and I became completely immersed in the process. The pain had taught me wisdom, through patience and taking pause to listen. I learned to trust the process, opening my heart to the freedom of what is with "I am who I am, and I am OK with it!" bridging the seemingly unbridgeable. It could not be understood in the mental realm or even explained. I had to experience it over and over in that present moment, like I had done in my goddess circling days.

The tantra philosophy teaches the yin and yang principles, just like I had learned in my macrobiotic teachings with Herman Aihaira in the early 1990s. Most notable was the balance between yin and yang, in relation to the percentages of acid and alkaline in the body, which was in constant flux. Choosing foods to keep the proper balance was the key in that game.

Yin and Yang

With regards to tantra, we all have feminine (yin) and masculine (yang) qualities within us, just varying degrees individually. In its simplest form, yin is a more receptive, open, and flowing expression of yourself. In contrast, yang is a more active, initiating, and strategic expression of yourself. When the two are in harmony, there is a joyous union and positive motion forward, an aliveness in a safe container. It is a marriage between life and spirit, consciousness and energy, or, as in the tantra tradition, Shiva and Shakti. When disjointed, life becomes a struggle, no longer in the ecstatic flow.

Through different tantra exercises, I learned how I could play with this "teeter totter" to expand beyond the thinking mind and into an observer role. Watching how I would move through situations, becoming aware of what role I was playing, and adjusting my role and response, if needed became the game for me. For instance, early in my rehabilitation, I worked with my occupational therapist on creating a meal schedule, writing out a grocery list, and going to the grocery store. We mapped out the route beforehand, of course. When we reached the store, there was a sign on the door that read, "Closed for inventory purposes. We will reopen tomorrow."

With dramatic fervor, I screamed and banged on the door with both fists, shouting, "No, no!" I started to cry. I turned and, cupping my head in my hands, slid down the door until my butt hit the pavement. My therapist kept telling me it was OK, but I launched into every direction. "You won't be here tomorrow to bring me back. I won't have any groceries for the week. I won't be able to eat," and on and on it went in my "PBA moment." It was truly the end of the world for me, although today it seems like comic relief. To deal with these types of moments, I learned to take a breath and then pause and engage the yang side of me. Yang took control of the situation and calmly created a new strategy. If I got emotional, it compounded the situation. So, best to take a step back, regroup, and try again.

There were times where I just had to be where I was. Before my head injury, I was an initiator, a leader, and very active, all qualities of the yang principle. After the direct hit, I had no choice but to surrender to my disability, be dependent on others around me, and be in more of a receiving mode, all qualities of the yin principle. I had to be in this phase of my life for over a year, realizing that rest was an intricate part of the process. It's hard to stay still and just "be" for that long.

Sketching became my expressive outlet for this temporary loss of yang aspects. Creativity, another expression of my feminine side, replaced it beautifully. It is interesting to remember how difficult it was to rebuild the yang part of my brain, with the constant reinforcement of cognitive and visual exercises. Through the months and years of practice, the persistent, deliberate recircuiting paid off as I regained an even more strategic analytical brain pathway, which then complemented my yin side.

Releasing Control and Surrendering

I was able to test this balancing act of yin and yang within me with various exercises during that week of my first tantra workshop with Margot Anand. One of the exercises provided a dual outcome, and it really pressed my buttons. It not only helped to balance my strong nature, but it also caused me to have to trust men again, or at least the man in front of me.

I chose a tall and muscular man for my partner, who outwardly exuded confidence and strength. His name was Jake, and he was wearing loose outdoor pants and two shirts: one long-sleeved against his skin, and one short-sleeved shirt over that. I needed someone to represent a strong authority to recreate that seeming submission I had fallen prey to, over and over again in my life. Jake, with a chiseled jawline and short, trimmed silver hair, towering over me with all his penile masculine authority—my projection, of course—fit that profile. It was that power over feeling and the sense of being trapped, the authority of the whole, a lifelong contribution of betrayal of men.

In the large convention center group room, we started first by standing across from each other, looking at each other intently, as did several other couples in the large circle. The usual sacred space ritual had already been performed, so knowing we were all committed to each other and the power of the present moment, it felt safe to continue the exercise. As the music played, we began a warm-up exercise by breathing up and down our own central spinal column, adding movement and sound while standing in place. We started to exchange breath from a standing position at first, and then we were instructed to sit across from each other and continue our breath exchange.

We sat on our firm zafus, which helped with a sitting posture. For a while, it was awkward trying to figure out how to coordinate our breathing. Emotional jabber in my brain all had to play out, and the voices of my past spoke loudly. "Why should I breathe with you?" "I hate you!" "You've betrayed me over and over." "You think you're so big and strong and can muscle me into anything you want, you fuck head!" There were some tears and even growls while I occasionally shifted my eyes away from my partner and then back again. It was really a stretch for me to sit and breathe with this "asshole," but I was committed to the process, as was he. I was able to transition the memories of these feelings from third person to this moment. Plus, I knew he was going through his own emotional drama in his mind that he was projecting on me, too. We were working together safely, in unconditional love, to move through whatever came up, with the use of breath movement and sound, with a highly skilled facilitator and her assistants. After a long time, the figuring out ceased, and we dropped from our minds to our hearts, the flow of air from one to the other progressing naturally.

The music shifted, and it was now a more playful part of the exercise. Many options were given at this point, and I chose to practice trusting my man in this part of the exercise. My partner sat, crossed his legs, and placed a pillow in his lap. I sat on his lap, facing him, my yoga pants stretching as I wrapped my legs around his waist and placed my hands on his firm, bulky shoulders. Oh, this felt so threatening and uncomfortable for me that my breathing picked up and we lost the rhythmic flow of our breath exchange. This is supposed to be playful, I thought, and I frantically raised my hand for assistance from a team member. A female assistant quickly came over, and I nervously discussed our dilemma.

Still in embrace, I articulated my goal for this exercise that I had shared with my partner Jake in the beginning of the session. I wanted to experience what trust felt like with men again, to connect with this man, to surrender to his strength, and to be supported by him. I thought this would be a great start.

The assistant had a loving demeanor and reminded me this was a playful exploration exercise. She suggested a couple of ways to lighten up and have some fun with Jake in our discovery process. With that, Jake and I did a playful hand dance, while I was still sitting in his lap. No longer focusing on our breath, we began a push–pull kind of movement where he held me securely with one hand around my waist and one hand on the middle of my back. He invited me to move with the music. I began to sway slightly back and forth, a bit intimidated at first, not wanting to relinquish control. But Jake smiled and said confidently, "I got you."

I tried again to just drop back and let him support and hold me, but the fear rose up. Again, I tried with tears in my eyes, "You don't have me. You'll let me drop straight back to the floor," I said, remembering the fuckheads who had let me down.

The memories came in flashes, each time I blessed the men and let them go. Each time, I gathered my inner strength until a slow smile began to form my lips. Jake picked up the cue, and he smiled back. "I will be your container. I got you. Now, dance with the music." His eyes met mine in a deepening gaze, and I knew he was there for me. I opened to his compassionate plea and laughed aloud, throwing my head back in joyous anticipation.

I began to move back and forth this time, undulating my body, and then rolling side to side with passion and fervor. Many times, as I danced in his arms, I felt my hair brush the floor, feeling completely supported and protected by him. Just as I felt the rush of energy of this exhilarating moment, I would feel the firmness of his hands on my body protecting me from any danger. Jake would swoop with me in any direction I chose, enjoying the dance himself. We became one couple, one union of ecstasy, now breathing passionately together. It was so easy and freeing, and we both delighted in the play until the music stopped. Our dancing session was over, yet we were instructed to lie together in a spooning fashion, Jake behind me, embracing my body with a gentle firmness.

I did it, I thought, in the comfort of Jake's arms. Oh, how good it felt to be held by a man who wants nothing more than to hold me. There are men of integrity, I secretly regaled, as we lay securely together in perfect unison for a few moments.

We took time to share all the different phases we had gone through individually and together during the three-hour exercise. It was amazing to hear my partner's story, his hang-ups, and his fears as he moved through the process. Jake confessed he had self-esteem issues because he was not as well-endowed as other males. He first became aware of this difference when he had to suit up for sports in the boys' locker room in school, noticing that some of his classmates were, as he stated, better equipped. Later, when he became sexually active, he was more aware of his physical difference. He needed to realize that his self-worth should not be based on his physical attributes and, in many ways, "small can be mighty." As the saying goes, "Size doesn't matter."

It takes great skill and presence to stay seated, yet each being vertically aligned to their own process, and still be working together to produce whatever is supposed to happen during the session. An awakening, an opening, an expanding into, a transformation can happen in any moment if we allow and trust the process. For me, I reached a place of trust with Jake, and that was the beginning of being able to access that sense of trust when faced with difficult situations or emotions. This is a practice I utilized every day.

The Rebirthing Story (2007)

Nestled in the mountains of Northern California, just off the Tahoe–Ukiah highway, rests the historical resort of Saratoga Springs that was established in 1871. It features centuries-old buildings and cabins, a large swimming pool, and featured cold mineral springs. The 260-acre facility, which once accommodated up to 250 people, included a stagecoach stop, a post office, a restaurant, and a dance hall. An on-site bottling plant made it possible to drink the healing waters, as well as bathe in them.

Long before it became Saratoga Springs, the Pomo Indians used this hidden valley for peacemaking and healing. Today, the valley still resonates with this energy, which enhances the experiences of all who come to Saratoga Springs. It is a safe and supportive place to follow your own path and nurture your body, mind, and soul. It is a place where you can simply be present. This sacred site has been used for centuries by Native Americans to connect with nature and their inner being. Most everyone who visits Saratoga Springs leaves with a renewed spirit and improved health just from walking the grounds.

Saratoga Springs has six batten and board cottages that are more than a century old and are important examples of the more modest accommodations these smaller resorts offered. Other structures supporting the importance of Saratoga Springs were the spartan hunter's cabins and the largest building of the grounds, sometimes referred to as the "Dance Hall." Very rare on any resort is the presence of such a two-story frame building with verandas, which were once common, but this is one of the very last to survive.

What a beautiful place to host another weeklong tantra workshop, I thought as I unpacked my belongings from the van. The drive was only eight hours from Santa Barbara, my longest yet, with plenty of built-in rest stops. I arrived with great anticipation of more healing and personal development. This tantra stuff was intriguing and, more important, it was working.

I stayed in an open-air cabin, which had no electricity, but was equipped with a full-size bed, a small desk for writing, and an armoire capable of hanging a week's worth of clothes. My cabin had screened windows and doors, beckoning the warm breezes during the day and cool dampness at night. With flashlight in hand, I made a quick 50-yard scurry to and from my cabin to the outdoor wooden-structure bathrooms and showers.

It was rustic and small, but I loved the privacy. I needed a safe zone from all the auditory and visual stimuli with the other workshop participants. As the days passed, I was able to quietly walk over to my cabin and take a nap to rejuvenate my flooded brain or skip an evening event to go to bed early. The week was filled with many exercises and small-group activities and proved to be very challenging because of all the stimulation.

On the last day of the awakening tantric journey, I sat with a couple of friends in the dining hall who were also on the tantric path. One woman, Asha, was a tall, well-toned African American with striking facial features, long brown hair, and cocoa eyes. She wore silky pants and a shimmering halter top accented with beaded jewelry and earrings. The other woman was just as toned and wore long dreads and colorful threads in her hair. She had the most crystalline blue eyes I had ever seen. Her name was Mia, and she wore a flowing blouse and skirt made of cotton from India.

As we ate a delicious vegetarian meal, we conversed about the week's adventure and how much had unfolded in the most unexpected ways through Margot's teachings. I was constantly coming to my edge, working through resistance, insecurities, and physical symptoms such as vertigo, with breath movement and sound exercises. I would pivot and choose the new path of Divine inner guidance and stay with that flow. It was always at a modified pace to accommodate my cognitive and visual issues.

I stood up to clear my dishes when I was abruptly met by our teacher, Margot Anand. I turned to greet her when she said she wanted to talk with me. Feet frozen in place, I obliged quickly and gave her my full attention. With a concerned look, Margot said, "The team and I have been watching you this week, and we think you are playing this disability card up too much."

Drawing in closer, I asked, "What do you mean?" I could feel the heat rising from my gut to my face. She said, "We've noticed you've been slipping out of class early to go to your cabin, or you're not showing up at all, which is putting a strain on the rest of the participants, especially those you are working with in a smaller group."

"I've been getting symptomatic from my head injury," I squealed in anger, "I have a disability!" In a matter-of-fact tone, she replied, "We're giving you an assignment for tomorrow afternoon's closing ceremony. We invite you to create a rebirthing ritual around this disability thing, at least 10 to 15 minutes long." With that, she turned and joined the rest of the "wisdom" team at their dining table in the corner of the lodge. Mission complete.

I was furious and turned to Asha and Mia in disbelief. They looked just as confused as I was but dared not interfere. There was something big happening here, so I took my anger and walked through the long meadow to the large heated swimming pool. Oh, how I detested Margot's words. I simply would not do it, and I would say no. I started resenting Margot with every step. Doesn't she know how hard I was trying?

I stripped down and jumped into the deep end, submerging my whole body, including my courtroom-filled mind, into the nurturing warm waters. My head was filled with thoughts of being judged, of standing before the jury—a cosmic coup! Oh, my God, that was stupid. My dizziness was amplified in the buoyancy of the moving waters that I had created! With legs and arms searching for the bottom, I floundered to the side of the pool and hung onto the side and rested my head on my folded arms until the waviness passed. Water dripped from my hair and chin as I looked at my wet arms clinging to the side of the pool. My body and legs dangled motionless in the water as I began to breathe from my belly, focusing on each inhale and exhale. In a few moments, I felt tranquility, and Margot's passionate words echoed in my mind, "Go with the current of ecstatic potential."

I looked up at the night sky to see the stars just beginning to twinkle at me as I shimmied over to the pool ladder and climbed out of the water. I grabbed my clothes and headed to my cabin. Calmer and a bit lightheaded, I dried off quickly because I was already starting to feel the chill of the night air. Not believing the task I was assigned, I lay in my bed with mixed emotions. I pulled the sheet and wool blanket close around my body, and pondered the question, "How am I going to do this? A rebirthing ritual?" I need help here!

In silence, I meditated as time and space disappeared. I awoke abruptly an hour later with a cosmic cornucopia of information. I fumbled in the cabin for a pen and paper and crawled to the desk chair to scribble the streaming consciousness of expression. When words stopped flowing, I read the whole message with sleepy eyes. It was the ritual I was to do the next day! I read it a couple times through, envisioning how it would look, and then turned the flashlight off and slipped back into bed.

One part of the ritual involved many of the other women in the workshop. Earlier that day, there was an animal speak exercise we were to do with Mia. I remember being a bit disoriented in this wild exercise, but Mia persuaded me to continue the process anyway. She was so compassionate and embodied her Divine Feminine side by being patient, seductive, and grounded, despite my anxiety and vocal gibberish. We all learned how to become different animals to express different emotions to correspond with where we were in the moment. I became a stir-crazy tiger and danced the dance with jungle music. I am glad I remained in the class because this wild animal exercise would be part of the live ritual presentation that I would perform the next day. I fell back asleep, happy to know there was a script written out, although I didn't know how I was going to pull it off.

The morning came quickly with the usual dynamic meditation at 7 a.m., followed by breakfast and the morning feedback session in the main lodge with the rest of the group, when I realized I had nothing to wear for the ritual. In a midmorning exercise, I discussed my dilemma with Asha, and she invited me to her cabin for a "dress for success" salon. Asha lived in L.A. and worked in the fashion industry, and she was excited to help me. During the lunch hour, I ran over to Asha's cabin so she could help me put together the perfect clothing combinations for my performance. I felt such an affinity with her and was happy to have her on my team. Time was marching on as I quickly walked back to my cabin with Asha's clothes. Sweating and out of breath, I realized it I was almost "show time."

I ran to the shower house in my sarong and tossed it on the grass just before I hit the shower to rinse off. Then, I pulled the clothes onto my half-dried body. I wrapped the long colorful scarf around my wet hair, like Asha had shown me, and tucked the ends in the front carefully while smoothing out the folds into a beautiful full headdress. I slipped on the wraparound silk drawstring pants and tightened them with a secure bow in front. Slowly, I slipped on the loosely fitting halter top and then pulled the long, beaded necklace over the headdress and let it dangle down to my breasts.

"There!" I sighed aloud. I looked just like Erykah Badu, the American singer-songwriter. "Badu" is of African American origin, and in English her name means "one who is strong, powerful." "Oh, Goddess," I mumbled in a frantic dance, searching for the scribbled notes from the nighttime cosmic cornucopia. I grabbed them off the disarrayed bed, shoved them in my book bag, grabbed my water bottle, and started walking quickly to the dance hall where the closing ceremony would take place. I noticed the large hall was already packed with participants, as I rushed passed the doors and to the back bathroom.

Several women were in there getting ready for their own performances. It was a variety show of sorts, apparently to showcase what we had learned and in appreciation for the performing arts therapy of it all. I began getting nauseated and disoriented with the flurry of activity and jumped into a stall just as someone was coming out. I vomited a couple of times, cleared my throat all the way to the back, and hocked a loogie smack dab into the middle of the toilet bowl, creating a ripple of water. "Arrgggh," I said, shrugging as I flushed at the same time, hoping no one heard me. But by the time I was finished, I had cleared out the whole place with the stench of my vomit and vibrating guttural throat sounds.

All was quiet until a man announced over a loudspeaker, "Our show begins in two minutes." He listed the order of appearance, and, quite shockingly, I was the first at bat! Unbelievable. I washed my face and hands nervously a few times and rinsed out my mouth with copious amounts of water. I pat dried with a paper towel until it tore into pieces. I held my belly and started to consciously breathe in and out and then walked out of the bathroom and over to the mock music studio area. I tugged on the shirt of the guy who was tending to the music to get his attention quickly. I shared two songs for him to play during my performance and told him where to cue up each one. Then, I sat on the floor with the circle of more than 40 participants.

Margot opened the ceremony by creating a safe and sacred space and honoring the elements, and then sat down, handing over the night to our minstrel emcee. I was immediately introduced and walked up to the front of the room and sat down on a chair facing the audience. I situated my sarong over my upper body with a quick toss over one shoulder.

My hands trembled as I held the microphone in one hand and the crumpled script in the other. In a mischievous tone, I said, "I invite you to close your eyes and keep them closed." I took a deep breath and blew out softly into the mic. More grounded, I continued: "Now, focus on your breathing, in and out, in and out, and take this journey with me. My name is Kathleen, tantrika extraordinaire. I sustained a traumatic brain injury nine years ago, and I have some cognitive issues, such as delayed processing, forgetfulness, dizziness from overstimulation, and ringing in the ears . . . wait, wait. I'm getting a direct channel from the cosmos." I beamed with curiosity as I held my hands and head up toward the ceiling.

"Oh, it's Margot Anand, and she has a message for me." I changed into Margot's voice, mimicking her French accent, and whispered softly into the mic with melodic splendor, "Those are the same symptoms you had going through menopause, Kathleen. Get on with it. You act like you're in the dark. It's not a part of your identity now."

I cleared my throat and continued in my own voice. "Oh, OK then, I won't do that anymore. I'll get on with it," I said, rather unconvincingly. "So, anyway, here I am, now in the fullness of who I am, and . . . wait, wait, I'm getting another transmission from Margot."

I changed back into Margot's voice and whispered in a singsong fashion, "You need to surrender to your Divine Feminine side, too!"

"Oh, so I'll let go of the disability crutch and step into my femininity more. Got it! Wait . . . what?" I stammered before changing into Margot's voice for her to add another request. "We want you to do a special ritual of rebirth around this." I emphasized the word *rebirth*.

"Hmm," I thought aloud. "This is becoming engaging. Well, if you want me to do this ritual, I will need to know what to say, some clothes, and some music . . . ." I barely finished my sentence when Margot's voice floated in like Glinda, the Good Witch of the North, with her billowing pink gown waving her star wand, in *The Wizard of Oz*. She said, "Embrace your ecstatic potential and seize the moment."

The music was supposed to start here, so I said, "Seize the moment," again, looked over at the guy, and nodded to cue the music. He was so mesmerized by my story that he had forgotten the uptake.

In seconds, India Arie's song, "You're Beautiful," began to play, filling the dance hall with a heavenly voice and melody.

"I invite you to now open your eyes." I stood and felt more confident. "My name is Kathleen Badu."

I put the mic down with a thud, with the script close behind. I closed my own eyes and felt my feet solidly on the ground. I swayed with the music for a couple of moments and then opened my eyes. I took the sarong off my shoulders, grabbing both corners with my hands, and moved the cloth in the air with a tilting action to the beat of the music as I sway from side to side. I flung the cloth in a spinning motion, and it flopped to the floor. My hands to the open air, I started dancing around the inner circle of the audience. As I came around a second time, the words of the song filled the room: "You're beautiful, you're beautiful." Then, I stopped dancing and stood tall.

I pulled the string of the silken pants to release the tension, and they dropped to the floor in one fell swoop, exposing my bare bottom and legs. I twirled, skipped, and stopped suddenly to lift my halter top over my headdress. With one hand, I flung it toward the audience on the right side, and it flopped right into Margot's lap. She laughed, and I continued dancing freely, naked, and barefoot. I stopped on the other side of the room where I began to display labor pains. I squatted while standing at the same time, breathed, and rocked my pelvis forward and back, with a wincing smile. I danced to the middle of the circle, continued my breathing, and yelled out in relief. I slowly unwound the sarong from my hair and laid it down on the floor, and then I curled up in a fetal position on it. I rested with my belly rhythmically rising and falling, my eyes closed, and with my arms around my knees.

The music guy picked up his cue, and started the next song, "Tumare Darshan," by Dema Premal, a Middle Eastern melody that celebrates the gift of being in the presence of the enlightened one. I smiled when I heard the melodic tempo of the accordion, with accentuating chords. The women from the wild animal session with Mia now picked up the beat. They are scattered along the perimeter of the circle and, one by one, wearing only sarongs, they entered the circle as their totem animals. They slithered like snakes, hopped like rabbits, crawled like lynx, pounced like tigers, lumbered like apes, and flapped arms like a raptor. They drew closer and closer to me with every downbeat until they surrounded me with their animal prowess. I stretched, lengthening my arms and legs, and yawned and grinned. They helped me stand in a melodic sway while they morphed back into women, uniting and dropping their sarongs to the floor.

The tempo of the music picked up and the women started to dance. We moved like busy bees in a small circle, spreading our sacred nectar to each other. I started the standing pelvic rocking and deep breathing with rolling anticipation. The Middle Eastern sounds coaxed the women to line up behind me, and they began the pelvic rocking and deep breathing, too.

The tempo accelerated with every pulsing beat, we were breathing more deeply and making sounds as we exhaled. Faster and faster our naked bodies undulated as we moved in one erotic rolling wave. We rose into bliss and a final crescendo of orgasmic laughter. We fell to the floor, like the line of Radio City Rockettes on Broadway, without the glamorous, eye-popping costumes, with continued laughter. Eyes met eyes, arms met arms, and we stood for hugs and to help each other find our own sarongs. We turned outward to the joyfully mesmerized audience and a standing ovation of cheers and whistles and then bowed graciously and shuffled off the floor with soft squeals of delight and pleasure.

I could hear the next act follow from where I was sitting in the bathroom. I think my montage was a bit longer than expected, but it was worth it. I wiped my body off with a towel, put on some yoga clothes that I had in my book bag, and headed back out to the circle to sit and watch the rest of the ceremony.

After the ritual, I felt a sense of freedom and wholeness. I did it! I had dropped not only my pants but also the ego, the judgments, and the armor and had kept breathing throughout the process. I moved beyond my own limitations and fears and the label of being disabled. I overcame the illusion of being crippled by this accident and I shattered the barrier of such emotional conditioning. It was a great practice in my opening to my inner guidance by meditating and connecting to the Divine within.

I went with the flow and kept the current of ecstatic potential moving forward. I felt the whole performance that night was truly just for me, with the cast of characters, the audience, the pivotal moments, and the act of consciously breathing. I reveled in the new me, raw and tender, with wonder and delight. I blossomed that afternoon as an ecstatic being, beautiful and free, witnessed by many.

At the end of the evening, I thanked Margot for her loving invitation that kept me on the tantric path. I told her that she was a constant demonstration of unconditional love and guidance, and I realized how essential it was for her to collaborate with the wisdom of the team. With this rebirthing performance, I had conquered the disability syndrome, an amazing feat for someone with cognitive and visual issues. From that day forward, I stepped into myself as an empowered woman with new hope. It was an extraordinary performance, an unforgettable night, and a new beginning.

CHAPTER 19

THE POWER OF FLOWERS

I stopped by Stargazer Hot Springs a few hours away, for a relaxing soak and integrate all that had happened at the tantra workshop in Saratoga Springs. It was such a big awakening. As nighttime came upon me, I felt the warm embrace of the sacred land and waters. I didn't want to leave, and I felt a strong urge to find out what one had to do in order to work and live here at Stargazer. Deep inside, I knew it was my time to be here; it just resonated within me.

The next morning, I spoke to a young woman who was the director of the human resources department, which was just a small office space in a cottage on site. We went over the ground rules, and then I filled out some paperwork, and she interviewed me on the spot. I had one more interview just before lunch with the maintenance manager, and we talked about an entry-level position as a cleaning woman in the auto shop. It wasn't what I had applied for, but it was the only job available at the time. I really wanted to work in the restaurant as a cook because I had some experience with food preparation. The human relations director said she would let me know in a couple of days if I was accepted to the Stargazer team.

There was nothing more to do, so I went down to the restaurant to have lunch. I ordered a salmon salad and an iced tea and gobbled it down with great anticipation. I was so excited about the prospect of working at Stargazer; I just needed to find living accommodations. With no housing available on the property, I looked for something affordable nearby. I grabbed a local newspaper and searched for rentals, circling a handful of them. There was nothing enticing in town, so I drove to the next town which had several rentals, all around a beautiful lake. I checked out a couple of stand-alone cottages, but nothing roused me. Plus, it took 45 minutes to drive to the lake, and I was not interested in a long commute.

I headed back to Stargazer discouraged, as it was already getting dark and all my efforts had led to nothing but a headache. I took a quick soak in the warm pool to relieve some stress and bought a sandwich and chips for dinner at the pool cafe, eating as I walked the long trail back to the campsite. I retired to bed early curled up on the floor in the back of my van, knowing I had to leave for Santa Barbara in the morning.

As I prepared for the long ride back, I stopped back at the restaurant for a cup of coffee and pastry. I noticed a bulletin board on the back wall, with a few flyers for different events pinned to the cork and a small postcard memo: "A-frame cottage in Deer Springs for rent." I couldn't believe my eyes. I called the number immediately and was able to meet the owner in half an hour. Magic happened just minutes before I had to leave this enchanting place.

The small community was just minutes from Stargazer and I could feel the excitement building within me. As I turned up the drive to the log A-frame, I felt goose bumps as I got out of my car and walked up the front steps. It was perfect, with a small screened balcony, a backyard, and a garage. The rent was steep for one person at $800 a month, plus utilities, but I could afford it with the extra settlement funds I had in savings.

There was a living room with a futon-like couch, a rocking chair, and a wood stove for romantic nights. There was a full kitchen, with a white, round wooden table and matching four chairs and a new black refrigerator, stove, and dishwasher, which I would never use. And the best part of all was the bathroom with a full-size bathtub and shower—so much bigger than in my trailer. There was an antique pedestal sink in a beautiful hue of mint green that matched the toilet and bathtub. I could already picture myself luxuriating and slathering in this tub like my sensuous friend, Dae, and I used to do together in her outdoor bathtub. The upstairs was an open loft, one side with a full-size bed and dresser, and the other side just had a small desk table and chair. Perfect office and music room, I thought. I put down a deposit, paid the first month's rent, and signed a yearlong lease that automatically flipped to a month-to-month contract. Done deal.

It was late fall as I walked the beach in Santa Barbara for the last time, ending the five-year head injury rehabilitation program. It was time for me to integrate into a smaller, more contained community and begin to work again for a paycheck. Plus, I had outgrown living in the trailer, where I felt like my head and hands and feet were sticking out the sides and roof.

I filled my Honda Odyssey van with some clothes and personal belongings, my accordion, a 12-inch black-and-white TV, and my two orange cats and drove to my new A-frame log home in Northern California. Adrenaline carried me through the long drive as I left the ocean to live in the forest. Fortunately, settling into my new home was easy because my friend Christine surprised me and came up for the weekend to help me unpack and help settle the cats. Jack and Maple Leaf had become quite mischievous with all the empty boxes to play in and running up and down the stairs to the loft. Maple Leaf was even more daring as he would lie close to the edge with his legs dangling between the balcony rails. Jack could be found hiding or sleeping in any one of the empty brown boxes.

Christine purchased some orange sheets for my bed upstairs, and she carried up the accordion for the music room. She also helped put dishes and favorite glassware in the cupboards, as I began the marking process that Lori had taught me with some sticky notes and a black Sharpie pen. It only took a day to get things looking like home, so we spent Sunday relaxing at the pools together, drinking smoothies, and visiting.

Christine spent a restful night on the futon, before she left the next morning to get back to her music kids' work in Palm Springs. I was starting my own job on Monday and didn't know what to expect or how my stamina would hold up in a new environment. Looking forward to my first day at work, I hopped into my new bed in the upstairs loft, with my cats close behind.

My manager, Mitchell, was a hunk: tall and muscular with wavy brown hair, a light tan, and a big, toothy smile. He wore blue jeans and a gray-blue long-sleeve, button-down work shirt, like an auto mechanic would wear, with his name, Mitchell, embroidered in white. He promptly gave me a work shirt to wear over my own shirt and handed me some gray work pants to try on in the back office. I certainly didn't look like a goddess, but I considered the auto shop my temple with great devotion and appreciation.

Mitchell was about my age and had a deep, sultry voice. I often heard him singing Beatles tunes while I worked at my usual duties in the auto shop. Sometimes, I joined in with higher harmonies. It was fun, and he encouraged me to have fun while I worked there, which was a bit difficult for me. I was an over-achiever back in the day, and I was compelled to do a good job. I worked steadily and diligently, detailing everything I cleaned, including the toilets. I rarely took breaks from dusting, vacuuming, and straightening the two offices and the greasy areas in the three-car garage. Mitchell would often tell me to slow down, sit down outside for a while, and stop working so hard. In the beginning, I worked only 10 to 12 hours a week, but I was certainly exhausted by the time I returned to my A-frame abode. Maple Leaf and Jack always welcomed me enthusiastically when I opened the front door.

After two weeks, I received my first paycheck for $58.60. I was elated. I was back in the workforce, earning my own money. Plus, the benefits were wonderful. I was able to soak in the mineral pools as often as I wanted, and I received an employee discount at the health food store and restaurant right on the property. The walking trails were endless, and magic abounded day and night.

I especially loved the weekly dances at Stargazer—lots of freestyle dancing to rhythmic music to which everyone danced unabashedly and unconditionally. There were no steps to learn, just everyone doing there their own thing to a driving beat. Sometimes it was held outside on a large wooden deck back by the meadow building under the stars, while other nights it was inside at the larger convention center to the front of the property.

There were always new weekly guests to mingle with and facilitators who came to teach their alternative healing classes. Dynamic vibrant musicians came from around the world to give concerts down at the straw-bale temple near the vegetable and flower gardens. The kirtan and East Indian bands were my favorites, with unusual instruments such as harmoniums, tablas, and sitars that created heavenly classical music and supported the chants.

The temple was designed and constructed by a group of creative sustainable builders, with help from the local residents. I went to the actual straw-plastering party one day. Deep wheel barrels were filled with straw and an earth-bonding composite, like clay and sand. Water was added from white construction buckets and allowed to absorb naturally into the dry mixture before we started churning it with our bare hands. Bare-bodied, too, we'd then take handfuls of the mushy mixture and spread it onto the wire-mesh structure, framing the interior, massaging it, and forming the walls.

I loved the primal camaraderie of spongy mud fun, with extra clay and straw dripping down our arms and legs and coating our bodies. By the end of the day, after squishing around in the newly formed temple, we resembled straw-bale creatures, with big smiles and white eyes. We took turns rinsing off the slimy goop with the garden hose.

About eight months into my work at the auto shop, I was soaking in the warm pool. I floated over to the large flower bouquet at the end of the cement pond and gazed into its colorful blossoms. The aroma was intoxicating as I pressed my nose right into an opening rose. I pulled back and noticed sacred geometry happening with the different flowers, stems, and greens. I was mesmerized at the deep beauty and tranquility the whole bouquet projected.

A woman in the pool quietly floated up next to me after noticing how intrigued I was with the large bouquet. "Do you enjoy the flowers?" she whispered softly. "Yes," I replied. "See how the colors complement each other and look at how they create a sacred flow of grace and art," I said, tracing my hand from one flower to the next. "It's fascinating to me how they all come together to make this whole." I took both hands and circled the bouquet from top to bottom, with a huge grin on my face.

Smiling, she asked, "How would you like to work in the flower department and arrange flower bouquets?" I wanted to let out a scream of excitement, but we were in the warm pool with strict rules of silence. "Yes, yes, yes," I whispered. She was the manager of the flower department and told me to meet her at the flower shed the next morning. I held my nose as I dipped my whole head underwater and bubbled, "Thank you," as loud as I could. When I came back up for air, she smiled and gave me a big hug before she slipped up the pool stairs and into the out-door showers.

Dana was an attractive, tall and slender blonde with a creative flair. She had attended a school in the performing arts in New York and loved to dance and teach yoga. Arranging flowers was a hobby, and she brought this expertise to Stargazer as their creative manager.

The next day, I ran over to the auto shop to tell Mitchell the good news, but, it was not so good for him. Happy for me, yet sad to see me leave, he requested I work in the auto shop another two weeks before I took on this exciting new job. We had such a good rapport at the shop that we cultivated a friendship during my stay at Stargazer.

The Flower Shed

As planned, I met Dana in the flower shed behind the restaurant, adjacent to the garden, in the afternoon. She trained me during the two-week transition period and taught me every-thing about flowers, fillers, greens, types of vases, and simple care for keeping the flowers healthy for a few days. I loved going to the flower shed each morning to arrange flower bouquets, and when I left the auto shop, I picked up a few more hours as a flower maiden. Each week, I created about a dozen medium-sized bouquets for the Stargazer offices, 20 small vases for the restaurant tables, and about a dozen one-stem vases for the massage rooms. I loved playing with the flowers, and it became my devotional worship.

After a year, Dana taught me how to purchase the flowers at a florist shop down the mountain in Santa Rosa, for the week's bouquets. The next morning, I was standing in the flower shed. My chest rose as I deeply inhaled the faint scent of freesia and it tickled my nose. My lips parted into a wide smile when I saw several buckets of fresh-cut flowers Dana and I had purchased the day before.

It was after my experience of gazing deeply into the warm pool bouquet that I surrendered to the passionate play of flowers. Welcoming hues of heart-shaped purple blossoms, brilliant yellow mums, sprigs of white tendrils, and glossy green ferns emanated their love to me like butter melting in the hot sun. Voices and low whispers disappeared in the warm pool, and an immersion into tranquility arose into emptiness and bliss. In that moment, I awakened to the blessing of becoming a flower maiden at Stargazer.

Finally, I had the courage to feel my own desires, and my inner expression seeped into the creation of my flower arrangements like the ambrosia of divine lovers. Birds of paradise mimicked the call of Kokopelli. At Easter, the Casa Blanca lily, a large white bloom with fuzzy yellow anthers loaded with pollen, invoked rebirth and resurrection. In the spring, green calla lilies, in the crown of the "goddess vase" bouquet of the hot pool, seduced the green man. And in the crown of the "cold goddess" vase, velvety royal-blue and sea-green plumes swayed and sang to fair maidens. On Mother's Day, large pink lilies with purple irises mingled with forget-me-nots to capture the essence of honoring our mother's favorite flower. And in the summer heat, flaming Asiatic lilies draped with red-orange honeysuckle danced under stars of Queen Anne's lace celebrating the longest day of the year.

Back to the cold plunge for meditation, the bouquet of large white mums and cheery gerbera daisies with dangling bluebells whisper sweet melodies, as the compassion of Kuan Yin outshone the moon and swept across the back of my neck. The leaves of the surrounding trees rustled in the wind and applauded existence. Sometimes, there were no themes at all, just the pure essence of the flowers: the lasting affection of colorful zinnias on the restaurant tables, the bursting splendor of yellow-orange sunflowers in the garden, the provocative lure of the creamy white gardenia blossom, or even the sweet pea flower, with its soft rainbow colors and sweet scent, offers comfort to those in sorrow. And beyond this, it was a completely unique experience in every moment to gaze on the flowers—brand new every time!

There were also unforeseen themes. When I walked into the cooler to choose flowers for a particular week, there was a huge surrendering of which flowers were supposed to come with me that day. I know this with all my heart because of many, many demonstrations, but this next example is purely magical and touching. A big smile, a big breath, and three steps, and I was in the large cooler! The flowers responded, their colors popped, and the freshest flowers were beaming and screaming with joy to me. Selecting the flowers each week for Stargazer was like scanning a crowded room, searching for a lover's eyes with magnetizing passion and pulsing anticipation.

A Rose Is a Rose

This day I was overcome with hundreds of roses majestically shining at me. All roses, I thought, but I have never done all roses. We simply couldn't afford them. I circled around and around and finally surrendered to the vibrating hues of pink roses. As I started to place the bunches on my cart, the flower attendant came in with a sign: "Rose paks, 3 for $10." I was happily stupefied! I grabbed three times as many as I had started with and returned to the flower shed.

The next day, I created the warm-pool bouquet featuring all the roses: light pink with darker-pink-tipped petals, fuchsia roses, pastel-pink roses, and dark pink roses with their sweet fragrance. The monochromatic theme was highlighted with stalks of pink snapdragons and gladiola, and even delicate pink wax flowers were sprinkled in to fill out the display. I continued with the cold-plunge bouquet, the "goddess head" vases in the hot and cold pools, all artfully created with pink roses and pink filler. Every bouquet made that week was adorned with pink-colored roses.

A few days later, I received a call from a friend who lived in Santa Rosa. She was very sad because her mother had just passed away. She rarely drove to Stargazer, but her daughters insisted they take a couple of days to soak and reflect in the healing waters. When she came into the pools, she was drawn to the flowers and began to cry. Everywhere she looked, the beautiful pink rose bouquets embraced her. She told me that her mother's favorite flower was the pink rose, and she felt the essence of her mother all around her. She was comforted knowing her mother was at peace and happy in a beautiful place.

By the time my friend finished telling me about her mother, I was in tears and feeling grateful to have gone with the flow of the call of the pink rose that day at the cooler. Who could have possibly known the reasoning behind the purchase of so many roses? Yet, standing in the cooler, I listened and acted, and in that letting go a miracle happened.

Small miracles happened each time I embraced the sacred vase and walked the path to the pools or Stargazer buildings. You could taste the joy the flowers would bring to all those who noticed . . . people bowing, nodding with delight, or just smiling and remarking, "They are so beautiful."

There also was the special silent ritual of presenting the meditation pool bouquet each week. In a crescendo of ecstatic bliss, my body tingled, and tears of appreciation flooded the waters every time I carried that large bouquet to its resting place on the ledge of the warm pool. I floated away from the flowers like a lingering kiss, and waves of liquid love and compassion rippled out to all those watching. Only the flowers existed.

Eventually, I began to manage the whole flower operation each week because Dana had taken on more responsibilities in her performing arts career. I even created a handmade manual of procedures for the flower shed maidens. With more responsibility came more hours on the property at Stargazer. The driving back and forth to the A-frame was becoming a drain and a drag, and I longed to live as a resident on the Stargazer property.

I checked in with the housing manager for living spaces on the property. There were several cute cottages and larger houses toward the back outer reaches of the land. The only problem was my two cats. With several housemates sharing space, it just would not work. And the cottages were occupied by long-standing residents, who have lived and worked there for several years.

I went to plan B, moving in with my new partner, Diana, a gifted singer-songwriter I met in the gardens near the flower shed. We enjoyed a very tantric love affair together, and she was supportive in helping me to practice healthy boundaries at Stargazer, especially with men. We went our separate ways after two years as I continued my tantric path.

Finally, I went to plan C, moving to the Stargazer property. I chose "independent lane" at the end of the main trail to the pools and across from the blue pine building where more intimate workshops were held. I was able to purchase a small trailer camper for $1,000 from a former resident, and one of the guys from the auto shop drove me in his four-wheel-drive truck to pick it up and drive it back to Stargazer. There, he unloaded the 15-foot trailer and secured it to its new resting spot at the end of the trailer park, complete with water and sewer hookup.

It was a bit small for the cats and me to live in, especially after enjoying the spaciousness of renting a three-bedroom ranch home with Diana and the enchanting A-frame before that. I certainly missed the luxurious large bathroom and a cozy fire on occasion at night, but what was simply magical was my walk through the forest on the dirt trail to the flower shed, about 20 minutes of pure enchantment. Sometimes I literally skipped down the trail. Other times I sang or just basked in the beauty of nature. I was happy because my dream of living and working at Stargazer had finally come true.

I never imagined I could be a flower arranger. It was a job that came about because of my passion and enthusiasm for something. It really wasn't work to me, and this spoke volumes to how I would proceed in my life. I will live from a joyous place, I thought, and this is how I will determine my success.

I enjoyed this set up at Stargazer another year until the drought kicked in. With no rains for months in California, Stargazer began to make rules about water usage to the residents because of the shortage, including laundering clothes off property, limiting shower times, and drinking spring water. The water tables were becoming dangerously low on the property, and fires were beginning to pop up everywhere. There was one I had to navigate from on my return to Stargazer with the buckets of flowers one afternoon. Upon reaching the top of the mountain, cars were backed up on the way into town. An out-of-control fire raged up the west side of the mountain, where emergency vehicles were helping people evacuate their homes. The fires were not close to the road, but I could feel the heat through my open van windows.

A couple of helicopters were flying back and forth over-head, carrying large sacks of water suspended from the bottom of their crafts. They would round the bend dumping the water atop flaming treetops and then return to a nearby pond and swoop down with great velocity to quickly retrieve more water. The copters would rise over the trees and past the road, spilling some of the water onto cars and windshields. The noise of the helicopters was loud and deafening, and the increased traffic confused my thinking.

When orange-and-red flames crested over the mountain, shooting high into the sky, it reminded me of a dragon rearing its head and spewing his flames with great force. Car horns sounded, and a policeman picked up the pace of maneuvering cars and trucks through a safe route. People began to panic, yelling and darting their cars to seemingly better positions in the line forward, as black smoke billowed and unfurled, making driving even more difficult. The heat was now intense, like opening a hot oven door, so I rolled up the windows and turned the air conditioning on high. I finally made it through the dangerous part of the fire tunnel.

Looking in my rearview mirror, I could see barricades going up across the street, and cars had to turn around and go back down the mountain to safety. Eyes back to the road, I drove through the Stargazer Hot Springs gate several miles away. I parked in front of the flower shed and hastily unpacked the buckets of flowers into the shed. I sat back in the car in disbelief and began to cry.

As the weeks went by, some fires in Northern California were contained, while others still burned. The air quality was poor, with a misty haze of fire smoke the norm every morning. I could hardly breathe as my lungs filled with light smoky air. I started wearing a bandana soaked in water around my mouth to filter out the smoke in the air I was breathing. I was growing weary of the constantly falling ash and of seeing cloudy, smoky nights instead of shining stars.

I was inside my trailer one afternoon petting my cats when I overheard two men outside talking. Apparently, it was the county fire marshal conversing with one of the property managers. The fire marshal was explaining that the manpower was dwindling to match the number of fires that were breaking out. And if a fire were to break out here, there would be less help from firefighters, and we would basically be on our own to evacuate. The marshal offered some good advice which was to start clearing trees and brush from existing buildings in an effort for them not to catch fire if a rolling fire came through the area.

At that point, I came flying out of the trailer. I asked the fire marshal how close the fires were in our area. Without wavering, he stated there were several fires in adjacent counties and that these fires basically surrounded the Stargazer property. Wind conditions would affect their speed and spreading power. It was a dangerous situation in my eyes, and the manager reported the news of impending danger and immediately rallied teams of residents to start up the chainsaws and clear space around the pools and other buildings in anticipation of any fire.

I was no longer in a safe zone and was completely out of my own comfort zone. I felt as though I was being choked out of this beautiful sanctuary I was living and working in. I needed more stability in my life and called on a trusted friend to help me.

On the Road Again

Maile, the stone diva, would see me through this intense situation. She had driven up from Santa Barbara with her boyfriend, unfettered by the rampant fires. She even took time to spend a few hours soaking in the relaxing pools of Stargazer before she meandered on the dirt trail to the trailer lane—a very good idea for what she was about to witness with me.

We were at my small camper trailer at the back of the Stargazer property, having some tea and talking, when I lost it. My heart rate picked up, and I began to rant that I couldn't breathe when I awoke each morning to smoke-filled mountains. I was pacing in front of the trailer breathing heavily when she grabbed me and pulled me down to the Earth. She held my hands and looked straight into my eyes. "What do you want to do, Kathleen?"

Anxiously, I yelled, "I don't know!" while shaking my hands out to my sides. I sat back on my heels and yelled again, "I want to pull my van up to this trailer, hook it up, and get the hell out of here!" Breathing less heavily, I sighed and pointed to the back of the trailer. "But I can't because the trailer is too heavy for my van to pull it."

Maile started breathing with me and helped me to slow my pace down even more. "You can sell it," she said calmly, "You can use the money to travel where you want to go." I stood, with my feet planted firmly on the ground now, as this was beginning to make sense to me. I didn't have to stay here, and selling the trailer would give me the necessary funds to move, but where? Maile and I walked back to the bench by the trailer and sat. She handed me my cup of tea as we soaked up the silence for a few moments.

I remembered Diana, who had left Stargazer a few months earlier with aspirations of a music tour and moved to be with her family in a small town in western North Carolina. She raved about the beauty of the mountains, the lush forests, and the cleansing rains. I would ask her, and with that, Maile and I took a long walk back to the warm pool for an evening soak. I felt comforted knowing a plan was formulating, and I was able to immerse myself in the calming waters once more. We met up with her boyfriend for a late dinner, and then we retired to our separate campers.

I had to see and feel this different mountain location for myself, so I contacted my cousin Lori and told her about my plan to move. She talked with her husband, Kurt, and they researched the area online. Kurt would accompany me on a five-day scouting mission to the Appalachian Mountain town near Asheville. Lori stayed behind to care for their children.

Sure enough, the forests were lush, plush, and bright green, with flowing creeks and streams. The air was clear, and I felt safe. On my first day there, I was sitting out on the front lawn of our rental and it began to rain. I just sat there and let the water pour onto me with droplets of delight, my body soaking up every drip.

The next thing I knew, a large mama Eastern box turtle came crawling up the lawn, passing me by to nestle in the dirt under the deck. That's it, I thought! This was surely a sign to move out here. Kurt experienced the same uplifting feelings of being in a more temperate rainforest climate and agreed that this would be a great place to live someday. Their days of living in a suburb of San Francisco would end in less than a year.

When I returned to Northern California, I packed up my things and put them in a storage unit just outside of town within a month. I loaded up Jack and Maple Leaf, a few clothes, and my personal items into the van and away we went, heading east across the United States. I was leaving California after 20 years of building a life in the Golden State. With the rising cost of living, sweltering temperatures, and raging fires throughout the state, I knew I was making the right decision to move where I could breathe easier again and where waters flowed freely. It beckoned to my golf teaching days and what I used to invite my clients to do, and that is within the power of choice. As Mary Poppins would say, "Once begun is half done!"

CHAPTER 20

WHERE FALLEN EAGLES SOAR

I traded the chaos of California for the tranquility of western
North Carolina in August 2008. I was motivated by the four
seasons, a moderate climate, welcoming rains, thunderstorms,
snow, and the lush, plush forests of the Appalachian Mountains.
But while driving across the plains of the United States on a four-
lane freeway, I developed a greater appreciation for the Native
American Indians. I had a vision of how they had lived in the
barren drylands but, more important, the mystery of how they
survived. Deep in my revere, I watched in amazement as a large
black feather dropped from amid the blue sky, kissed the middle
of my windshield, and then disappeared under the car. It
happened so quickly, yet I saw it in slow motion. I felt honored
by this gift. I only wished I could have pulled over fast enough to
retrieve the feather. I would later realize the true significance of
what this feather symbolized.

Six nights and seven long days later, after driving more than
2,000 miles, I settled into my new garage-top studio apartment,
nestled in the mountains, right near the town hall. There was no
town center, although there was a large pavilion where the
residents would play bingo every Thursday night. I could see
rows of picnic tables filled with people and their colorful
dopplers, ready to strike their numbered paper. I could hear the

bingo numbers being called by a man's voice on the microphone from my 6-foot by 4-foot balcony. Such a welcome!

My first project at the little apartment was to immediately screen in the porch so the cats could claim this bachelor pad and put the litter box outside for them to use, which kept my place smelling a bit better. Although there was always a strong smell of gasoline or oil or something in the apartment, it reminded me of my days working in the auto shop. I realized I really was sitting right on top of a two-car garage, and the landlord was often working on a car engine or lawnmower. He was a stout man who always kept busy.

There was an old, worn stuffed chair with a broken leg that rested in the corner of the balcony, which was a perfect nap time retreat for the cats. I enjoyed sitting out there, too, with a small wooden kitchen chair I'd bring out from the small living room. Yes, there was a small rectangle wooden table with these two chairs in the back living room in front of the large bay window. A velvet tan loveseat flanked the other side, with an old Magnavox television set atop a makeshift shelf in the corner, with black cable wires coming out the backend. A torn braided rug rested in the middle of the room, separating the furniture pieces. There was a matching tan recliner in the other corner near the front door, boasting a sturdy steel screen door, which I often left open for a wafting breeze.

In the hallway leading from the living room to the bedroom, there was a yellow kitchen sink, some counter space with a microwave oven, a small refrigerator, and two cupboards filled with plastic plates, bowls, and cups. I was literally in the hallway washing dishes or preparing food. I don't care for microwaves, so I spent a lot of my mealtimes dining out at local restaurants and eating some good Southern cooking. Across from the hallway was the bathroom with a full, stained white ceramic bathtub, toilet, and old walnut vanity sink.

This two-room apartment was built in the 1970s, and the decor reflected it, with lime-green shag carpeting throughout, even in the bathroom. It felt more like a Motel 6 than my new home. It was just a landing spot, I kept reassuring myself. Within a short time, I walked into a local real estate office to start the process of looking for a more permanent place to live. I often sat on the balcony in my wooden chair and tried to visualize the place where I wanted to live. I'd gaze straight up into the nearby mountains, setting my intention with all my heart.

I walked and hiked daily, discovering several easy trails not far from my apartment. Once again, it felt good being in nature and appreciating the lush, plush trees; the babbling creeks; the bountiful plants; the colorful flowers; and many species of birds and other wildlife and remembering the big Eastern box turtle that greeted me that summer day. The newness lifted my spirits for a while, although I was starting to feel a little depressed and homesick for my friends in California. I had left so abruptly, barely saying good-bye to the many friends I had made up and down the state.

On the downside, I was eating greater quantities of rich foods in my new habitat. Although I was walking, I was not as active as I was in California and gained more than 50 pounds in the following months. My cousin Lori and her family had not moved here yet, so I fell into a deeper depression without family nearby. I began thinking of my tantra days and picked up Margot's book, *The Art of Everyday Ecstasy*, and started rereading it in the evenings. I came across a chapter on third chakra development and the spotlight of being my own source of personal power. I had fallen into a black hole and needed to pull myself out of this, balancing the yin and yang principles of will and pleasure once more.

While sitting in daily meditation, I started by simply visualizing the golden sun filling my solar plexus with radiant light beams. Then, I challenged myself with an assignment that was offered in the book, a self-empowerment project, to help me practice further strengthening the solar plexus energy center, building confidence, and boosting my will power and spirits.

On my strolls in the forest, I would stop for a while, contemplating what theme I would choose for such an all-consuming project. I would just watch the trees sway or the clouds drift by, keeping an open channel for any clues stirring inside me. I heard an orchestra of birds singing and watched a party of little woodpeckers up in a tree canopy guarding their nests. Something was happening, and that something had to do with the birds!

In the simple act of standing, watching, and listening, with a heartfelt desire to serve in some way, I had visions streaming through about birds. What kind of birds are those? Where do they come from? How many species are there? Where do they sleep, and why do they come to our feeders?

In the county library, I researched the migration area in North and South Carolina. I went to the local mom-and-pop bookstore which carried several local authors' writings on birds, bird watching in the area and conserving bird habitat. I even went to the local visitor centers and chambers to gather whatever information was available to the public. I studied and wrote copious notes for over five months about bird species, their habitat, the local organizations, and birding clubs and prayed daily to the great eagle spirit for guidance.

I was immersed in the project as it had a flow of its own, and I was enjoying the ride. I created a binder filled with scripts, an outline, pictures, and flyers. I also created a vision board, a beautiful collage on a large poster board of cuttings from bird magazines. (See Figure 9: Birding Vision Board.) A PowerPoint presentation was constructed, with the help of a bird enthusiast and an active member of a civil organization and later presented to the chamber and the town.

I created an altar in my bedroom on a small dresser facing east, with a picture of an Indian woman holding a white feather above a conch shell that had smoke rising from it, with an eagle above her and a wolf below her, a hawk feather that smelled of the wind, a talking stick, two postcards of Native American Indians, and a Native American Indian arrow, among other things. It was important to me for these items to be handmade by Indians. I wanted to feel the authentic energy of the red people, not the yellow people.

There were only two places in the Cherokee Indian Reservation that I knew of where such items existed. The Qualla Boundary is territory held as a land trust for the federally recognized Eastern Band of Cherokee Indians, who reside in western North Carolina. The area is part of the Cherokee historic territory. This sacred energized altar helped keep me focused and in tune with its direction and purpose of appreciating the natural world.

I was a visionary, documenting and initiating eight components of a whole birding project emerging from my research. I became the project consultant for envisioning Maggie Valley as a real bird sanctuary and birding community. Although Maggie Valley was already considered a bird sanctuary, the meaning would be slightly different, adding much more than not being able to shoot birds in this town. I wrote a series of press releases, which helped the whole project gain momentum and visibility, and even our congressman attended a couple of the project ceremonies.

My most visible accomplishment was the creation of the Great Smoky Mountains Audubon Society (GSMAS), with local log pioneer hotel owner Ed Jones, where "Maggie" happened to be born, nominated as president. The community got its name from Maggie Mae Setzer. Her father, John Sidney Setzer, founded the area's first post office and named it after one of his daughters, Maggie. I was named vice president, but I was not responsible for the policy side with the Audubon Headquarters. Ed was a genius in this area, while I was much better at the creative stuff. I helped organize several presenters for our club during the first couple of years, drawing on the talent and experience of local wildlife and birding organizations. They included live bird and wolf events, Haywood Community College backyard habitat experts, bird-watching field trips, and elk and firefly tours. The club had over 500 members, with about half in Haywood County where I lived.

The territory of the GSMAS included eight counties that surrounded the Great Smoky Mountains, straddling the border between North Carolina and Tennessee in the Great Smoky Mountains National Park. World renowned for its diversity of plant and animal life, the beauty of its ancient mountains, and the quality of its remnants of southern Appalachian Mountain culture, this is America's most visited national park. The motto of GSMAS became "Stand–Watch–Listen," as that is how the project emerged within me.

The first project of the GSMAS was to secure the trail signs of the North Carolina Birding Trail (NCBT) up in the Haywood Group of the Mountain Trail Guide (July 2010). Maggie Valley is the epicenter of the six Haywood County Group Birding Sites of the NCBT. The first signs would be placed at Lake Junaluska, a winter birding hotspot and part of the NCBT, in July 2010. The locations were in the secluded wetlands area, near the conference center, and near the west gate walking entrance. The public and press were invited to meet at the welcome center for this momentous event.

One day, I was walking around the lake, where we had put up the birding trail signs, to help filter out distractions of some surfacing challenges with the project. I had just walked a labyrinth, an ancient pagan ritual, which was incorporated into part of the landscape of a Methodist church there on the property.

Filled with deep peace and surrendering, I stood at the edge of the lake and gazed outward into the hazy gray horizon.

Something black was moving toward me with a very large wingspan. As it flew directly above me, I saw its white head. It was a bald eagle! My whole body trembled. Tears of joy streamed down my cheeks, and words like *magnificent, honor,* and *respect* came to life. The presence of this raptor was a sign to me that all would be well with the birding project. I was on the right path. The representation of the eagle is that of a higher vantage point, the connection to the Divine. It is the ability to stay connected to Source and yet remained balanced with the realm of the Earth. I took it to heart and gathered my courage that day, rising above any seeming obstacles.

The second component of the birding project was to nominate an NCBT site in Maggie Valley, which was Cataloochee Ranch and its many acres of conservation land near the Smoky Mountains. The site became official in March 2012 and was commemorated by a ceremony and reception for this accomplishment. Other components of the birding project included heritage, a visual experience down the main road, marketing, advertising, ecotourism and agritourism, mountain migration station and turtle park, and a birding festival. Some of the components were well underway and making a difference in awareness and appreciation for our natural resources in the mountains, especially the birds, to whom I dedicated this project. "A dedication to those who settled this valley and those who walk in their footsteps."

As a visionary, I wanted to bring the other mountain Audubon chapters together. I created the history-making "Audubon Mountain Council" with three other mountain chapters attending the inaugural meeting at Cataloochee Ranch in 2011. This meeting marked the first real effort to bring the western mountain chapters together for common interests and prospective goals in the future.

All had been going well until just days before the annual Great Smoky Mountain Trout Festival in April 2011. My heart sank, and I dropped to the floor and cried when I read the news in a local paper. There was a photo of the sheriff holding a juvenile bald eagle from wing to wing with his white head drooping. The dead eagle had been found at the festival grounds, apparently shot down by a human. Rumors and speculation heightened when reward signs were posted in local business storefronts looking for leads as to who would do this.

A couple of weeks later, I expressed my sorrow at the local community fire. Under the night sky and comforting flames and glowing ambers, as I shared my story to the circle of how the eagle's death had shaken me to the core, my voice trembled. Several offered the possible meaning behind such a happening. One woman began to shake a rattle, while another began to sing softly about the eagle rising and soaring. I dried my eyes and rose to sing the words with outstretched arms to twinkling stars amid a dark sky. Another woman stood and then another. The song grew louder, my own voice strengthened, grounded in the Earth. Stimulated and fueled by the fire, meaning resonated within my body, and I knew I had to rise and be the eagle in my own life. I rose above my own thoughts of judgment, blame, sorrow, and despair regarding the perpetrator, the town, the community, and the GSMAS. The urge to do something became unbearable. With our next general meeting approaching in July 2011, I sat down and wrote out a dedication to the eagle.

The Maggie Pavilion was packed that evening with nearly 70 people humming and buzzing in celebration of our one-year anniversary and our official acceptance into the Audubon family. There was cake and coffee, and a large screen displayed a continuous slideshow of all the events, people, and fun we had our first year, accompanied with the music of "What a Wonderful World" by Louis Armstrong playing in the background. Our butterfly presenter, who had traveled from Raleigh, North Carolina, was anxious to begin his PowerPoint presentation. The heat and humidity soared as a GSMAS representative welcomed everyone and made some announcements. She then nodded to me, and I made my way to the front of the pavilion to read the following dedication of our fallen friend.

As I began reading the words, there was a deafening silence, and someone even turned off the blowing floor fans. A picture of an adult eagle from a Lake Junaluska sighting was the lone photo on the large screen. (See Figure 10: Lone Eagle.)

> *How many of you walk at Lake Junaluska? And how many of you have seen this bald eagle around the lake? It is truly a rare and beautiful sighting, isn't it? The eagle soars gracefully from the height of the clouds and sees the world from the higher vantage point . . . the bigger picture.*
>
> *Tonight, I would like to honor this eagle and the juvenile eagle whose life was taken just a couple of months ago, not very far from here.*
>
> *Wisdom comes in many strange and mysterious forms. Let us always look higher to touch the sun with our hearts, and to learn to love the shadow as well as the light. When we see the beauty in both, we take flight like the eagle, who majestically soars once more.*
>
> *The gift is freedom and following the joy our hearts desire. Please, let us take a moment to pause and reflect on the bald eagle. Thank you.*

Months passed with more clarity and confidence; and it wasn't until December 2011 that I realized the true confirmation of my own growth, when magic filled the air.

I was walking the loop around Lake Junaluska with my friend Robert just days before the winter solstice. Robert was one of the first friends I met in Maggie Valley. We met in a sports bar, sitting near each other on bar stools while watching a football game, eating hamburgers and fries and indulging in a cold pint of beer. He was an attractive and fit man, a little older than me, who worked for the park service.

Robert was very knowledgeable about wildlife and the parks and forests in the area. We easily struck up a conversation and then agreed to walk or hike daily together on different trails in the area, talking nonstop about everything wild. He was also one of the most trusting, compassionate, and caring men I had ever met and would do anything for me in a time of trouble. He hugged me like a big bear, and although he had several solid core values, our destiny was to be very good friends.

We had just crossed the footbridge when I enthusiastically said, "Wouldn't it be wonderful to see the bald eagle again?"

Robert countered by shaking his head and looking down, "The juvenile was shot, and the other adult eagles are probably dead, too."

I stopped in my tracks and turned to face my negative friend. "Robert, you just gotta believe."

He replied, slowly looking up to meet my eyes, "Well, I want to believe they're still around."

Off in the distance, an object was flying toward us. My heartbeat quickened as the raptor came closer. "It's the eagle! It's the eagle!" I shouted, jumping and pointing.

"No, that's an osprey," Robert said in his deep, commanding voice. Then, a couple came running up in their Christmas sweaters exclaiming in a joyous spirit, "Do you see the eagle?"

I laughed and confirmed, "Yes, we do!"

Well, other people started gathering, and I watched that eagle cross the lake and then start to circle back. "He's coming back! He's coming back!" I proclaimed.

With heads tilted back, all eyes were to the sky. The eagle flew directly above all of us as if to say, "Yes, I am a bald eagle, and I am here!" He disappeared around the bend as quickly as he had appeared, leaving everyone high from his presence and witnessing a truly beautiful gift of the season.

As I think back, it is quite possible the eagle was really a *she*, and even more so could be the mother of the juvenile that had been shot. There have been several sightings of two bald eagles playing and preying at Lake Junaluska. I was so high from seeing the eagle once more that I was compelled to share this story with the community fire circle later that month. The teaching of great eagle spirit had come full circle: birth, death, and rebirth. I had never stopped serving the eagle spirit, even though the road was quite challenging at times, for it had never really been about me. I was just a messenger.

The eagle reminded me to soar in my own life again, keeping my head to the sky, the higher vantage point. And the feather that fell from the sky became the pen in my hand. I have since learned that in the Native American Indian tradition, the gift of a feather is given for one's journey. And the symbolic meaning of the turtle, as in the large Eastern box turtle that welcomed me to Maggie Valley, is for the "spirit of the people."

I worked on the MBSBP for three years as an act of goodwill, with my focus on staying with the integrity of the natural world and our connection with her. Other components morphed into spin-off projects, while others are still waited to be birthed. Unfortunately, the GSMAS folded in 2016 due to a lack of volunteers. Our seven amazingly dedicated board members had served their positions well for several years, though could no longer carry the responsibilities.

The birding project helped me to build more than confidence, I put my whole body, mind, soul, and heart into it. I was not paid for any of my services, nor did I expect to be compensated. It was inherently rewarding and filled my days with passion and excitement of what I would discover next and who would I meet and play with on the project in all its many facets. In a small way, I felt as though I had contributed to the whole of life.

In a broader sense, the birding project helped to spotlight the value of the land and waters and their ecosystems without placing an economic value on them. It was a win–win with the townspeople because everyone loved nature and the birds. My motives were heartfelt and from a place of integrity. Plus, the information that was being transmitted was from a Divine Source, not by me, which is a great demonstration of co-creation with God at its best.

After completion of such a multidimensional project, the prospect of taking on more complex and challenging projects seemed more attainable. I proved to myself that I could handle multiple levels of information, albeit the whole process was exhausting and exhilarating, like hanging onto the tail of a tiger.

CHAPTER 21

LET'S GET PHYSICAL

The birding project increased my self-confidence by giving me a sense of accomplishment and awareness in my new community. Interspersed with the birding project responsibilities, I began a more serious campaign for purchasing a new home. I could no longer live in such cramped quarters above the garage workshop, with the stench of gasoline and smoking engines wafting up my nose.

I searched for homes with a Real Estate Agent within a 15-mile radius of a quaint surrounding area, including where all the golf courses were. I even considered homes on fairways, but those days were over; I didn't want to be reminded of my injury from the golf ball incident in Sebastopol. From meadows to mountaintops, I viewed one-story and two-story structures, constructed of bricks and sticks, for eight solid months. I almost gave up. But all was not lost, as I learned a lot about the community.

Within 24 hours of almost giving up, my agent called and suggested that I look at a quaint 750-square-foot cottage just a mile from my apartment. So, I put on my sneakers and walked the distance with an optimistic attitude. I had nothing to lose and something to gain.

When I rounded the sharp, steep S-curve and headed up the street, I felt excitement stirring within my body. As I walked

261

farther up the hill on an evergreen-lined street, I heard a babbling creek. I stood for a moment, breathing heavily from the grade of the slope, and proceeded slowly. Then I saw it, a little white cottage on a ridge, nestled amid tall trees. I picked up my pace because I knew instinctively that this was the dream house I had envisioned for myself. Coincidentally, it also happened to be the spot in the mountains that I gazed at from my garage apartment. "Sometimes you don't have to go looking any further than your own backyard," as Dorothy said in *The Wizard of Oz*.

I walked up the stone driveway and discovered a spring cradled amid a grouping of oak trees. Immediately, I noticed another creek running alongside the spring that traversed farther up the hill, and another creek that cut down below in front of the house. Impressed with my findings, I walked back over to the driveway and under the carport to peek through the windows of the little cottage. To my delight, it was a completely renovated two-bedroom, one-bath home that had an obvious abundance of love and care.

I turned my attention back to the lot as I walked along a three-foot stonewall that stretched the length of the backyard. When I rounded the corner of the house, I dropped to my knees on the lush grass when I saw the million-dollar view. I stared in awe and with great appreciation at the forest, creeks, and mountains in the rising mist. I stood and strolled over to an old wooden bench swing, just like my grandparents had at their house, and sat down. I pulled out my flip phone (yes, the only flip phone still in existence), and called my Real Estate agent. My long search was over—I signed the sales contract within 24 hours. I gave myself this special 50th birthday present in June 2009.

The cottage was furnished, so I could move in as soon as the closing papers were signed. I was relieved to own a home again. The last time had been 15 years earlier, before my accident, when I was a golf professional in Palm Springs. This place felt safe and had a very sacred vibe to it. It would become my sanctuary and writer's haven.

There wasn't much maintenance to do, except for screening in the porch for Maple Leaf and Jack. I hired a local contractor to do the work because the porch was much larger than in my previous residences. There was a large adjoining deck off the front of the house, complete with two white rocking chairs. For the *pièce de résistance*, the carpenter installed a picket fence along the perimeter of the backyard, painting it a soft sage green, to add a little privacy to a circle of four steel outdoor chairs and an in-ground firepit.

The cottage had a small kitchen, which I set up to be quite functional, with a spice rack over a small stove. I hung pots, pans, and utensils on a steel triple shelf to the right. The cupboards were metal painted white and had the brand name "Beauty Queen," which was an omen of how I would feel living there. I enjoyed the yang aspects of Artemis the archer, with the yin pleasures of Aphrodite, the Goddess of love. I had been signing my handwritten letters and cards to family and friends with the tag, "Your Artemis, Your Aphrodite," since my days in Sebastopol and the goddess gatherings. I felt my dream home offered me a perfect balance of both.

The living room was large enough to accommodate a couch and two recliners that faced south and afforded a view of the mountains through the large picture window. Playing keyboard instruments has been a wonderful high-interest hobby since the accident, allowing me to exercise my brain with creative expression. I enjoyed playing music in the privacy of my own home, with unbridled abandon, so I positioned my accordion and a Casio keyboard near the picture window for easy accessibility and stacked my music books and sheets on the shelf nearby.

For lighthearted humor, I played "Somewhere Over the Rainbow" and "If I Only Had a Brain" from *The Wizard of Oz* and select songs by Barbra Streisand, along with the exceptional repertoire of music from around the world, selected by my Santa Barbara accordion instructor, Ross. My curious cat, Jack, would be mesmerized by the musing melodies and would jump on the keyboard and literally turn it off when he had had enough of my playing. Unfortunately, his time at the cottage was short-lived, and in a few years he passed quietly in the comfort of the backyard grass and a setting sun. He was 14 years young.

The two back rooms were about the same size. I staged one as a bedroom with windows looking south at the million-dollar view. I designated the other room as an office. The stacked washer and dryer were tucked in the bathroom, and a full-size bathtub sat near the window for evening soaks before bed.

Punches and Kicks

I was learning a new way of life in the mountains, far from the shores of the Pacific Ocean. My lifestyle habits had changed a bit, most noticeably with body image. This was due not only to being depressed about moving away from a life I had built with true and dependable friends but also to the new environmental stimuli. I had to learn and relearn routes to grocery stores, banks, and activities farther away than this little town. I used tools and strategies that Dr. Smith, my neuropsychologist, had shown me in Santa Barbara, although it felt like I was starting over again. I kept her updated on my progress from time to time, with a letter like this one written in the summer of 2012:

> *Dear Dr. Smith,*
> *I am still using several strategies originally learned from you; for example, card game sorting exercise (blacks/reds, reds, hearts/diamonds, etc.) to get down to one variable. I play brain word games every day, such as Scrabble; finding the words game, crossword puzzles are*

not so fun, visual exercises such as near and far, tracking (which I have learned to do in nature, following hummingbirds doing circles, watching green worms on their long strings hanging from a tree, following butterflies, etc.; balance exercises such as working on a half ball, yoga (modified), and if I am near an ocean walking in the sand and for added difficulty was sure to bring on nausea, I watch the waves. I understand the value of using two of the three stabilizers: visual, auditory, and kinesthetic to help me stay grounded; breathing exercises daily to increase circulation in the brain and body.

I use ear plugs for restaurants and other places with over stimulation. I "mark" when I walk, hike, and drive. I just started hiking in the mountains and forests this year and always with someone. There are many variables to navigate, so I follow a person from behind, using the butt strategy. It's a great mark, but it makes me aware of the terrain and I cannot look around a lot. I still have problems looking left and right, so I must be consciously aware of my head movements.

I drive short distances, but never at peak traffic times. Sometimes, I can listen to the radio when I drive, but it's situational to what I have been doing that day. That's the case with everything. I still pretty much follow the format from my daily activity sheet we had started so long ago. I use an appointment book to write down everything, including building in one- or two hour-long naps a day. This is necessary, so I can move through the whole day; otherwise, I fade quickly and my recovery time is longer. This daily activity format foundation gives me a better chance to accomplish tasks, but sometimes I forget to look at the appointment book, especially when it is covered accidentally by papers or a book or sweater or something! I just pick up where I left off, and it eventually gets done.

I still use egg timers when I cook, although sometimes I forgot I was cooking on the stove, and then I smelled the burning food from the living room or bedroom and I ran to turn off the stove and start again. I usually can do just one thing in the morning and one thing after my nap in the afternoon. The morning is still my best time for two or three hours. I can go to the grocery store, bank, gas up, then come home, eat lunch, and take a nap. It's best for me to stay home in the afternoon, but I can work in the yard, write, or work on a project. If I have plans to go out in the evening, I don't schedule anything the following day, so I can use the time to recover.

After reviewing my daily life, I realized just how many strategies have become the norm for me. I have been able to expand some threshold levels a little bit, but the stopper is usually the visual aspect from the brain. It can take me out in less than five minutes! The debilitating symptoms return immediately: disorientation, dizziness, non-speech, confusion, and even drooling. I am down for the count, and sometimes require assistance for these days.

I must avoid vibration of fluorescent lighting, computers, and action movies. I don't have a TV and I only watch select movies from Netflix, no fast flipping of anything, overhead fans, fireplaces/pits, crowds of people, etc. I still wear a visor or ball cap and sunglasses to diffuse some of this.

A few months ago, I had severe vertigo for a couple of weeks. I went to a doctor for a vertigo treatment, a sports physical therapist, which helped, but not completely. It took a few more weeks of moving very slowly as if I had a neck brace on. I don't even know how it happened. There have been other milder cases, but, in general, I have been able to stay under threshold levels, so this debilitating experience does not happen.

I'm starting to fade already just writing this up. I need to turn off my computer and rest. Reading is the same way. So, now I truly realize how much structure you gave me so many years ago! I remember how long it took to get over what had happened and how it literally changed my life forever. How could anyone really understand this journey? I am attempting to write a book about my experience. Finally, I feel I'm up to the task.

One last thing, I have been practicing martial arts in a classroom setting for the last two years at a modified pace. My coach says it will take me twice as long to earn a black belt, but he believes I can do it. I'm half way there, though not so sure I will make it as you have to know all of the forms, which have too many variables to comprehend. I don't really care about a black belt, though I continue to practice. We'll see what happens.

I appreciate you and your work so much. I have a good quality of life because of your expertise and efforts. Thank you again!

Kathleen

As you can see, a person with a traumatic brain injury must deal with a lot of daily challenges. Although watching multitaskers today with their fast-paced technology that changes every three months could be just as challenging! This is normal for me, whatever normal is! Here is the good news. I persevered in my Blue Dragon Tae Kwon Do class, although I did not take the class to achieve black-belt status. I took the class to increase circulation for a blood-clotting problem and to lose weight, and that I did, in fact, over 60 pounds! My blood consistency was also just fine.

After a few months in my Tae Kwon Do class, my instructor, Head Master Sa Bum Nim Marshall Hale, a fourth-degree black belt and a student of the late Grandmaster Young Soo Do, asked me why I was not testing for colored belts each quarter. I shared my reasoning for attending the class and took him up on his invitation to at least take the first testing for yellow belt.

The first form, or *poomse*, was called "The Beginning of the Universe" and represented the element "Heaven," with 18 moves, including two kicks and nine punches. A poomse is a pattern of prearranged Tae Kwon Do moves consisting of blocks, strikes or punches, and kicks. The testing location was the basketball court/gym at the local fitness center where anyone could watch, especially from the walking track above, that circumferences the gym. I don't get nervous, but I was on this morning. I was up first, with other students who were testing the same form, about 10 of us all together, including a couple of teenagers and one younger child. I completed my form with deliberateness and grace and then moved onto the "break." We each had to do a sidestepping kick and break a board, held by two advanced students. Channeling all the nervousness into the board, I did it on the first try.

After the whole testing session, which was composed of eight groups that matched each of the colored belt levels, there was a ceremony. Master Hale presented each of us individually with a certificate and the colored belt we had just tested for and passed. I was overcome with emotion when he handed the certificate to me and helped me take off the white belt and put on the yellow belt. This was the first time since my accident that I had performed a sport in public and in front of a live audience. I was so happy for this small achievement, and with new inspiration, I was on my way to progressing through the different belts to black belt.

The journey was long and challenging. As the eight forms progressed, they became more difficult with more motions of kicking, blocking, and punching. Now, there were 22 to 25 moves, delivered with precision and in unison with the rest of the group, which always seemed to go at a faster pace than me. I was constantly asking the group to slow down but to no avail. My brain would flood out, and I would have to stop for a few moments to try to regroup. Plus, many times, double vision would kick in because of the fluorescent lighting and a shiny wooden floor reflection.

I talked to Master Hale about my dilemma, and he suggested working one-on-one with other students in the class to pick up my pace. I did, and it was very helpful. But I also did something that I enjoyed even more: doing my forms in my living room with music. I would learn the form slowly and then add music with a bit faster tempo and try to keep up with the music. It also felt like more of an art form to me, than a series of steps to be memorized for military purposes. This harkened back to the familiar Zen approach. It also gave my brain a different channel to work from, more from the right brain, or at least a better combination of the two spheres.

I hated some aspects of the class, such as sparring, but I loved self-defense moves. Sparring is when two students would practice their skill level of punching, kicking, and blocking against each other: a fight for points in a contest or a fight out in the streets of the real world. I tried not to complain too much, as I was always reassured this was an invaluable part of the teachings of Tae Kwon Do, as you never know when you may need the tools learned and, more important, the action and reaction required to defend and protect yourself or others.

Interestingly, I attended a Christmas service in the city with a man I was dating at the time. Victor was a tall, handsome, muscular massage therapist, with a big heart and a big smile. I had to drive down the mountain almost an hour to get to the auditorium, while Victor only had to drive across town. We met for a beautiful holiday program, and then he stayed to usher for the next service. We parted at the door with a hug and a sloppy, wet kiss, then I walked to my car down the street. Instead of getting into my car, I took a quick walk around the block to get some circulation going before I hit the road for the long trek back up the mountain.

I noticed some young men across the street near a bar, so I angled to the left side of the street to avoid the whole scene. I walked briskly in my black stilettos and long black-and-gold cloak, enjoying the cold night air, when I suddenly heard footsteps trailing behind me. My armpits started to sweat, and thoughts raced through my mind: make a run for it or turn and face these predators.

With summoned energy, I swiftly turned and landed in the ready stance, motioning my arms up, with one arm coming down with a fist-striking motion and the other resting at my side, fist in ready position for punch. My heels struck the ground with lightning speed, and my long cloak swirled around me like actor Keanu Reeves in *The Matrix*. "May I help you?" I asked in a firm and controlled voice, as my coat whooshed across my legs.

There were three men, staggered one behind the other about three feet apart. I looked directly into the first man's eyes when I spoke. The two guys behind him turned and ran off, leaving just the one. He had his hands in his pockets, and within several tense seconds, he mumbled, "I don't believe this." He turned, quickly walking to catch up with his other friends.

Huh, I thought for a moment. Just the act of confidence and knowing what I would do was enough to scare these three guys

270

and send them on their way. I quickly changed my mind about sparring! I walked to my car and drove to my home that night feeling grateful for all that my Tae Kwon Do students and Master teacher had taught and practiced with me.

It would be another two years before the anticipated black-belt testing day. I had learned to work daily with many of the other red-belt students in the class, and I even had a couple of tutorial sessions with Master Hale to move through some tougher sequences. We were now a family, moving through this together, and I felt such a warm sense of belonging with this group. They were always there for me and for each other.

Black-belt testing was a long grueling day, with group warm-up presentation, sparring demonstrations, exhibition kicking and punching boards, and the long-awaited poomse and breaking boards testing. There was a large crowd in the gymnasium that day and night to witness the mastery. The final poomse, called "The Foundation of Life," represented the element "Earth" with 24 moves, six kicks, and 12 punches. This was my favorite form sequence because of the graceful moves and kick combinations. I practiced this over and over daily with a couple of the other red-belt students at the gym for several weeks. That night, the audience watched this beautiful poomse performed by all 10 of us in unison. I passed this part of the test with ease and presence.

Board breaking was next. I had to break three boards, with a double spinning kick—a move that I had taken a bad fall on practicing just a few months before the testing. I wore a full soft red helmet for the kick that night, just as a precaution. There were six of us going to break-board test, and we all sat on the floor with are boards stacked in front of us, as we awaited our turn. There were three black-belt judges, including the Grandmaster Tania Habayeb, who had flown in from Florida. She was a well-toned woman with short brown hair, who looked much younger than her years. She had done a couple of self-defense demonstrations for the crowd earlier, which displayed her six-degree black-belt status. Now, she was observing and judging the breaks.

The first two students broke their boards on the first or second try, and I was up next. Master Hale took the three stacked boards and held one side tightly, as another student held the other side tightly. Then, two other students put both hands on each of the holders individually as to brace the force and momentum which the kick would create. I counted my steps, practicing the motion of the double spinning kick a couple of times to get the right footing. Eyeing the extended boards, I narrowed my focus to the middle of the board, and then, in a sweeping motion, performed the kick extending my leg and clipping the top of the boards with my foot. A miss ... my helmet slipped in the spin.

I took a couple of breaths and tried again, this time striking the boards but not enough to break them. I tried again and again but could not break the boards. The crowd was restless with my attempts as I walked and paced for a few moments. I noticed the Grand Master held up her index finger to me, meaning this was it. I had only one more time, one more try. I was heated, my adrenaline was racing, and I unbuckled the straps of my red helmet and threw it to the ground. I motioned for the boards to be put in position once more, and I took my stance. I summoned the life-force energy within me. Visualizing through the boards, I leaped into the double spinning kick and pressed my foot straight through all three boards with a mighty *crack*.

The crowd went crazy and stood up and applauded. I held my arms up and pumped my fists yelling, "Yesssss!" Then, I did the traditional bow to the judges and the Grand Master. I watched as the rest of my group had their experience with the breaking of the boards. In the end, we all passed.

The ceremony was sensational, with the taking of the red belts off and then the tying the black belts around our waists. Certificates were handed out, and then something quite unexpected happened. There was a final award to be given, an award that had not been given out in many years. It was the Spirit Award, and that award was given to me. I was elated and honored to receive such a prestigious award. After over four years, I knew, on some level, I had earned it but not alone. Everyone in my group that night had helped me to get where I was, including Master Hale. I thanked all of them, my Tae Kwon Do family.

I continued my Tae Kwon Do classes for a few more months before I became committed to other priorities. I practiced my punches and kicks at home in the living room or backyard to keep in shape, especially my reflex and sequencing skills.

This whole escapade was certainly not only about the journey but the prize at the end, too: a black belt, renewed confidence, the spirit within, and a healthier and well-toned body. Plus, it's OK to ask for help. It was certainly more fun and beneficial to combine my efforts of rehearsing alone, with the collaborative efforts of the group ensemble.

Reclaiming My Divine Feminine

With this latest accomplishment under my belt—my black belt, that is—I felt safe, secure, and settled as the owner of my writer's cottage. Now, I was ready to reflect, grow, and feel more comfortable with my own identity. So, I set my arrow of intention with pointed vision and returned to what had worked before: continuing the transformational workshops with Margot Anand, albeit this time in France, and her methods of sexual healing and awakening.

In subsequent workshops, I began the sexual healing journey by revisiting the original site of the trauma: the pelvic floor. I worked with men in the sacred workshop setting, where they, too, were healing their own past wounds. I had my own vagina monologue running ("she speaks from between her legs"), and I was listening! My yoni was able to speak out against the men, old hurts, and old pain and release the anger I had built up toward them. I moved beyond the limiting clouds of guilt and shame because of her voice. I liberated the woman in me with every exercise and every yoni pump. She even touted her own names, like trying on hats in a boutique, such as Shakti Woman, Juicy Plum, Changing Woman, and Purple Iris. It was interesting to hear the other "talking yonis" of the women in the group, as all those flapping lips had similar experiences growing up.

After there was no more to heal, I learned how I liked to be loved, what made my yoni feel good, and what I liked and didn't like. The next few years, I expanded into my sexual spiritual pleasures, as the Divine Feminine, practicing and playing with several male tantric partners from around the world, including India, Ukraine, Germany, Sweden, England, Africa, Italy, and Brazil. I now understood love, sex, and intimacy with them. (This was the fun part!) I trusted men in relationships again because I was attracting and interacting with men who also were on the tantric path. I shared a new mutual connection with them, a powerful presence with an open heart. This was the truest balance of yin and yang (Shakti/Shiva), not just within myself and with women lovers but also with the pleasure of men. I was experiencing an ecstatic new dance of passion and play.

I had reclaimed my Divine Feminine aspect, as Margot had instructed me to do in the rebirthing ritual, by immersing myself in the experiential waters. This could not be intellectually healed from a therapist; I had to do the physical work and follow the natural unfoldment. "OK, now I'm doing this. It's hard, but I'm going to continue." It was OK to be right where I was. I didn't try to push the river or hang onto the sides of the riverbank. I just followed the flow of my life by embracing and living the Divine Feminine. I was living my ever-evolving "ecstatic potential."

Bows and Arrows

With my reclaimed sexual identity, I paid tribute to Artemis by turning part of my backyard into a private archery range. I purchased a long bow at an American Indian shop. It was handmade with three different types of wood (bamboo, orange sage, and hickory) with a buckskin hand rest. The bow came with wooden green arrows with real turkey feathers (known as *fletchings* in the archery arena), and a blunt point for target shooting, not critter shooting. I kept the arrows inside a handcrafted buckskin quiver strapped over my shoulder. I set up three or four straw bales at different distances atop the long stone wall, marking off the number of yards from my target line back up against the cottage.

I remembered Dr. Smith, my neuropsychologist in Santa Barbara, explaining the importance of taking up a new sport since golf was no longer an option. There were just too many variables with 14 different golf clubs, 18 different target journeys, and all the other factors of the golf swing, not to mention the outdoor elements. I considered my options and enthusiastically settled on archery. It was the ideal replacement for golf because it involved only one target (the big yellow bull's eye), one bow, one arrow, and one stance. This I could finally do, with great accuracy and focus, repeatedly. It was fun to put on my quiver with its colorful arrows, take my stance, then slowly draw an arrow out of my quiver, and place it on the string, called "knocking the arrow."

The best part of the process was the empowering feeling of the draw. I grounded myself into the Earth through conscious breathing. Exhaling into the Earth with a firm foundation, inhaling while drawing the energy up from the Earth and into my body simultaneously, as I lifted the bow and slowly drew the arrow back to its anchor point at my lips. Exhaling gently from my heart and then releasing my fingertips from the bowstring, the string whirrs, allowing the arrow to fly to its intended target, as I brush my ear and touch my shoulder with my hand to full finish position. It was an exhilarating and primal act that was oddly familiar to me, and I know I had experienced it before.

I practiced this sovereign control of technique over and over until becoming one with nature, the target, myself, and the "artless art" of transcending the steps into the realm of emptiness. This, to me, is exactly what happened when I was so mesmerized by the flower arrangement at the warm pool at Stargazer. It is how I created the flower bouquets from this state of unconsciousness, an inspiration of the moment. This Zen approach was the feeling place of performing my golf swing. It was more about vitality and spiritual awareness than technique or the people who were watching. It did not depend on the latest equipment, such as golf clubs or golf balls, but on the presence of mind.

Shivas Irons, a mystical golf pro from Michael Murphy's novel, *Golf in the Kingdom*, used only a shillelagh, a stout, knotty stick with a large knob at the top, and an old *feathery*, which was a golf ball made of feathers wrapped in leather, to outdistance any man who challenged him with traditional golf clubs and golf balls!

The act of releasing the arrow is likened to snow falling off a bamboo leaf, as described in Eugen Herrigel's book, *Zen in the Art of Archery* (New York: Pantheon Books, 1953), which I read in 1999. It must fall under the weight of the snow. This is how I had always practiced archery. One day, I had a delightful experience with this in shooting my traditional recurve bow and cedar arrows with an archery colleague. We shot from 20 yards, then 30, 50, and 75 yards, each time I allowed this same ritual of highest tension to "fall," despite how far we moved back, and I still hit the target on the straw bales. (OK, I missed a few times short before I got the right distance down!) I became more enthusiastic with this internal ceremonial act, proceeding even farther to 90, 100, and, finally, 120 yards away, just missing the target by inches, although

I was not attached to making the mark. It was the imitation of performing the shot from that exquisite state of emptiness, nowhere attached to any place, in particular. I ran with wild delight, hooting and hollering all the way to the target, quite pleased with my performance! Watching the arrow fly filled me with the same satisfaction I felt when I hit a golf ball a long distance. Pure ecstasy.

CHAPTER 22

THE BIG SIGN

I felt I was ready to work on a career again, but what? I was on my way into town to run some errands in the late spring, when all of life was bursting forth, the greening magic of flowers, plants, birds, bunnies, and bees. I could smell the freshly cut grass, which brought me back to the links once again. I found my car just turned itself around to a golf course I had just passed on the outskirts of town. I parked the car, got out, and with curious wonderment, strolled along the path that led to the clubhouse. The first tee was right in front of me, its fairway extending down to some trees, and to the right was a large putting and chipping green, freshly manicured.

I continued up a cement driveway, lined with colorful flowers and plants, and to the back of the golf shop where rows of golf carts rest. One of the young high school boys had taken a part-time job, cleaning out golf carts, so I watched for a moment and chatted with him. Then, I proceeded into the golf shop and chatted with an older guy behind the counter. He was answering the phone, taking tee times, and checking golfers in at the cash register. They seemed quite busy for a low-profile public country club. I asked him where the head pro was. He said he was out on the course somewhere, so I went over to the golf carts, sat in the driver's side of an empty cart, and wrapped my hands around the steering wheel, thinking of fond memories back in Palm

Springs—like the time I flew out of the golf cart! It was early morning, and I was one of the first golfers out on the links, with a golfing pal driving our golf cart. We had already hit our tee shot and had headed down the fairway at great speed. My golfing pal took a sharp turn on the still-dewy grass, and I unexpectedly slipped right out of the passenger side with my club in hand and plopped onto the wet grass. I took a good tumble but hopped back in the cart as he circled back and onto where my ball had landed, still laughing along the way.

I chuckled when I saw a man in golfing attire a little older than me, pull up in a golf cart. "What's so amusing?" he asked with a big smile as he parked the cart in front of me. I responded, "Fond memories of golf when I lived in Palm Springs," as I hopped out of the cart to shake his hand. "My name is Kathleen, and I am a former golf professional." He obliged and said his name was Mr. Frederick and that he was the long-standing head golf pro at the club.

That started a long conversation with this most pleasant man who was intrigued by my story and genuinely wanted to help me get back into golf again. By the time I left, I had a job. It was a part-time job, where I would work as a helper at the front desk, answering the phone, greeting customers, and preparing golf carts, if necessary. It was a minimum-wage job, but I was delighted to be "back on course."

After a couple of months, I learned the layout of the course and started understanding my job responsibilities, Frederick invited me to begin teaching at the golf course, which included going out with the ladies' golf league on Friday mornings. I was thrilled at the prospect of teaching golf again, but was a bit slow to respond because I didn't know if I could take on any more. I was only working 12 hours a week, but all the extra environmental, auditory, and visual stimuli were starting to overload my brain, especially when I worked behind the counter and greeted all the members on league days and then the public in the afternoon. Compound that with trying to understand and work the cash register became a bigger problem, as I often would miscalculate and charge customers incorrectly, resulting in another employee having to take over. The members were always understanding, but I was shrinking on the inside. Luckily, my good humor seemed to carry me through the situation.

My enthusiasm ruled, and I accepted Frederick's invitation to teach. My first assignment was to help him on Tuesday evenings with a Junior Girls' Golf Clinic. Now, that was fun! I was a great helper, as he was the head teacher, and I just followed through with the instructing of some of the junior gals. With parents standing nearby, safety was always a priority. My favorite part of the clinic was when we worked on putting with the girls, as the short game was my forte. More than this, the playing area was well contained and more defined, with an immediate goal of sinking that putt. The girls were so wide-eyed and attentive, and watching their excitement and putting the ball into the cup was just precious.

On Fridays, I began to meet the women of the Ladies' Golf League, before they would tee up, to give them a golf tip to work on while out on the course. I started off by being terribly late the first morning, so I never showed for the session beforehand. Not very impressive, but I did meet them out on the back nine to show them some chipping tips.

It became quite a juggling act for me, as being out on the course was making me feel unsafe because of the extra stimulation. I also took a golf cart to drive along the 10th fairway to get out to the small teaching green, which exposed me to navigating golfers and golf carts and watching when they would hit their golf ball to the next green. It was that motion of constantly looking left and right that would tax my brain and leave me feeling a bit disoriented. I was constantly trying to get marks and stay focused.

Once I made it to the teaching area, the experience went much better. I was remembering all the teaching techniques I used and having such a good time with the clients. I really connected with them, and they usually left very satisfied with new tools to keep their golf performance positive. I continued teaching part-time for a few months, but I realized other responsibilities were not getting done, and it was taking a toll on my health. I would return home fatigued and unable to perform many of my daily routines, such as cooking meals, taking care of my cats, and attending to various household chores. I enjoyed being with the people again and helping them with their golf game. And the extra cash helped pay for the gas to get there, along with some needed groceries, but it wasn't worth the setbacks. My brain was getting too flooded.

I worked at the golf course for only one season, knowing it was just too much for me. I had to give it another try to convince myself that I could not return to a career in the golf industry. It was a part of my past, and now it was time to move on. It was 2015, and I felt like I was a wayward ship bobbing up and down on the sea, looking for land and a port to dock at. All I saw was a little blip. A smudge in the distance. Then, slowly the smudge stretched into a line across the horizon, and there it was: "Land, land . . . resurrection!" Not quite; it sounded like another movie with actress Cate Blanchett in *Elizabeth, the Golden Years*.

Coming into the bay, I spotted several different ports to drift into, several different possible directions I could go with my career at that time in my life. Minister, archery instructor, tantra coach, amazing wife, speaker, author, golf instructor, or even strolling with my accordion downtown, playing an occasional tune for tips. Some of these I had already tried part-time, but they were unrealistic due to the cognitive and visual issues I experienced.

282

I couldn't choose one lane and so I bobbed up and down on the restless sea waters until one day when I stirred with anticipation. I was ready to sail into a port; I didn't know which one, but I was ready to get on with it. Besides, I was feeling tipsy. I wanted a meaningful and fulfilling career path that provided me with enough income to financially sustain myself and that I was able to do. So, I asked for help. I looked at the open sea and asked for a sign from God. "Please dazzle me with a big sign that I cannot mistake nor ignore!"

Then, I kept my eyes and ears open, hoping my prayer would be heard and answered. I didn't wait long before a sign presented itself to me in a unique way. I was on a flight from California to Utah en route to Asheville, North Carolina, near my home. I was sitting in an aisle seat in the front row when a tall man boarded the plane—a very tall man. I offered my seat to him so he could stretch out his long legs during the flight. His legs stretched all the way into the cockpit!

This man was 7 feet 4 inches and a former athlete like me. I was intrigued by his manner and eloquent way of speaking and found out he was a member of the National Speakers Association (NSA), a nonprofit association dedicated to providing education and networking opportunities to individuals who deliver information and words of inspiration to audiences through the spoken or written word. He was on his way home from a big speaking gig and shared with me his story about how his basketball career ended and how speaking became his new career. His name was Mark Eaton, and he was an NBA star and a former center for the Utah Jazz, playing against superstars like Michael Jordan, Kareem Abdul-Jabbar, and Larry Bird. Well, my heart was beating really fast now, and my armpits felt moist as I asked several questions on how he did it.

Mark shared with how he, at the age of 21, had no experience, talent, or interest in basketball. Yet, he went on to become an All-Star who achieved success beyond anything he ever thought possible. He described his rags-to-riches basketball odyssey, which originated from being a car mechanic right out of high school to a rising NBA star, because of his height, by being the acknowledged master of one facet of his sport: the blocked shot.

"One variable!" I exclaimed as I almost jumped out of my seat. "I can relate to this," I said to him in a calmer voice with widening eyes.

Mark continued his story, as he played through his limitations, ignored the ridicule of his offensive shortcomings (not being a better scorer), and concentrated on honing the aspect of the game that he was best at, shot blocking, until he became one of the very best who ever played the game. He was at the center, the very core, of the franchise's rise from last place (where it was the season before he arrived) and the brink of extinction to its then-current level of dynamic success. When he arrived, the Utah Jazz were perennial 50-game losers; when he left, because of an ailing back injury, they were perennial 50-game winners.

Mark explained how he challenged himself and his beliefs and found the courage to keep going and achieve success beyond anything he ever thought possible. His advice to me now was to join my local Toastmasters Club right away and practice speaking and listening with this group for a year or so.

He stated it was most important for me to be authentic, which I completely agreed with, and I shared it was one of my strengths already. Mark advised me to take it a step further by being myself on the platform—naked. Well, I could agree easily with this one! But stopping to think for a moment, I realized it also meant to be who I was in that moment, even if it meant speaking more slowly because of the brain flooding. That would be OK because I could only be where I was, and that would level the playing field with the audience. As I showed them my vulnerability, they would open up to me, no longer feeling inferior and being receptive to my message.

Mark's final question was, "What are you asking people to believe?" Another easy question for me to respond to because of my golf career days. This is one of the High-Five principles I taught my golfing clients, and that was to "believe in yourself" because I had to believe in myself to make it through the challenges and survive a traumatic brain injury. I could reassure them if I could do it, so could they.

Next, Mark recommended that I become a member of NSA to achieve a higher level of speaking education and profes-sionalism. He confided that he traveled and spoke to about 50 to 60 different audiences a year! Wow, I thought, now that would be impossible for me to do. No way I could travel that much and be cognizant. I'd be like the walking dead but not walking. Moving past the quantity of gigs, I sat slightly turned toward Mark at the edge of my seat and, curious, asked, "How many speeches do you have in your back pocket for all these audiences?" I thought he would respond by saying maybe 20 speeches or so.

"Just one," he said. "One outstanding speech," he repeated confidently, looking directly into my eyes.

"One?" I exclaimed as people seated near me looked at me with disdain. "One good speech," I pondered aloud. Looking at Mark, I proclaimed with conviction, "I can do that; I can give one good speech over and over." Softly and pensively, I repeated, "One speech," as I looked away and out the window, settling back into my seat.

In that instant, the lights came on in about a real career that I would be able to do and that I could eventually make enough money to sustain myself and more. The real possibility existed now, with the words that came from Mark's mouth in that moment. I felt the plane begin its descent, and I thanked Mark for sharing about his life from down to up. We then talked more casually about his ranch and his love for horses before the plane landed with a thud onto the airstrip.

I couldn't wait to get home, but I still had a connecting flight to catch. The epiphany lingered, and I pulled out my little note pad from my purse and quickly wrote down some notes of my connection with Mark . . . literally and figuratively speaking, he was the big sign! This was a very big sign, indeed. I couldn't ignore this man who stood 7 feet 4 inches. My prayers had been answered, and the Universe had dazzled me far better than I could have ever imagined.

CHAPTER 23

BLAZING A NEW CAREER PATH

I got started on Mark's advice as soon as I arrived home, looking at all the Toastmasters Clubs in my area online. I visited five clubs in the weeks that followed before deciding to join the one that met at lunchtime. Perfect for me, as driving to the venue would not be at a peak time during the day, and I could take a nap after class.

My first meeting was held on the third floor of the town's visitors' center. I had a blast getting to know about 15 people who were at different levels in the Toastmasters program. I was even called on in table topics, an improvisational short speech, because I accepted the invitation to play with the rest of the group. I delivered the best table topic, explaining how with conscious breathing, I stayed focused on drawing my bow and arrow and releasing it to its target. With such early success, I was invited to give my ice-breaker speech the following week. Sometimes you can jump too quickly out of the blocks! I left a bit apprehensive as performance anxiety reared its ugly head.

I wrote out my speech with pen and paper during the days that followed. I even cut out part of the article I wrote about my traumatic brain injury that was published in the *Santa Barbara Family Life* magazine in 2002. "My very young, vibrant, and motivated life, as I knew it. changed in an instant." I pasted it with white glue on page three of five-and-a-half pages. I stapled them all together, without having the time to rewrite it neatly.

When it was my turn to give my speech in class, I nervously placed my stapled paper on the lectern and proceeded: "Members and guests, my name is Kathleen Klawitter, and I love life and I love people." I continued reading the best I could, although the scribbled writing and arrows pointing to the next section to read became a bit distracting. I clung to the script, speaking slowly with frequent starts and stops, though managed to look up occasionally and give my speech in the five to seven minutes allotted for the icebreaker. I finished with a call to action, for all them to help me become a better speaker. The members applauded me with cheers and smiles, and I felt relieved. I had done it! After the class, I was immediately appointed a mentor.

Elaine was a short, savvy woman who was a veteran of Toastmasters. She congratulated me on my first speech and asked to see my stapled script! She chuckled and said next time would be easier. She asked me why I didn't type my speech. I honestly don't know why, but it brought back the memory of when I did the speech read for the Klawitter Golf Classic at Sandpiper Country Club. "Déjà vu." It was the same way I had put together that speech.

Well, that was the last time that happened as Elaine went out of her way to help me prepare for my next two speeches. They were typed out after Elaine and I had reviewed speech script. They were well rehearsed, sometimes in front of Elaine first at the visitor center. In my fourth speech, I threw my notes in front of the class and went to index cards! A dramatic demonstration to help me give my speech more like a story instead of reading it. It was a challenge, but I knew I had to start recircuiting that new pathway in my brain to eventually be able to do a speech without any notes at all.

I was well on my way, attending and participating in Toastmasters each week for over a year, and then I joined the National Speakers Association (NSA). This was the original guidance that Mark had offered, and I kept in contact with him a couple times via email to share my progress in practicing my speaking and listening skills. My learning curve initially with the NSA would be different in that I would receive tips and strategies through webinars of professional speakers on the NSA website. I would be able to listen to webinars over and over to learn key aspects of speaking effectively, such as using pauses, body language, and anecdotes to illustrate key points. I went to the state chapter conference, where I met some very dynamic speakers in the business.

I also was invited to share my story in an article I wrote for NSA's *Speaker* magazine, "Triumph Over Traumatic Brain Injury." My article was selected for the June 2017 "brain issue," marking the first time a new member's story had been featured in the publication. This would be my calling card to exposure of a new career, as the annual NSA Influence Convention was just one month away. People would recognize me if I were there. But how to get there was the dilemma. I applied for a registration grant to attend NSA's 2017 Influence event held at Disney World in Orlando, Florida, and was one of five to be accepted. Lucky me, I got to go to Disney World!

I believed that by attending the event, I would have the opportunity to network in person with some of the most prestigious professional speaking people in the world. I wanted to learn from them, watch them, talk with them, and be inspired by them. And, indeed I was. I found the tribe that would help propel my career, and I would deepen into a professional family I could count on and grow with. To my delight, Mark Eaton was one of the keynote speakers, as he was presenting the sports celebrity workshop, which I attended. We reconnected and had lunch together, where we recounted my journey. Mark and I came full circle, two years later. (See Figure 11: Kathleen Klawitter and Mark Eaton at NSA Influence 2017.)

I met some of the most receptive and supportive colleagues in those four days. Lisa Brown, another budding comeback speaker and fundraiser from Ohio, invited me to sit in the front row with her and watch the featured keynote speakers at a morning general session. The second keynoter, Vinh Giang, a magician who shared his secrets of how he can influence his audience with his topic "Mindset Is Everything," asked a handful of attendees—including me—to come up onto the main stage with him. It was no coincidence that I played the brain game with this brilliant master of illusion.

My first Influence, and my first appearance on a main stage in more than two decades, was exhilarating, with about 1,500 people in the audience. I was comfortable and jovial being alongside this dynamic professional speaker as he asked me some questions. It almost felt familiar, as I breathed with confidence with this unexpected endeavor. The only thing that bothered me was the lights. They were so bright, I had trouble focusing on the audience. I wanted to see their faces and eyes and connect with them. Plus, the intense brightness caused me to squint my eyes a bit. What a "gleaming insight" to have for when I would someday speak on this stage, or any other main stage in my speaking journey. I would have to figure out a way to diffuse the lighting, without wearing sunglasses or a visor!

Some of the other professional speakers I met and had in-depth conversations with were those who had been in that triumphant "comeback" category, including Patrick Sweeney, who defeated leukemia; Elaine Pasqua, Certified Speaking Professional (CSP), who survived her parents both dying from AIDS; John Register, who overcame a leg amputation; and Libby Gill, who overcame a family history of mental illness and suicide. They all persevered, going through major transitions in their lives and reinventing themselves, becoming extraordinary professional speakers with profound messages. This gave me more than hope, because here were the most amazing people living out their greatest destinies. They had transformed themselves, and now the green light was lit for me to follow in their footsteps!

I was leaving the main conference center to go to my hotel room, when I met another remarkable speaker/coach named Gordon Viggiano, who had a stroke. He had emailed me before the Influence event, after reading my article in *Speaker* magazine, and wanted to connect at the conference. Gordon was nine years out from his stroke and still worked diligently with his dis-ability.

We met after a break-out session near the main group center and talked on a hallway bench for about 30 minutes before I realized the time, needing to dash and get ready for the Cavett Awards Banquet. Cavett Robert, CSP, Council of Peers Award for Excellence (CPAE), founded NSA in 1973, with the spirit of the organization built around ideas of mutual support, shared success and giving back, instilling an atmosphere of cooperation, not competition.

I took a breath and stayed with Gordon longer, as I was so touched by his quiet and innocent demeanor. He talked about my being a professional golf instructor and asked about some help with his golf game. Yes, he still plays golf, albeit using only one arm to swing his club! Astonished with his willpower, I took off my jacket and scarf and showed him a couple of basic putting tips, demonstrating right there on the carpet of the hallway. He was very attentive. I was so elated, I took the time to be with him that late afternoon. It was a heartfelt connection and one that stayed with me. We parted with a long embrace, and then I scampered to my hotel room to get ready for the big gala affair. Gordon wished me well and was impressed I could go to the bustling event, as he could not. I turned with a smile and said, "With earplugs and marking, I'll get through, I hope!"

I made it to my hotel room out of breath, still brimming over my conversation with Gordon, and quickly showered. I pulled over my head the floor-length mango gown with understated elegance. I had borrowed it from Aphrodite Dae. I blotted on some makeup and some gold hoop earrings and quickly styled my hair. I slipped on my bronze fashion sandals before I ran out the door of the Swan Hotel and over the long walkway to the main center hall at the Dolphin Hotel. There must have been a passing thunderstorm as the cement was wet and the air humid. Amid some lingering periwinkle clouds, sun rays cast a resplendent double rainbow in the distance. My feet splashed to a halting stop and I stood in silence. Cousin Lori, my heroine, had passed away a few days earlier and her service was today. I know with all my heart this was her glowing spirit shining down on me. How wonderful to have her blessing at this most exuberant time in my life!

I felt like Cinderella, as I walked through the flowered archway and into the large decorated center. More than 100 round tables were draped with white linen cloths, fully dressed in fine china and glassware, lit with tall glass candles, and adorned with vases with fresh flowers. The room filled with conversation and laughter, as professional photographer captured fond memories.

Everyone was dressed in their finest, some men in tuxedoes and women in long, elegant gowns while others remained in casual business suits or cocktail dresses. The evening flowed with the flare of the Academy Awards, with entertainment from creative NSA members, who opened as The Village People, performing the famous "YMCA" dance number, while the audience sang along with the appropriate arm gestures. The entertainment segment was followed by a delicious gourmet dinner and an awards ceremony recognizing some of the outstanding speakers of the year. It was surreal for me, as I had never imagined my first NSA Influence convention would be so extravagant and fun. I left the gala event high on the whole affair, strolling barefoot down the long outer walkway with my sandals in my hands. Before I reached the Swan Hotel entrance, a loud crack of thunder commenced with a shower of brilliant fireworks right above my head! I laughed in wonderment while thinking, "All for me?" A perfect ending to a perfect evening and a perfect new beginning!

Applause! Applause! Applause!

Inspired by my convention experience and fueled with mojo, I continued my dedication to Toastmasters. I had joined the Toastmasters Club to help me become a better speaker. What I found out was so much more. It was a consistent weekly "in-person" thread that kept me polished and sharp, similar to how my neuropsychologist kept it together and on track for me during my rehabilitation.

Toastmasters is a program where I must be present and listen; I have a role, a task to do for that meeting, such as time-keeper, grammarian, evaluator for a speaker, or even toast-master for the class. I got to practice my improvisational speaking with table topics, an exercise that kept my brain neurons firing. In practicing and giving my speeches, most any-thing I did was applauded: throwing my speech notes; clutching my notes back; becoming my alter ego of a French maid, "Je ne comprende pas!"; doing the waggle bee dance; breathing and laughing together; and even tearing up together. The members of my group took me in as family and supported my every task, and I reciprocated where I could with them. The practice arena was challenging, revealing, fun, and productive.

After being in Toastmasters for almost two years, I completed a milestone on January 30, 2017, with my speech, "Triumph over Tragedy." I gave a 10-minute inspirational speech—my story on how I survived and thrived after a traumatic brain injury, at a "fearless" speech craft event put on by our Toastmasters club. I was the keynote speaker, in front of an audience of more than 30 people.

The opening was strong with a question posed to the audience: "Have any of you had the experience of having everything going your way, you are on top of your game, you're in the zone, you're making a difference, and then suddenly you have it all taken away?

"Toastmasters, members, and fearless guests, I have . . . and in a big way."

I went on with the speech describing the "direct hit" of the golf ball. "My entire career, everything I had worked for was gone. Everything I lived for was shattered," I explained, standing confidently in front of the audience. I continued with the painful and challenging journey of rehabilitation, with a new direction in life. "Along the way, I have learned something quite profound; the brain is magnificent, resilient, and changeable." I followed with categories of my strategies and brain training, giving a couple of examples. I was on a roll, enjoying the spotlight once again, connecting with the audience, and feeling the positive flow of energy between and around us.

"The way I access information is different and ever-evolving, especially in how much I practice these skills and strategies. The more I have practiced, the stronger the new pathway or brain circuit becomes. It is the most important task for me to do, just as if I were tending to a flower garden. I awake each morning with great appreciation, for I get to begin a new day. I originally had to change my brain out of necessity, but now I get to create my life with passion, power, and purpose. I am human proof it can be done! I want to speak to audiences and organizations about how they can be courageous and fearless when met with obstacles in their lives."

Approaching the end of my speech, I proclaimed a call to action to my engaged audience: "Sometimes life takes an unexpected turn; and you may lose everything. Yet, you too can come back, for you have the power and resources within to overcome any challenge or obstacle."

With great enthusiasm, I delivered my last sentence: *"Be courageous and believe in yourself more than anything in the world!"*

Loud applause broke out, along with positive cheers. I turned to the toastmaster with a huge smile and a thank-you before handing the meeting back over to him.

It was a triumphant moment as I not only had met the requirements for the competent communicator award in Toastmasters, but after over 20 years, there I was on stage again, doing what I loved best: inspiring and uplifting people to their own highest potential.

I had found my port, my new direction in life. I was moving on a steady course now with a new career in speaking emerging, and becoming an author was close behind.

Encore Performance

I returned home that afternoon to recount the momentous occasion. I had finally come full circle from the days before my accident, as a successful golf entrepreneur and motivational speaker and consultant, to an emerging author and speaker. I went to my backyard sanctuary to give thanks and appreciation for the long, long adventure; standing tall with outstretched arms and loving the land, waters, and wild things, I began to breathe with life.

I did my conscious breathing ritual with utmost devotion. I gave the essence of my spirit to the rising sun, the mountains, the flowing waters of the creek below, and the standing people (trees). Softly, I intimately blew this Divine air with all the love in my heart, and then slowly inhaling, I took this Divine air back into my lungs, every cell of my body, my soul, and I felt the bursts of love and joy and magnificence of all that was before me, and I am at once ecstatic and at peace. Then, I exhaled again exchanging this immense state of appreciation, of being, softly spraying my bliss back unto the Earth, land and waters and wild things, and with the next inhale, it all came back unto me with spiraling magnitude . . . entwined, swirling, infinity rings rising as mist from mountains to sky, ascending with such grace, such fluidity in perfect balance, we are one flowing column of love.

My body quivered with delight, and I bowed to all that was before me, with one hand on my heart and the other extended out, turning to each of the four directions. Then, I reached both hands up to the sky, bowing with a sweeping motion to the Earth, brushing the grass with my hands on the way back up and ending with both hands on my heart and one last big breath of appreciation. Exchanging breath is one of the most intimate acts I continue to do. I returned to my little cottage, feeling lighter and renewed. I sat down at my keyboards, rustling music sheets to find and play a tune that no longer haunted me:

Said a scarecrow swinging on a pole, to a blackbird sitting on a fence,
Oh, the Lord gave me a soul, but forgot to give me common sense,
If I had an ounce of common sense. . .
Well . . . I would while away the hours,
conferring with the flowers,
Consulting with the rain, da-da da-da da-daaa!
And my head I'd be scratching, while my thoughts were busy hatching,
"If I Only Had a Brain."

I continued to play with gusto and sang along where I could, missing notes here and there, with the tempo slowing but never stopping.

Oh, I could tell you why the ocean's near the shore,
I could think of things, I never thunk before,

and then I'd sit, bump, bump, and think some more!
"If I Only Had a Brain."

When I finished playing the song, I turned the keyboard off, still softly humming the melody. I swiveled around on the music stool and stared out the picture window unto the mountains, reflecting on my life now. Maple Leaf, my faithful companion of 20 years, sat purring on a couch pillow and looked up at me, still loving and attentive to me as he had always been. I started humming a different tune, Whitney Houston's 1986 hit song "Greatest Love of All." I rose from my stool and began to do my ecstatic dance with happy feet and waving arms, moving in time with the rhythmic beat of unbridled bliss.

I decided long ago, never to walk in anyone's shadows
If I fail, if I succeed
At least I'll live as I believe . . .
Because the greatest love of all
Is happening to me
I found the greatest love of all
Inside of me . . .
Find your strength in love . . .

Dancing the colors of my life, as an emerging feminine force, I share my creative transformational journey to uplift and inspire all of humanity.

Now, that's a new Direct Hit!

FIGURES

Figure 1: In Perfect Love and Perfect Trust

Figure 2: M. Lonlee

Figure 3: Illusions

Figure 4: Moon Salutation

Figure 5: Strawberries

Figure 6: Green Peppers

Figure 7: My Arrow-Making Yogini

"Arrow-making Yogini"

Kathleen
September 2001

Figure 8. Brain Anatomy

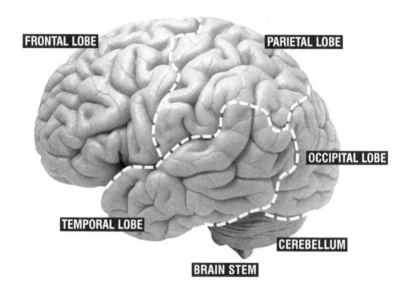

Figure 9: Birding Vision Board

Figure 10. Lone Eagle

Figure 11: Kathleen Klawitter and Mark Eaton at NSA Influence 2017

ACKNOWLEDGMENTS

I am very grateful to the following people who have contributed in different ways and on multiple levels to the healing of my traumatic brain injury and my new way of life.

My loving parents, the late Don Klawitter and my mother Carole Klawitter, along with other family members, especially my sister, Kim Klawitter, and my late cousin Lori Kroothoep.

The many friends who supported my healing journey and encouraged me to share my story with the world.

To my Californian and European tribes, sacred sisters, and sky dancing partners, who contained the space, churning the energy which allowed me to revel in my dark and ecstatic selves and really go there.

I am deeply grateful to Dr. Cheryll Smith, neuropsychologist extraordinaire, for her expertise, devotion, and unwavering patience with my traumatic brain injury recovery. She taught me strategies and tools that have continued to help me survive on a daily basis so I can lead a good quality of life, despite my challenges.

The late Cork Milner, author and teacher in Santa Barbara, California, who, in 2002, helped me realize the importance of writing about my head injury. He guided me in writing a prologue that would later be morphed into the first chapter.

This book would not be possible without the fierce dedication of my highly organized and jovial friend, Caroline Reis, who plunged into heaps of handwritten papers, notebooks, and articles, typing everything into the computer for me and then creating an expanded book outline in 2012.

Great appreciation to my collaborator and editor, Barbara Parus, who believed in me and saw the depth and grander picture of my life, skillfully transforming and rebuilding a fragmented manuscript into a compelling, full-length journey. I am thankful for her unwavering clarity and extensive and meticulous expertise in making sure every piece of vital information was extracted from my brain since our collaboration began in 2016.

My heartfelt thanks to those who endorsed my book: Vicki Noble, Nabil Doss, Margot Anand, Scott G. Halford, Patrick J. Sweeney III, Laura Cornell, Mark Eaton, and Libby Gill.

To my Toastmasters and National Speakers Association colleagues who continue to support and applaud me every step of the way.

Special thanks to graphic design artist, Bill Van Nimwegen, for his magnificent book cover design.

Finally, much love and appreciation to my two beloved orange cats, Jack and Maple Leaf, who were unforgettable furry companions of my adventurous life since 1998. They were loyal "Guardians of the Goddess," providing amusement, pure joy, and unconditional love.

ABOUT THE AUTHOR

KATHLEEN KLAWITTER

Kathleen Klawitter is a former LPGA golf instructor who was a pioneer in the body–mind–spirit approach in the early 1990s. Kathleen has a BA in psychology and has almost thirty years of experience in holistic modalities including Science of Mind, women's studies, Eastern philosophy, and Earth-based spirit-uality.

Although Kathleen suffered a traumatic brain injury and is considered disabled, she became a black belt in Tae Kwon Do and was honored with the seldom-bestowed Spirit Award. In 2017, she moved up to Advanced Toastmaster, winning a Toastmaster's International Area speech contest. The same year, she became the first National Speaker Association (NSA) Academy member to be featured in *Speaker* magazine for her article "Triumph Over Traumatic Brain Injury."

Kathleen's leading-edge thinking, enthusiasm, and state of well-being offer proof of her willingness to live life as a joyous adventure. As a traumatic brain injury survivor, even when faced with relearning how to read, write, and drive, she looked at life with profound optimism and found constant comfort in nature and Spirit.

Kathleen is a romantic at heart and loves dancing in the living room, under the full moon, or on the ballroom dance floor. She also enjoys candlelight dinners, strolls on the beach, stargazing, yogurt blueberry masks, and playing Scrabble without keeping score.

In her memoir, *Direct Hit,* Kathleen transports readers into her real-life stories with a visceral experiential journey, leaving them uplifted, empowered, and ready to seize the moment. With refreshing candor, she regales readers in how she reprogrammed her brain using some of the most innovative methods and strategies. This author is ferocious about not believing in appearances and embodies the "live your ecstatic potential" philosophy. Her vivid tale exemplifies the immense capacity of the human spirit.

Motivated by this inspired reclamation of her life, Kathleen passionately shares her transformational journey as an emerging feminine force, speaking to audiences everywhere.

For questions or to book a speaking engagement, contact Kathleen through her website, www.KathleenKlawitter.com.

You either control your mind or it controls you.
There is no half-way compromise.
~ Napoleon Hill

CPSIA information can be obtained
at www.ICGtesting.com
Printed in the USA
BVHW042132050220
571548BV00006B/21

9 781733 039307